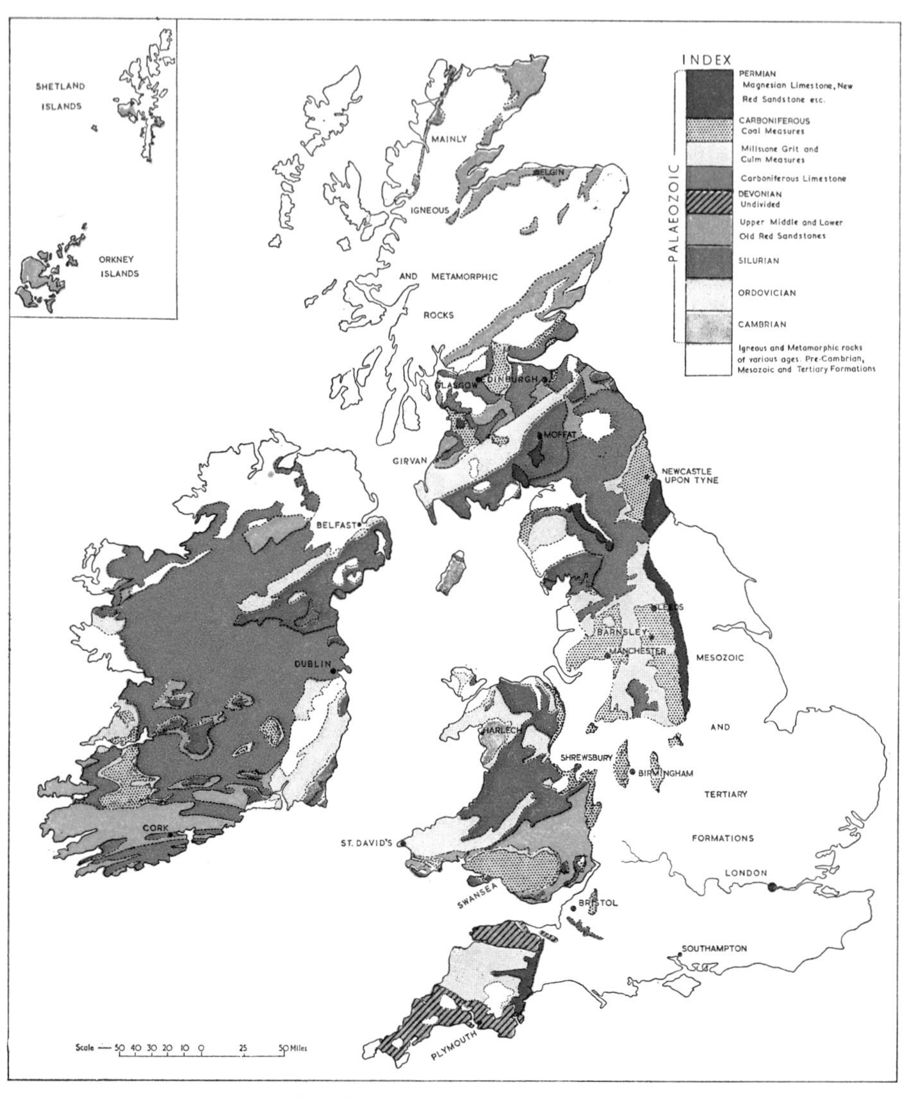

Distribution of Palaeozoic Strata

British Museum (Natural History)

BRITISH PALAEOZOIC FOSSILS

THIRD EDITION

London
Trustees of the British Museum (Natural History)
1969

Price Thirteen Shillings (£0·65)

First Edition 1964
Second Edition 1966
Third Edition 1969

Printed in England by Unwin Brothers Limited, Woking and London
(B8000)

Contents

Preface

The publication of *British Palaeozoic Fossils* brings to a conclusion an enterprise that was started some years ago by my predecessor, the late W. N. Edwards, as related in my preface to the first volume of the series published, *British Caenozoic Fossils*. The aim in view is there explained as 'a series of handbooks illustrating British fossils . . . issued in response to repeated requests for a simple and inexpensive book to enable the young, or those without experience, to know what fossils they may expect to find or, even more important from our point of view, to identify for themselves those they have collected.' Simple in illustration the three books certainly are, the text too, so far as a somewhat esoteric subject will allow, but if their inexpensiveness is a little less obvious, it is certainly through no fault or desire of those who have compiled them. Indeed, the cheaper they are and the more widely distributed they become, the more likely is the final hope to be realized, that collectors may identify for themselves those fossils they have collected, for it would be more than disingenuous to pretend that our purpose was entirely altruistic.

This Palaeozoic volume covers by far the longest period of the three, some 375 million years against 155 million years in the Mesozoic, and a mere 70 million in the Caenozoic; and during this vast period of time, some 217,000 feet (41 miles) of rock were deposited on the earth's surface in various parts of the world.

Illustrating the life of such an immense period within the limits set by a handbook of this nature presents considerable problems of selection, not made easier by the frequent distortion and indifferent preservation of many of these ancient fossils, the earliest of which take us back 600 million years, virtually to the beginning of macroscopic life capable of preservation.

Four hundred and forty-three species of animals and plants are illustrated, which is seventy-eight more than in the Mesozoic volume, but they represent a much smaller percentage of the known forms.

Before the Palaeozoic era the rocks have yielded only obscure traces of fossils such as sea-weeds, jelly-fish, horny brachiopods and worms; yet even in the earliest Palaeozoic strata invertebrate animals such as molluscs, brachiopods and trilobites, were both varied and well developed and, indeed, the era saw the beginning of most of the groups of animals and plants that exist today (and of some that do not), but not necessarily in their present highly developed form.

The first finds of back-boned animals, primitive creatures known as Agnatha, came from Ordovician rocks, followed at some distance of time by those of the true fishes and then the amphibians and reptiles; but mammals and birds were Mesozoic 'creations' (see the Geological Time-scale, p. 21) as were the flowering plants. Land-plants were already present about the middle of the era, and there is evidence that in the Devonian period the land was clothed in vegetation; and the rich coal seams of the succeeding Carboniferous period are ample proof of the luxuriance of the peculiar evergreen vegetation of the time. Winged insects appeared in variety, among them the egregious cockroach, testifying that an ancient lineage is no guarantee of nobility.

As in the previous volumes, much of the preparation has been carried out by Mr C. P. Castell, and Dr W. T. Dean has written the introduction and is responsible for the rather complex stratal tables. Dr Dean has been massively aided in regard to the Carboniferous and Permian correlations by Dr H. M. Muir-Wood, with a useful contribution by Mr J. Ferguson; while Dr H. W. Ball's knowledge of Devonian and Old Red Sandstone stratigraphy, like that of Mr H. A. Toombs, has proved of invaluable assistance.

Outside the department we have received capital advice from the Director of H.M. Geological Survey, Dr C. J. Stubblefield, F.R.S., and from his staff, in both London and Leeds. Moreover, in Leeds we had the further advantage of the wide experience of Mr Selwyn Turner, and of the knowledgeable commonsense of Dr Dorothy Rayner. Dr J. E. Robinson of University College, London, too, was most helpful. To all these, our kind friends, we willingly acknowledge our indebtedness, and if we have not always been able to follow all their advice in detail, it is only because we have had sometimes to select from varying shades of opinion.

With few exceptions the excellent illustrations are the work of Miss J. C. Webb and Mr D. Erasmus. The cover, like those of the preceding volumes, was designed by Miss Audrey Weber.

The frontispiece is, of course, based on the fine 25 miles to the inch map of H.M. Geological Survey, but at this reduction justice is not done to it, and the colours have had to be altered.

ERROL WHITE
Keeper of Palaeontology

15*th June*, 1963

Preface to Second Edition

The demand for this handbook has proved exceptionally brisk and, in spite of a specially large printing, the original edition is nearly exhausted.

It is satisfactory to record that no major criticism of the contents has been received, not even of the stratal tables, which are always subject to varying and strongly held opinions. Some adjustments have been made—the term Middle Ordovician has been dispensed with and modifications of the boundaries of the Lower Carboniferous Divisions include the elimination of Zone D_3.

The plates are the same and the alterations in the text and explanations are mostly just refinements of nomenclature.

ERROL WHITE
Keeper of Palaeontology

19*th January*, 1966

Introduction

The two previously published handbooks of this series of three dealt with the British Caenozoic and Mesozoic fossils respectively. The name Palaeozoic (literally Ancient Life) is applied to the rocks which were formed before the Mesozoic Era, about 225 million years ago, but subsequent to a point in time now generally accepted as being about 600 million years ago. The latter is of great significance in Palaeontology because it marks the beginning of what we know as the Cambrian period, and it is in Cambrian rocks that we find remains of the earliest-known organisms possessing hard parts capable of fossilization. That is not to say they were the earliest forms of life. The manner and date of the origin of life on our planet are largely matters of speculation and present enormous problems which may never be satisfactorily solved. Traces and impressions of what were presumably soft-bodied animals have been found, though rarely, in rocks whose age is of the order of 800 million years or more, but it is a remarkable fact that the beginning of the Cambrian period is marked by the advent, world-wide in extent, of undoubted fossils of marine animals. The rocks formed before this time are grouped together for convenience as Pre-Cambrian, but they represent a far greater span of time than has elapsed since the beginning of the Cambrian. The study of Pre-Cambrian rocks presents problems of great complexity and does not concern us here, but mention of such rocks will be made from time to time on account of the effects of their outcrops on the deposition and distribution of later strata.

The 375 million years following the beginning of the Cambrian period form collectively the Palaeozoic Era, and it is the object of this handbook to illustrate representatives of the animals and plants living during that time, which was equivalent to more than one-and-a-half times that occupied by the combined Mesozoic and Caenozoic Eras. The study and interpretation of Palaeozoic rocks and fossils offer a great challenge to the geologist and palaeontologist. Many of the animals found belong to groups which are now completely extinct, and we are thus unable to compare satisfactorily their structure and habits with those of living representatives. During their long history many of the older rocks have undergone several periods of earth movement, as a result of which the contained fossils have often been distorted and their extraction and interpretation thereby made difficult. The Palaeozoic rocks have been subdivided into six Systems, successively the Cambrian, Ordovician, Silurian, Devonian, Carboniferous and Permian, representing periods of 100, 60, 40, 50, 80 and 45 million years respectively. For convenience these six are generally formed into two groups of three Systems, termed Lower and Upper Palaeozoic. Although the Palaeozoic rocks occupy such a large span of time in relation to Mesozoic and later strata, the number of fossil species illustrated in this handbook is not so large in proportion. This is in part due to the difficulties encountered in obtaining well-preserved specimens suitable for illustration, and is also a reflection of the additional work required for a fuller understanding of our Palaeozoic strata and their fossil contents.

The whole of Britain west of a line running roughly north-north-east from the Devonshire coast near Exmouth to the coast of County Durham near Hartlepool is composed largely of Palaeozoic rocks. These strata do not crop out at the surface over the south-eastern half of England, but their presence in that region has been proved by means of boreholes penetrating the overlying cover of Mesozoic and Caenozoic rocks. The oldest Palaeozoic rocks belong to the Cambrian System, so-called after Cambria, the ancient name for Wales, where they were first studied in detail. There is a threefold subdivision of the beds into Lower, Middle and Upper Cambrian and they rest on Pre-Cambrian rocks, from which they are separated by an unconformity or break in deposition. In the Midland and Welsh Border counties they form relatively restricted outcrops comprising mainly sandy strata, some of them now compacted into quartzites, laid down near the fringes of a shallow sea. Examples of poorly fossiliferous basal quartzite occur in Shropshire at The Wrekin, in Herefordshire at the Malvern Hills, and in Staffordshire at the Lickey Hills. Farther west, in North and South Wales, the Cambrian rocks are much thicker and represent deposition in deeper water. Fossils are not, on the whole, common, but by means of the trilobite remains the vertical succession of strata has been subdivided into a series of 'Zones' characterized by particular genera and species. The remains of these extinct arthropods outnumber those of all other fossil groups from the Cambrian Era, and the trilobites of the Anglo-Welsh area show close affinities with corresponding faunas in Scandinavia and other parts of Europe. Although many different fossils have been recorded from the Cambrian rocks, specimens are not always easy to find and extract, and especially in Wales they have frequently been distorted by the numerous earth-movements which have taken place since the animals were buried on the sea-floor. The fossiliferous Cambrian horizons in Shropshire and Warwickshire are not, in general, well exposed, and much of our knowledge of them has been established only as the result of prolonged research and excavation. Fossiliferous Lower Cambrian limestones occur at the tiny village of Comley in Shropshire, where they are overlain by Middle Cambrian sandstones and Upper Cambrian grey and black shales with brachiopods. A somewhat similar succession is found in the Malvern Hills, where the black shales have yielded trilobites near the village of Whiteleaved (or White Leaf) Oak, whilst in Warwickshire fossiliferous Middle Cambrian shales occur near Nuneaton. Elsewhere, fossiliferous Middle Cambrian rocks may be examined on the coast of South Wales to the east of St David's, Pembrokeshire, where the cliffs at Porth-y-rhaw, near Solva, contain occasional large specimens of the trilobite *Paradoxides*. In the Upper Cambrian, outcrops of the Lingula Flags, so-called on account of the abundant brachiopod *Lingulella* (previously *Lingula*) *davisi*, are widespread and fossiliferous in both South Wales, near St David's and Haverfordwest, and North Wales, near Dolgelly and Portmadoc.

In Scotland the Cambrian rocks form a restricted outcrop confined to the North-West Highlands and only the Lower Cambrian is represented, consisting of a basal quartzite followed by what are known as the Fucoid Beds, dolomitic mudstones and shales with worm tracks. The trilobites obtained from the shales include the genera *Olenellus* and *Olenelloides*, which are unknown from corresponding strata in England and Wales. They apparently inhabited a separate sea which extended westwards to Greenland and eastern North America where similar fossils have been found.

Above the topmost Cambrian strata in England and Wales lie the rocks of the Tremadoc Series, named after Tremadoc in Caernarvonshire. As there is a local unconformity above these strata in their type-area, some British geologists have included the beds within the Cambrian System, but others, as well as most non-British workers, prefer to place them within the lowest part of the Ordovician System (a convention followed in this publication) on account of the Ordovician affinities of the Tremadoc faunas. The term Ordovician is inevitably associated in many readers' minds with the well-known controversy involving the eminent geologists Sedgwick and Murchison about the middle of the last century. With Sedgwick working his way upwards through the Cambrian succession of North Wales, and Murchison working his way down through the Silurian succession of the area farther east and south-east, it was almost inevitable that the two should conflict, with the unfortunate result that certain strata were claimed by both geologists as Cambrian or Silurian. Lapworth's compromise solution, whereby he erected a new system, the Ordovician, named after the ancient British tribe of the Ordovices dwelling in the

Welsh Borderland, has since found general favour, although occasionally one may still encounter older British text-books, as well as more recent foreign publications, in which only Cambrian and Silurian are used. Although the terms Lower, Middle and Upper Ordovician are sometimes used, it is more usual for geologists to divide the Ordovician rocks into six Series as follows:—Tremadoc, Arenig (after Arenig Mountain, Merionethshire), Llanvirn (after Llanvirn, Pembrokeshire), Llandeilo (after Llandeilo, now Llandilo, Carmarthenshire), Caradoc (after the Caradoc Hills, near Church Stretton, Shropshire), and Ashgill (after Ash Gill, near Coniston Water, in the Lake District.)

The rocks of the Tremadoc Series in the type area comprise dark slates and mudstones containing trilobites which include the genera *Angelina*, *Asaphellus* and *Shumardia*. Notable localities occur near Portmadoc and Penmorfa, Carnarvonshire. This series also marks the first known occurrences of the extinct animals known as graptolites. In the rock these appear typically as single- or multi-branched colonies, sometimes replaced by iron pyrites and generally flattened by compaction of the sediments in which they occur. At one time or another they have been linked by palaeontologists with numerous other animal groups, but are at present regarded as having affinities with the hemichordates, a primitive group allied to the vertebrates. There were two main groups of graptolites, first the so-called dendroids, mesh-like conical forms, for example *Dictyonema*, which appeared in the Tremadoc Series and ranged sporadically through to the Carboniferous, and the true graptolites, such as *Didymograptus* and *Monograptus*, which ranged through the Ordovician and most of the Silurian in Britain. The graptolites were marine in habitat and some of the species have been found to be of extremely wide lateral distribution. This, coupled with the fact that they underwent rapid evolution and marked morphological change during their long history, makes them very useful to the geologist as zonal fossils. To the west of Portmadoc there occurs a widely-distributed thin horizon of dark grey shales, weathering brown, known as the *Dictyonema* Band, in which the dendroid graptolite of that name is found abundantly, preserved in iron pyrites. The stratal equivalents of the Tremadoc Slates of North Wales are well represented in the Midlands and Welsh Borders, where they occur in Shropshire as the Shineton Shales, at Tortworth, Gloucestershire as the Breadstone Shales, in the Malvern district as the Bronsil Shales, and near Nuneaton as the Merevale Shales. These strata form soft, easily-eroded shales and mudstones which contain, especially, graptolites (*Clonograptus*, *Dictyonema*) and trilobites with some cystids (*Macrocystella*) and worms. The exposures in the brook-section at Sheinton (present-day spelling of Shineton) have been a classic collecting ground for many years and contain numerous well-preserved trilobites. Some years ago a bore-hole at Calvert, in Buckinghamshire, showed the existence there of similar rocks underground.

In South Wales rocks of Arenig age occur in the neighbourhood of Whitland and include dark mudstones and shales, some of which contain characteristic graptolites of the genus *Didymograptus*, whilst on Ramsey Island, off St David's, there are outcrops of both graptolitic strata and others, the *Neseuretus* Beds, which contain brachiopods and the trilobite *Neseuretus murchisoni*. The Llanvirn Series is well developed in South Wales, the type succession being situated near Abereiddy Bay, north-east of St David's. The rocks are black mudstones and shales in which graptolites are not uncommon, and the south side of Abereiddy Bay is well known for the occurrence there of large numbers of the so-called 'tuning-fork' graptolite *Didymograptus murchisoni*, strikingly preserved as white films on a background of dark shale matrix. Elsewhere in South Wales graptolitic shales of Llanvirn age are to be found around the towns of Narberth, St Clears and Whitland as well as Llandrindod Wells farther north. In west Shropshire the Arenig Series begins with an almost unfossiliferous quartzite, the Stiperstones Quartzite, but this is succeeded by a large thickness of dark mudstones and shales in which graptolites, brachiopods and trilobites occur. Fossils may be collected from several localities in the Minsterley district, whilst the beds cropping out beside the church at the hamlet of Shelve are famous for their graptolite fauna, which includes numerous dendroid forms. The succeeding Llanvirn strata of the district are somewhat more varied in type, including some volcanic rocks, but they contain both graptolites and trilobites and may be seen at Betton Dingle, near Meadowtown. The trilobites in this part of the succession are closely similar to contemporaneous faunas known from Czechoslovakia (so-called Bohemian faunas) and must have lived in a sea connecting both regions.

In North Wales the Arenig Series crops out in the vicinity of Portmadoc and Bangor, Caernarvonshire. Fossils are not usually abundant but near Arenig Station, Merionethshire, the so-called '*Calymene* Ashes' contain numerous brachiopods and the eponymous trilobite *Neseuretus* (previously *Calymene*) *murchisoni*. The Skiddaw Slates of the Lake District form extensive outcrops centred roughly on Derwentwater and Skiddaw itself, but the rocks, mainly shales and mudstones, have been extensively folded and cleaved, and fossils are not easily collected. However, numbers of graptolites have been found, some of them in a good state of preservation particularly in the vicinity of Keswick and Mungrisdale, indicating that most of the succession belongs to the Arenig and part of the

Llanvirn Series, whilst the Tremadoc may also be represented in the lower strata.

We noted earlier that the Lower Cambrian fossils of the North-West Highlands are of eastern North American type. No fossils of undoubted Middle or Upper Cambrian age are known from the Highlands and the Lower Cambrian beds are there succeeded by a poorly fossiliferous series, the Durness Limestone. The few fossils known from the latter include trilobites, gastropods and cephalopods. They indicate that the affinities of the limestone lie with the Canadian Series (early Ordovician) of Greenland and eastern North America, a relationship which was paralleled yet again, during the Middle Ordovician, in the Girvan district of the Southern Uplands.

It will be seen from the accompanying stratigraphical tables that the Llandeilo Series is equated with only one graptolite zone in the Ordovician succession. However, the beds are often highly fossiliferous and near the town of Llandilo (modern spelling of Llandeilo) in Carmarthenshire they have been subdivided on the basis of the contained trilobites, the trinucleid genus *Marrolithus* being particularly important in this respect. Characteristic fossils may be collected from mudstones and impure limestone bands at quarries in Dynevor Park, as well as at Llan Mill, near Narberth. Elsewhere in South and Central Wales the Llandeilo Series crops out around the spa towns of Builth Wells and Llandrindod Wells in Radnorshire, the rocks forming a succession of dark shales and mudstones in which graptolites (*Diplograptus*, *Glyptograptus*) and trilobites (*Cnemidopyge*, *Ogygiocarella* and *Trinucleus*) are often abundant. Farther north fossiliferous Llandeilo strata of generally similar type may be examined at the village of Meadowtown in west Shropshire where they contain abundant trilobites with subsidiary graptolites and brachiopods. There are restricted outcrops of Llandeilo strata containing characteristic fossils in the Berwyn Hills, in the general area of Llanrhaiadr-ym-Mochnant, Denbighshire. These, however, are some of the most northerly occurrences of Llandeilo fossils in England and Wales, the rocks of this age being either absent or represented by the great thickness of igneous rocks forming the Borrowdale Volcanic Series of the Lake District.

The transition from the Llandeilo to the Caradoc Series is continuous and observable at relatively few places. In the area south-east of the Pre-Cambrian and Cambrian rocks forming the Church Stretton Hills in South Shropshire the only Ordovician rocks developed are those of Caradoc age, but a few miles farther west, in the Shelve area of West Shropshire, there is a remarkably full development from the Tremadoc to the Caradoc. The Caradoc strata of south-east Shropshire are famous for their fossils, and the rocks were laid down on the bottom of a shallow sea in which brachiopods, trilobites, polyzoans and ostracods flourished in large numbers. The basal beds are said to be diachronous, that is to say they were not all formed at the same time, owing to the gradual encroachment of the sea over the shoreline of earlier rocks. The valley of the River Onny cuts through almost the whole Caradoc succession of the district, and the highest beds yield large numbers of the trinucleid trilobite *Onnia* at the well-known section in the river bank south-west of the village of Wistanstow. Outside Shropshire, fossiliferous Caradoc strata are developed over much of North Wales, but we may profitably single out the Berwyn Hills, the Lleyn Peninsula around Pwllheli, the Bala district and the neighbourhood of Welshpool. The last includes the famous 'Trilobite Dingle', more properly Bron-y-Buckley Wood, with its large fauna of trinucleid trilobites, especially *Salterolithus caractaci.* The igneous rocks of Snowdonia belong to this series, and they too sometimes contain shales and mudstones with trilobites and brachiopods, for example at the summit of Snowdon. The higher Caradoc beds of North Wales are graptolitic shales, whilst the whole succession in South Wales is made up almost entirely of dark mudstones and shales in which graptolites are the chief fossils, though an impure limestone with corals occurs at Robeston Wathen, Pembrokeshire. The North of England has fossiliferous Caradoc beds well exposed near the villages of Knock and Dufton in Westmorland, and a narrow outcrop of strata runs diagonally across the Lake District from near Shap Fell in the north-east to Millom in the south-west. The latter rocks yield poorly preserved trilobites, brachiopods and corals at several localities and are overlain by the beds of the Ashgill Series, here forming a parallel outcrop. In Scotland Caradoc beds are developed in the Girvan and Moffat districts of the Southern uplands. The Moffat succession is made up of graptolitic shales containing genera and species which are found in the Anglo-Welsh area as well as elsewhere, but near Girvan the beds, which are often highly fossiliferous at Balclatchie, Dow Hill and Ardmillan, contain trilobite-brachiopod faunas closely similar to those of the eastern United States, and bearing almost no relationship to contemporary Anglo-Welsh faunas.

As already noted, the Ashgill Series has its type area near Coniston Water and fossils may be found at several points along the Lake District outcrop, particularly near the village of Torver, Lancashire. Elsewhere in Northern England characteristic faunas can be collected at the hamlet of Keisley, south-east of Dufton, Westmorland, and at Cautley, near Sedbergh, Yorkshire. Farther north the Girvan district has produced several prolific localities, one of the best known being Thraive Glen, where the large fauna includes trilobites, brachiopods and echinoderms, some of which are illustrated here. In North Wales fossiliferous Ashgill rocks occur at numerous places, including Rhiwlas, near Bala, Merionethshire; Bryn Hendre and Deganwy, near Conway, Caernarvonshire; and various points around the Berwyn Hills, such as Glyn Ceiriog. In South Wales they are well exposed around St Clears and Haverfordwest. The faunas of shelly type in the Ashgill rocks were much more cosmopolitan in character than those of preceding series, and broadly similar assemblages are found not only over the Anglo-Welsh area but also in Scotland, Eire, Scandinavia, Poland and Czechoslovakia.

Before leaving the Ordovician rocks, mention must be made of an interesting horizon which, although strictly speaking, should be included in the Trias, nevertheless belongs with the Ordovician, and to a lesser extent Devonian, as far as its fossils are concerned. Exposed in the cliff-sections a short distance west of Budleigh Salterton, on the South Devon coast, is a bed containing rounded pebbles of liver coloured quartzite. Some of these contain well-preserved trilobites and brachiopods belonging to species otherwise unknown in Britain. The fossils and their enclosing matrix can be matched exactly with those of an horizon in Normandy known as the Grès de May, and the Budleigh Salterton pebbles represent the products of erosion of a land-mass lying south of Britain during the Triassic period. Similar pebbles have also been recorded from the Bunter Sandstone (Trias) in the Midlands, around Birmingham.

The Silurian System was first named by Murchison in 1835 after the Silures, an ancient British tribe inhabiting what is now the Welsh Border region between Shropshire and Montgomeryshire. It is perhaps best known from its development in the agricultural country of Shropshire south-east of The Longmynd and the Church Stretton Hills, where the rock-succession is composed mainly of thick mudstones and shales alternating with extensive developments of massive and nodular limestones. The latter are more resistant to erosion than the intervening shales and so give rise to the topographical ridges or 'edges'—Wenlock Edge is the best-known—for which the county is famous.

Over much of the Anglo-Welsh region the time interval covering the later part of the Ordovician and the beginning of the Silurian coincided with pronounced earth-movements—the so-called Taconian Orogeny—as a result of which the highest Ordovician and lowest Silurian strata are absent from some districts. Just as the Ordovician rocks are subdivided into a number of Series named after places in the Anglo-Welsh region, so the Silurian rocks are divided into three Series, namely Llandovery, Wenlock and Ludlow. A complete succession of Llandovery strata occurs in relatively few parts of the British Silurian outcrop. In the neighbourhood of the towns of Llandovery and Haverfordwest in South Wales the earlier Llandovery beds comprise in the main sandy mudstones containing large numbers of brachiopods and some trilobites. They are well exposed along the valley of the River Cleddau near the Gasworks at Haverfordwest, Pembrokeshire. In the Southern Uplands of Scotland mudstones of Llandovery age, often highly fossiliferous, occur around Newlands and Mulloch Hill, north-east of Girvan. All these strata represent deposits formed in shallower parts of the sea, but the rocks laid down in the deeper waters of the same sea are of a different facies, comprising a thinner succession of dark shales and mudstones with graptolites (especially *Monograptus*), often abundant and beautifully preserved in iron pyrites. Graptolitic beds of this type are to be found in North and Central Wales, and in the Lake District, where good specimens of *Monograptus* may be collected at Skelgill and Browgill, both near Ambleside, as well as from other parts of the outcrop. The Llandovery beds of the Moffat district, Dumfriesshire, are also essentially graptolitic, contrasting with the shelly development of Girvan and so following the general pattern of distribution existing in the Southern Uplands during part of the Ordovician.

Outcrops of the highest Llandovery strata are more widely distributed than those of the earlier beds and often highly fossiliferous, containing numerous brachiopods, trilobites and corals. In South Shropshire there is an interesting development of conglomerates and limestones with the brachiopod *Pentamerus*, resting on Pre-Cambrian rocks around the margins of The Longmynd. The beds were evidently deposited very close to the shore-line of a sea in which The Longmynd was either an island or an area of very shallow water. Farther south, fossiliferous beds of both similar and later age occur at May Hill, near Longhope, Herefordshire; at Tortworth, Gloucestershire, where the solitary button-like coral *Palaeocyclus* is abundant; and in South Wales at Marloes Bay, Pembrokeshire. In the Welsh Borders the highest Llandovery strata are shales which pass upwards into the rocks of the Wenlock Series, comprising a lower group of shales, followed by a thick group of massive and nodular limestones. These two horizons, known respectively as the Wenlock Shales and Wenlock Limestone, are typically developed around Much Wenlock. Parts of the Wenlock Limestone represent a development of reefs, and large quarries in the vicinity of Much Wenlock and along Wenlock Edge yield especially corals, polyzoans, and brachiopods. To the east, the Wenlock Limestone of Dudley was a classic source of fossils and large numbers of beautifully preserved brachiopods, trilobites, corals, polyzoans and echinoderms were collected during the 18th and 19th centuries, particularly from the outcrops at Wren's Nest Hill. Unfortunately for present-day collectors most of the fossiliferous limestone was removed by quarrying and used as a flux in the smelting of local Coal Measure ironstones, but some fossils are still obtainable from the adjacent strata. As one moves west from Wenlock Edge the Wenlock Limestone dies out and is replaced by a more graptolitic development of strata, for example at the Long Mountain, near Middletown, Shropshire, although an interesting development of slightly earlier geological age, the Woolhope Limestone, with numerous corals, is found near Old Radnor. The graptolites from the Wenlock Series include easily-recognized species such as *Monograptus priodon*, in which the thecae are of conspicuously hook-like form. Generally speaking the Wenlock faunas are widely distributed, and often have marked affinities with their Scandinavian contemporaries. Rocks and fossils of this series have been proved at depth in boreholes in the south-east of England, whilst in parts of North Wales, as well as the Lake District, the rock succession contains coarser sediments in which fossils are less common. Wenlock strata are present in the Southern Uplands of Scotland but the beds are highly folded, and the fossils are mainly graptolites with smaller numbers of trilobites and brachiopods.

The rocks of the Ludlow Series are best known from their type-area around the old town of the same name in south Shropshire. The succession there, which follows upon the Wenlock Limestone, was at one time divided simply into three parts, the Lower Ludlow Shales, Aymestry Limestone and Upper Ludlow Shales, but modern refinements in stratigraphy have resulted in the introduction of several new terms. The Lower Ludlow Shales are soft, graptolitic shales, easily eroded and forming the valley of Hope Dale; good exposures are not plentiful, but fossils can be collected at Upper Millichope, five miles south-east of Church Stretton. The succeeding Aymestry Limestone forms the well-known scarp of View Edge, and its north-easterly extension parallel to Wenlock Edge. The limestone is often highly fossiliferous, containing large numbers of brachiopods and corals, but its most spectacular development is seen in the large quarry at Weo Edge, overlooking Craven Arms, where it is composed almost entirely of the valves of the large brachiopod *Conchidium knighti*, though whole specimens are rather difficult to extract. The shaly strata about the horizon of the Aymestry Limestone contain the last-known British graptolites, though the group survived into the Devonian elsewhere. The succeeding beds, previously known as the Upper Ludlow Shales, are often rich in shelly fossils, particularly brachiopods such as *Camarotoechia*, *Dayia* and *Protochonetes*. The rocks may be examined at numerous points along the dip-slope behind View Edge; by the road from Craven Arms to

Ludlow; at Ludlow itself, especially near the Castle; and at localities around Bringewood Chase, near Ludlow. Researches during recent years have shown that the Ludlow rocks of the Welsh Borders and adjacent districts were laid down in the shallower, marginal or 'shelf' areas of the Silurian sea, whilst farther west, in Central Wales, the rocks represent deposition under deeper marine conditions, the so-called 'basin' deposits. The fauna of the basin rocks differs in many respects from that of the shelf deposits and contains more graptolites and molluscs. Limestone horizons are generally absent and the strata, which are considerably thicker than those of the border counties, consist mainly of siltstones and flags, but despite the differences in lithology enough characteristic fossils have been found to effect a reasonable correlation. Ludlow strata of this type form large outcrops in Wales, but particular mention may be made of the areas around Usk and Builth Wells. A conspicuous feature of the rocks both here and in the Denbighshire Moors of North Wales is the presence of curious contorted strata, and these are interpreted as having been formed by the sliding and slumping of layers of unconsolidated muds along gentle slopes of the sea-floors. Farther north, in the Lake District, a large thickness of Ludlow strata is developed, forming a wide outcrop extending north-eastwards across the area, parallel to those of earlier strata. The rocks are exposed in the neighbourhood of Windermere, Kendal and Kirkby Lonsdale, and comprise slates, grits and flags in which fossils, particularly brachiopods similar to those of the Welsh Borders, occur, usually in bands.

Over most of the British Isles the period of time about the end of the Silurian and the beginning of the Devonian was marked by pronounced physiographical changes which were reflected in the types of sediments laid down. Earth-movements, forming part of what has been termed the Caledonian Orogeny, caused uplift of the region now embracing Wales and neighbouring areas together with parts of Scotland. As a result, the Silurian marine deposits of Wales and the English Midlands were supplanted by either terrestrial strata or beds laid down under deltaic or semi-fluviatile conditions. With these changes in lithology the marine animals of the Ludlow Series were replaced by assemblages composed essentially of inarticulate brachiopods, gastropods and primitive fish-like ostracoderms which probably lived in fresh and brackish water. The deposits so formed comprise large thicknesses of mainly arenaceous strata to which the name Old Red Sandstone was applied last century by Murchison to distinguish the beds from the later New Red Sandstone, of Permian and Triassic age. In the absence of the more useful marine invertebrate fossils the stratigraphy of the Lower Old Red Sandstone is often difficult to elucidate, but the succession has been divided into a number of Stages and Zones, named after places in the Welsh Borders and characterized by different genera and species of ostracoderms which have proved of great value in correlating the rocks not only in Great Britain but also with other parts of Europe and as far afield as Greenland and North America. These animals were not true fishes; they carried an armour-like covering of thick plates, and were distantly related to the present-day lampreys and hag-fishes. In the Midland Valley of Scotland the transition from marine conditions of deposition began somewhat earlier than in the Anglo-Welsh area, and near the town of Lesmahagow, in Lanarkshire, strata of Upper Silurian age are of shallow-water type, passing upwards into typical Old Red Sandstone, and have yielded ostracoderms as well as numerous arthropods, including the eurypterid *Pterygotus*. In parts of the Welsh Borders the base of the Old Red Sandstone is marked by an interesting, though irregularly distributed, deposit known as the Ludlow Bone Bed. As the name implies, it consists essentially of fish fragments and teeth, embedded in a loose, weathered matrix and showing signs of having been rolled around and abraded on the floor of a shallow sea. The bed crops out at Ludlow and at intervals along the north-west side of Corve Dale, a valley running north-eastwards from near Ludlow. Other localities for collecting Old Red Sandstone fishes are distributed over the Clee Hills of Shropshire, though specimens are not common, whilst across the border in Wales, large outcrops of Old Red Sandstone form the hills of the Brecon Beacons. *Cephalaspis* and *Pteraspis* are perhaps the best-known genera of Old Red Sandstone ostracoderms, whilst the horny brachiopod *Lingula* and the large bivalve *Archanodon* may be locally abundant. In Cornwall the corresponding beds, which are well exposed in Bude Bay and on the south coast around Polperro, have been highly distorted by earth-movements and are known as the Dartmouth Slates. The ostracoderms in them occur in an extremely tattered condition and their fragments were originally described as sponges!

Only traces of Old Red Sandstone occur in the north of England, but the series is well represented in Scotland, and Dura Den, near St Andrews, is a classic locality in the Upper Old Red Sandstone once noted for fossil fishes in an excellent state of preservation, representing the inhabitants of a small lake which had quickly become filled up. The Orkney and Shetland Isles, together with the neighbouring parts of the mainland, also afford good outcrops of Old Red Sandstone, Only the middle and upper parts of the series are represented, comprising mainly sandy beds showing shallow-water characteristics, and the remains of fossil fishes may be locally abundant, for example at Thurso and other places in

Caithness. These were true fishes, related to the living lung-fishes and coelacanth.

At the same time as most of the Old Red Sandstone was being laid down in England and Wales, the south-west of England, including Devonshire which gave its name to the Devonian System, was covered by a sea which extended eastwards into Europe, in particular Belgium, north France and Germany. In south Devonshire, limestones are well exposed along and near the coast in the neighbourhood of Torquay, for example at Hope's Nose, and contain numerous corals, brachiopods and trilobites whose affinities are with corresponding faunas in Germany. Some of the Devonian strata of south Devonshire include thin limestones together with other beds indicating muddier conditions of deposition, and their fauna, whilst lacking corals and certain brachiopods, contains the cephalopods known as goniatites, and some trilobites. The former group, so-named after the angular form of the septal sutures—the lines marking the junction of the shell with the septa dividing its interior into separate chambers—bear the same relation to Upper Palaeozoic stratigraphy as do the ammonites in the Mesozoic, and have enabled the rock-succession to be divided into numerous stages and zones which may often be correlated over large distances. Fossil localities are numerous in South Devonshire, but we may perhaps single out the Chudleigh, Newton Abbot and Torquay districts, whilst Mudstone Bay and Saltern Cove, both near Brixham, are well known for their goniatites. Outcrops of marine Devonian rocks extend also into Cornwall, where fossils, including goniatites, have been found at several localities around Padstow. The Devonian strata of north Devonshire represent an intermediate type of succession comprising marine rocks with alternations of Old Red Sandstone type, sometimes with fish and plant remains. Some of the marine strata in the Ilfracombe district contain brachiopods (*Stringocephalus*) and corals (*Heliolites*) whilst at Fremington the Pilton Beds have yielded trilobites, brachiopods and goniatites, and represent a process of sedimentation which was continuous during late Devonian and early Carboniferous times.

The Carboniferous System derives its name from the fact that it contains all the important coal-producing strata of Britain. Despite this, however, there is a great variety of rock-types involved, ranging from pure limestones to sandstones and coals. The thickness of rocks is considerable, and in North America the equivalent strata have acquired the status of two separate systems, the Mississippian and Pennsylvanian. The British Carboniferous succession may be divided approximately into three parts, to which the somewhat generalized names of Carboniferous Limestone, Millstone Grit and Coal Measures, indicative of the typical lithologies, have been applied in ascending order. The Carboniferous Limestone corresponds broadly to the Lower Carboniferous, whilst the Millstone Grit and Coal Measures constitute the Upper Carboniferous, though problems have sometimes arisen regarding the exact position of the boundaries. As in the case of other systems, the Carboniferous rocks have been subdivided into Stages founded on palaeontological criteria and named after the places where the strata are best developed. Amongst others, the names Avonian and Dinantian have been used for the Lower Carboniferous, but it is now more usual to divide the succession into two parts, successively Tournaisian and Viséan, named after districts in Belgium. Similarly the terms Namurian, Westphalian and Stephanian are used for the Upper Carboniferous.

Outcrops of Lower Carboniferous rocks are widely distributed over much of the British Isles, the rocks in the main comprising large thicknesses of grey limestones, deposited in seas of moderate depth which covered most of England, North and South Wales, and were linked with extensive contemporaneous seas in central Europe. Considerable lateral variations in rock-type occur, and these in turn are reflected in the types of fossils present, but in general there are large numbers of corals, brachiopods, polyzoans and algae. The so-called compound corals are important rock-formers in the more massive types of limestone, and their colonies are made up of numerous individual corallites growing together, each corallite being cylindrical or polygonal in cross-section. *Lithostrotion* and *Lonsdaleia* are abundant, widespread genera. Brachiopods are often prolific in the Lower Carboniferous, belonging to numerous genera and families, and frequently of stratigraphical value. The productoids and spiriferids are the most noteworthy. Cephalopods, particularly the goniatites, and trilobites are subsidiary in numbers, but often important stratigraphically.

Probably the most famous of all British Lower Carboniferous sections is that exposed along the gorge of the River Avon at Bristol. The lowest Carboniferous strata, which overlie Old Red Sandstone, crop out at the Avonmouth end of the gorge, and one moves through successively higher beds towards the Clifton Suspension Bridge. At the beginning of the century the area provided the setting for Vaughan's classic work on the Lower Carboniferous succession, which he subdivided into a number of zones, founded on coral and brachiopod genera. Palaeontological refinements since then have necessitated detailed changes in our conception of Lower Carboniferous stratigraphy, but the basic framework of Vaughan's zones remains. The massive limestones of the Avon Gorge have been extensively quarried, so that exposures are numerous. Characteristic fossils, especially corals and brachiopods were formerly abundant, though their extraction from the fresh rock is now often difficult. The lower Carboniferous outcrop continues south-westwards into the Mendip Hills where the strata are overlain by Jurassic beds, the normally intervening strata being absent. Exposures of fossiliferous limestone are abundant, but particularly fine sections may be examined along the Cheddar Gorge and at Burrington Coombe nearby. West and north of the Bristol district the thickness of Lower Carboniferous rocks gradually diminishes, and in the Forest of Dean, in Gloucestershire, as well as on the eastern side of the Clee Hills of Shropshire, the rocks are thin and more arenaceous in character, indicating that they were laid down under shallower marine conditions along the margins of a land mass, to which the name St George's Land has been given, comprising most of what is now Wales and extending westwards as far as south-eastern Ireland. In the Forest of Dean, fossils may be found near Coleford and Mitcheldean, whilst at the Clee Hills, sandy limestones in Oreton quarries, near Farlow, yield many brachiopods as well as fish fragments, chiefly the teeth and spines of primitive sharks. In South Wales, Lower Carboniferous limestones and sandstones form a rim enclosing the area of the South Wales Coalfield, but are not encountered again in the Principality until one reaches North Wales, where extensive outcrops of fossiliferous limestones occur in the vicinity of Llangollen, Llandudno and the Vale of Clwyd, and are represented to a lesser extent farther west, on Anglesey. These North Welsh outcrops extend eastwards into the North Midlands, where they are well developed in Derbyshire, especially around the towns of Matlock and Castleton. The rocks here consist mainly of limestones with shelly fossils and subsidiary shales containing goniatites, and represent marine strata deposited on the north and east sides of St George's Land. Among the many interesting features of the Derbyshire strata are the existence of local volcanic rocks, known as toadstones, and the presence in the Lower Carboniferous rocks of some of the few commercial oil deposits in Britain. Near Castleton, for example at Treak Cliff, and at Dovedale, there occur pure, poorly-bedded limestones, sometimes forming small conical hills, in which a locally abundant and specialized fauna of thick-shelled brachiopods and molluscs is found. The structures have been termed knoll-reefs, and they represent the remnants of deposits formed not far from a coast-line, and occupying a position analogous to many present-day reefs. Corals, with the exception of the genus *Amplexus*, are generally absent from the knoll-reefs. Travelling north from Derbyshire one does not encounter Lower Carboniferous outcrops again until one reaches the Pennines in the region of Skipton, whence they continue unbroken into Berwickshire. Over the southern part of these outcrops the Lower Carboniferous consists largely of massive grey limestones which form well marked topographical features and abundantly justify the name Mountain Limestone which was applied to them during the last century. However, the details of the rock-succession differ considerably, as do the faunas, from those farther south, and there are also marked lateral variations. Dark shales containing the stratigraphically important goniatites are well represented, particularly in the Bowland (or Bolland) Shales of the Bowland Forest area on the Yorkshire–Lancashire border, whilst knoll-reefs are an important feature of the geology of the Clitheroe–Settle district, where they form conspicuous topographical features. As in Derbyshire the knoll-reefs are highly fossiliferous, for example at Coplow Quarry, near Clitheroe. The reefs are believed to vary in their mode of formation, some representing mounds of débris on the sea-floor, surrounded by contemporaneous shales, whilst others are remnants of a once continuous deposit, since eroded and with the intervening spaces filled by shales of later age.

The highest Lower Carboniferous rocks of the Northern Pennines comprise what is known as the Yoredale Series, so-called after the old name of Wensleydale. The rocks represent deposition under a particular set of conditions rather than a definitely restricted horizon, and their age is somewhat variable, so that they sometimes bridge the boundary between Lower and Upper Carboniferous. One of the most interesting features of the Yoredale rocks is the manner in which a particular cycle of deposition is repeated several times, a process known as rhythmic sedimentation. In this case the cycle consists of the ascending sequence of limestone, shale, sandstone and coal, and indicates initial deposition under marine conditions, followed by shallowing so as to produce conditions suitable for plant life which provided the raw material for the coal. Fossiliferous limestones of this group are well exposed in the valleys of Wensleydale and Swaledale, as well as on the neighbouring high ground. When traced into the Bowland Forest area the beds of the Yoredale Series are found to pass laterally into the Bowland Shales. Lower Carboniferous rocks are well developed in the north of England, where good sections are exposed along the Northumberland coast, near Alnwick and Berwick, as well as in the Midland Valley of Scotland. Generally speaking the succession, which is often highly fossiliferous, differs from that found elsewhere in the British Lower Carboniferous in that it includes numerous thin limestone horizons. The strata of the Midland Valley are economically important and contain the so-called Oil Shales, from which crude oil is obtained by distillation, as well as commercial coal deposits. Additional coals occur higher in the Carboniferous succession, coeval with certain of the Anglo-Welsh Coal

Measures, of Ammanian age (see Tables), whilst Central and Southern Scotland were the scene of intense volcanic activity throughout much of the Carboniferous period.

The rocks of the Millstone Grit are typically developed in the north of England as a series of alternating sandstones or 'grits' and shales, the former giving rise to the characteristic escarpments in the topography west and north-west of Bradford and Leeds, as well as in parts of Derbyshire. The sandstones were deposited in shallow water, in the delta of a large river flowing from a land-mass to the north or north-east. On the other hand, the shales represent deposits of marine muds laid down when the area was periodically submerged below sea-level and they contain the fossils of marine animals, in particular those of the goniatites (e.g. *Reticuloceras*) which, as in the Devonian rocks, have proved of great value in correlation over wide areas. Sometimes the goniatites are preserved as three-dimensional moulds in nodules, but they are more commonly found as flattened impressions in black shales, though the details of the surface ornamentation are often well preserved. Profitable collecting grounds are to be found in Derbyshire, at Edale and near Castleton; in Lancashire, near Preston and Whalley; and in Yorkshire, near Hebden Bridge, Keighley, Lothersdale, Marsden and Todmorden. Strata of Millstone Grit age are well developed around the margins of the South Wales coalfield, where they are separated by a marked stratigraphical break from the underlying Lower Carboniferous rocks.

From an economic standpoint the Coal Measures form the most important part of the geological column in Britain. The coals themselves form only a small fraction of the thickness of rock present, and the series represents the fossilized remains of deltas and forest swamps in the fringes of land areas occupying what is now the Highlands of Scotland and also extending from east to west across the centre of England and Wales. Similar conditions prevailed over much of north-west Europe, but in the Mediterranean region and eastern Europe the equivalent strata are marine deposits. The forests of the Coal Measure swamps probably thrived in a warm, moist climate, and several plant groups were represented. They included giant club-mosses or Lycopodiales such as *Lepidodendron* and *Sigillaria*, together with horse-tails or Equisetales (*Annularia* and *Calamites*), tree-ferns or Filicales, and a group of seed-bearing fern-like plants, the Pteridosperms, exemplified by *Neuropteris*. Attempts have been made to sub-divide the rocks stratigraphically, on the basis of their included fossil plants, into a number of stages and 'floral zones'; these may be used fairly successfully over short distances, but have generally proved less reliable for correlation than fossil invertebrates. As might be expected the Coal Measure forests supported an insect population, the remains of which, including large dragonflies, have sometimes been found. Vertebrates were also present, and included fishes and amphibians together with the first representatives of the reptiles. The streams traversing the swamps often contained large numbers of bivalves which have been likened to present-day fresh-water forms such as *Unio*. The Coal Measure bivalves, which include the genera *Carbonicola*, *Anthraconaia* and *Naiadites* amongst others, lived in water which need not necessarily have been fresh, and they were probably able to tolerate a certain degree of salinity. Their remains have proved of great value in correlation, and the Coal Measure succession has been divided into zones on the basis of the various genera and species. The swamps were low-lying and underwent occasional submergence, when marine strata were deposited. The latter, known as Marine Bands, are relatively thin by comparison with the other beds but contain marine fossils, for example brachiopods together with goniatites such as *Gastrioceras* which enable more precise correlations to be made. Sometimes the goniatites are found uncrushed, preserved in nodules which are known to the miners as bullions. The fauna of the marine bands may also include fish remains, whilst horizons containing the brachiopod *Lingula* suggest brackish conditions of deposition.

As a result of extensive earth-movements at the end of the Carboniferous period, the rocks formed during that time were folded into a number of troughs and basins which form the principal coal-fields at the present day. Open-cast workings afford facilities for collecting fossils in place, but as coal is mostly mined in Britain it is to the tip-heaps of waste material that the collector must turn for most of his specimens. Exploitation of coal resources has been carried out on such a large scale that it is impossible to give here a comprehensive list of fossil localities, but in the Bristol-Somerset coalfield the Radstock district is well-known for its fossil plants, whilst in the South Wales coalfield the districts of Aberdare, Caerphilly, Merthyr Tydfil and Pontypridd, amongst many others, have yielded abundant floras and faunas. The Coal Measures of Coseley in Staffordshire, and Coalbrookdale, near Ironbridge in Shropshire, have long been famous for their beautifully preserved fossils, including brachiopods (*Brachythyris*) and arthropods (*Euproops*) as well as plants. In the northern counties fossils of both marine and non-marine type may be obtained in Yorkshire at Baildon, near Bradford, and Horsforth, near Leeds; in Lancashire, near Bolton and Wigan; and in Staffordshire near Burton-upon-Trent. As yet we have made no mention of the Carboniferous rocks in the far south-west of England. The entire Carboniferous succession in Devonshire, a structurally complicated region, is made up of cherts and shales together with some bands of poor quality coal known locally as culm, hence the name Culm Measures which is sometimes applied to the rocks. Though much of the succession is unfossiliferous, some of the beds contain goniatites, bivalves and trilobites which have facilitated a correlation with corresponding strata in Northern England and North Germany. Lower Carboniferous strata of this type crop out to the south-west of Barnstaple, where they include the well-known fossil locality of Coddon (or Codden) Hill, and farther south-west, in the Bideford region, they pass upwards into Upper Carboniferous beds containing occasional plant remains.

We have already noted that the end of the Carboniferous Period in Britain coincided with extensive earth-movements. In consequence of these, non-marine conditions prevailed over the region and the rocks laid down comprise marls and sandstones containing no organic remains. Thus began the prolonged arid or semi-arid conditions which continued through the Permian and into the Triassic period of the Mesozoic and produced the deposits known as the New Red Sandstone, a series of events analogous in some ways to those which led to the formation of the Old Red Sandstone some 170 million years earlier. Although the British Isles are well endowed as far as outcrops of Carboniferous and earlier strata are concerned, Permian rocks are comparatively poorly represented and those available afford few opportunities for the fossil collector, though they are interesting geologically and often important economically. The most fossiliferous British Permian strata are found in the north of England and include, in particular, the Upper Permian of County Durham. The Marl Slate at Ferryhill is a fissile sandy limestone which has produced well-preserved fossil fishes, for example *Palaeoniscus*, and plants of a type similar to those found at the corresponding horizon in North Germany. The highest Permian rocks of County Durham are made up of extensive limestone deposits, not the more usual types of limestone which are predominantly calcium carbonate, but the so-called Magnesian Limestones, in which much of the carbonate present is magnesium carbonate. Certain of the Magnesian Limestones contain curious structures, sometimes superficially resembling fossils but in fact inorganic in origin, whilst others are associated with large-scale deposits similar in form to present-day reefs. The latter sometimes yield fairly well-preserved brachiopods, such as *Pterospirifer* and the spinose productid *Horridonia*, together with bivalves and polyzoans. The beds are exposed in the Sunderland district, as well as on the coast farther south-east. In the Pennine region the Permian succession consists predominantly of sandstones with impersistent beds of coarse conglomerate known locally as Brockrams. These beds are unfossiliferous, but an associated bed of sandy shales exposed near the village of Hilton in Westmorland is well known for its fossil plants. The underground evaporite deposits of north-east Yorkshire, comprising minerals formed by the evaporation, under arid conditions, of shallow, semi-isolated stretches of sea-water, are found in Permian rocks, whilst in parts of Scotland there occur igneous rocks of the same general age. Over most of the country, however, the Palaeozoic era closed with the formation of the New Red Sandstone, almost devoid of fossils and passing upwards without any significant break into the earliest Mesozoic strata.

W. T. D.

GEOLOGICAL TIME-SCALE†

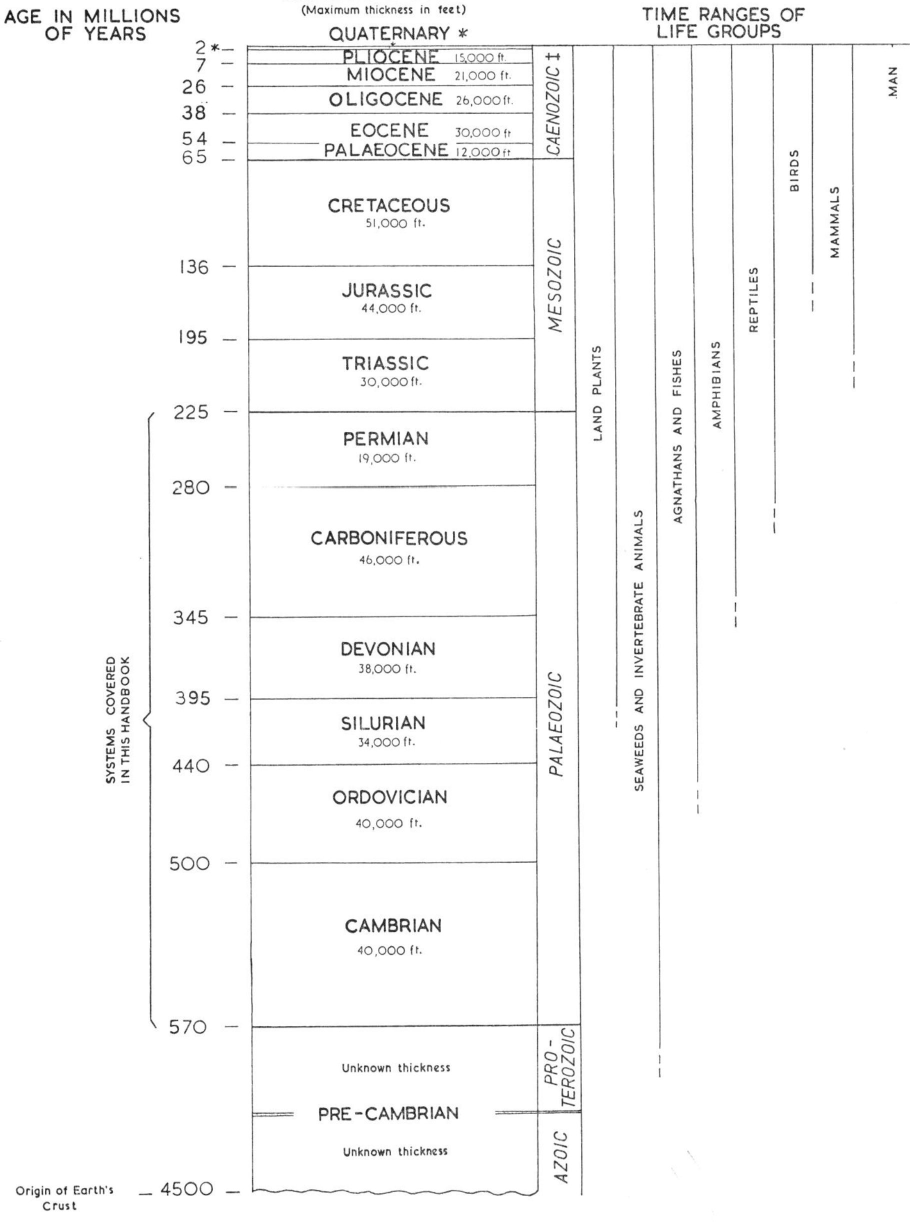

† Time-scale approximate with probable error of ± 5% throughout
* Quaternary (Pleistocene and Holocene) 6,000 feet +
‡ Caenozoic = Tertiary (Palaeocene - Pliocene) + Quaternary
Column proportional to time-scale

Stratigraphical Tables

of

British Palaeozoic Strata

I. Cambrian

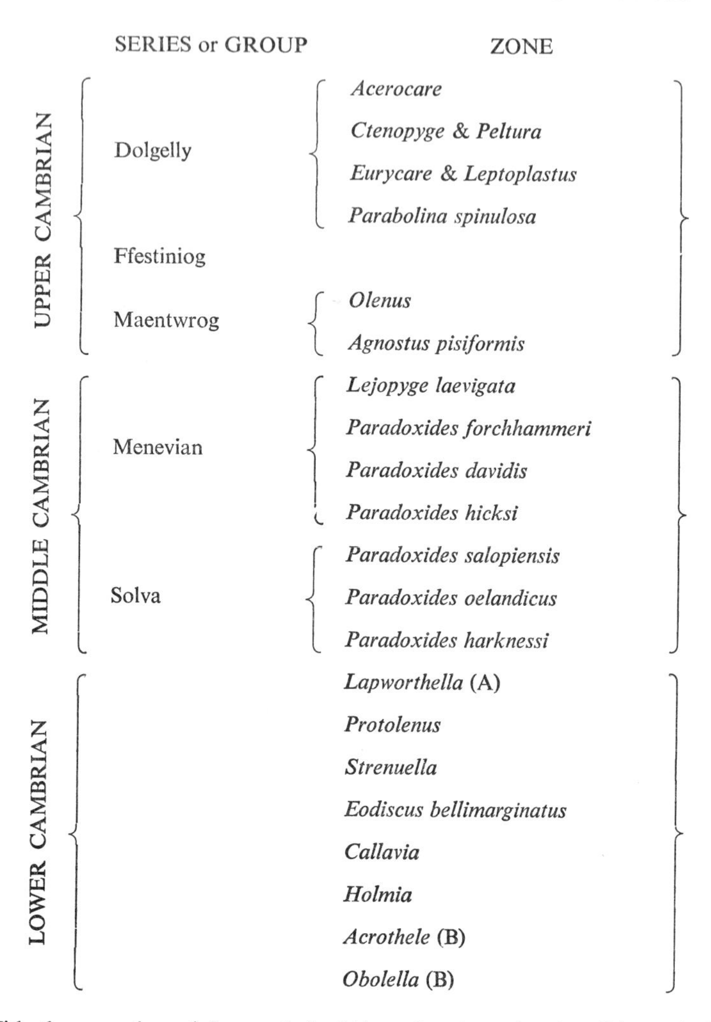

	SERIES or GROUP	ZONE
UPPER CAMBRIAN	Dolgelly	*Acerocare*
		Ctenopyge & *Peltura*
		Eurycare & *Leptoplastus*
		Parabolina spinulosa
	Ffestiniog	
	Maentwrog	*Olenus*
		Agnostus pisiformis
MIDDLE CAMBRIAN	Menevian	*Lejopyge laevigata*
		Paradoxides forchhammeri
		Paradoxides davidis
		Paradoxides hicksi
	Solva	*Paradoxides salopiensis*
		Paradoxides oelandicus
		Paradoxides harknessi
LOWER CAMBRIAN		*Lapworthella* (A)
		Protolenus
		Strenuella
		Eodiscus bellimarginatus
		Callavia
		Holmia
		Acrothele (B)
		Obolella (B)

With the exception of *Lapworthella* (A), assigned to the Annelida and the trilobites. Only the Lower Cambrian is represented in north-west Scotland, where cannot be applied. The succession there comprises: Basal Quartzite, Pipe Rock,

System

TYPICAL BRITISH STRATA

Lingula Flags (North & South Wales)

Orusia Shales (Shropshire)

Whiteleaved Oak Shales (Malvern Hills)

Monks Park, Moor Wood & Outwoods Shales (Nuneaton)

Harlech Series (*pars*), Menevian Beds,

Nant-pig Mudstones (North Wales)

Menevian and Solva Groups (South Wales)

Abbey, Oldbury and Upper Purley Shales (Nuneaton)

Upper Comley Sandstone (Shropshire)

Harlech Series (*pars*), Hell's Mouth Grits (North Wales)

Caerfai Beds (South Wales)

Wrekin Quartzite, Lower Comley Sandstone and Limestones (Shropshire)

Malvern Quartzite, Hollybush Sandstone (Malverns)

Park Hill Quartzite, Camp Hill Quartzite, Lower Purley Shales (Nuneaton)

inarticulate brachiopods *Acrothele* and *Obolella* (B), all the zonal indices are
the faunas are of North American type and the zonal scheme outlined above
Fucoid Beds and Serpulite Grit.

Stage	Zone	Symbol	Beds
	Upper *Caninia*[2] Zone	C_2S_1	Lower Clifton Down Limestone, Lower Cromhall Sandstone (Bristol district); *Caninia* Shales and Dolomite (South Wales); Whitehead Limestone (Forest of Dean, Gloucester, and Chepstow); Lower Red Beds and Pebble Bed Group (Breedon, Leicestershire); Weaver Hills Beds, Cauldon Low Limestone with '*Productus humerosus*' (North Staffordshire); Castletown Limestone in part (Isle of Man); Reef Limestones of Bolland, Salt Hill, Coplow, Clitheroe (Lancashire); Slaidburn (Yorkshire); Embsay Limestone (Yorkshire); Fell Sandstone Series [C_2S_1], Cambeck Beds [C_2] (North Cumberland); Gastropod Beds, Orton and Ashfell Sandstone in part (Westmorland).
TOURNAISIAN	Lower *Caninia*[2] Zone	C_1	Black Rock Dolomite & Gully Oolite (Bristol district); *Caninia* Dolomite and Oolite, Main Limestone in part (South Wales); Chatburn Limestone in part (Lancashire); Eshton Moor Beds (Yorkshire); *Solenopora* Beds (Weaver Hills, Staffordshire; Westmorland); Cementstone Series (North Cumberland & Northumberland); Main Algal Series, Bewcastle Beds, Lynebank Beds in part (Liddesdale, North Cumberland and Roxburghshire); Shap and Ravenstonedale Dolomite Series (Westmorland); Cementstone Group in part (Scotland); Randerstone Limestones (Fife, Scotland).
	Zaphrentis Zone	Z_1 & Z_2	Black Rock Limestone in part (Bristol); Main Limestone in part (South Wales); Fish Beds (Bristol, & Clee Hills, Shropshire); Cementstone Series in part, Lynebank Beds in part (North Cumberland); Pinskey Gill Beds [Z_2] (Westmorland); Cementstone Group in part (North-east England & Scotland).
	Cleistopora[1] Zone	K_1 & K_2	Lower Limestone Shales (South-west England & South Wales); Shirehampton Beds, Palate (Fish) Bed, Bryozoa Bed (Bristol); ?Skrinkle Sandstones (Pembrokeshire); Cefn Bryn Shales (Gower, South Wales).

[1] *Cleistopora* now *Vaughania*. [2] *Caninia* now replaced by *Syringothyris*. [3] *Seminula* now *Composita*.
[4] Coral-brachiopod Zone D_2 is approximately equivalent to Cephalopod-bivalve Zone P_1 (see p. 27)

V. Carboniferous System (*continued*)

Upper Carboniferous, Goniatite/Non-marine Bivalve Zones

	DIVISIONS		GONIATITE ZONES	NON-MARINE BIVALVE ZONES	CHARACTERISTIC BEDS IN GREAT BRITAIN
COAL MEASURES	STEPHANIAN	Westphalian D	*Anthracoceras* Zone A	*Anthraconaia prolifera*	Upper Coal Series (South Wales); Radstock Group (Somerset & Gloucestershire); Erbistock Beds (North Wales).
	MORGANIAN			*Anthraconauta tenuis*	Highest Upper Coal Measures (Kent); Upper Coal Measures (South Wales); Barren Red Measures (Somerset & Gloucestershire); Ardwick, Keele and Newcastle Beds (Midlands); Thin limestones and coals (Lancashire); Highest Barren Red Measures (Ayrshire).
		Westphalian C		*Anthraconauta phillipsi*	Upper Coal Measures (Kent); Upper Coal Measures generally; New Rock and Pennant Sandstone Groups (South Wales); Red Beds (Yorkshire & Nottinghamshire); Etruria Marl (West Midlands); Barren Red Measures (Scotland).
	AMMANIAN			Upper *Anthracosia similis*-*Anthraconaia pulchra*	Top of Middle Coal Measures generally; Cwmgorse Marine Band marks upper limit of zone (South Wales); Main '*Estheria*' and *Edmondia* Bands (Yorkshire & Nottinghamshire); top of Productive Measures (North-east England); Barren Red Measures in part (Scotland).
		Westphalian B		Lower *Anthracosia similis*-*Anthraconaia pulchra*	Middle Coal Measures generally; top of Productive Measures (North-east England & Scotland). Several probably equivalent marine bands mark the upper limit of zone: Cefn Coed, Gin Mine, Dukinfield, Mansfield, Chance Pennystone, Bolton, Charles, Overseal, Ryhope and Skipsey's Marine Bands.
				Anthraconaia modiolaris	Lower part of Middle Coal Measures and upper part of Lower Coal Measures generally; Amman Marine Band (South Wales); Clay Cross Marine Band (Yorkshire & Nottinghamshire).
		Westphalian A	No goniatites known	*Carbonicola communis*	Lower Coal Measures generally; Low '*Estheria*' Band (Yorkshire & Nottinghamshire); base of Productive Measures (North-east England & Scotland).
			Gastrioceras Zone G_2	*Anthraconaia lenisulcata*	Carbonate Nodule Beds (Devon); Ashton Vale Group (Somerset & Gloucestershire); Farewell Rock Group in part (South Wales); Upper Gwespyr Sandstone (North Wales); Alton and Pot Clay Marine Bands(Yorkshire, Derbyshire & Nottinghamshire).

MILLSTONE GRIT	NAMURIAN	*Gastrioceras* Zone G_1	Rough Rock Group (England generally); Farewell Rock Group in part (South Wales); Lower Gwespyr Sandstone (North Wales); possibly represented by upper part of Roslin Sandstone (Scotland).
		Reticuloceras Zone R_2	Thick shales (South Wales); upper part of Holywell Shales (North Wales); Middle Grits Group (Yorkshire & Derbyshire).
		Reticuloceras Zone R_1	Culm in part (Devon); Basal Grits (South Wales); Holywell Shales in part (North Wales); Kinderscout Grit Group (Derbyshire); Cayton Gill Beds, Upper part of Sabden Shales (Yorkshire & Lancashire); not represented (North-east England & Scotland).
		Homoceras Zone H	Culm in part (Devon); Basal Grits (South Wales); part of Holywell Shales (North Wales); Sabden Shales in part (Lancashire); Congleton Edge Beds (Cheshire); part of Edale Shales (Derbyshire); not represented (North-east England & Scotland).
		Eumorphoceras Zone E_2	Plastic Clay Group (South Wales); Cefn y Fedw Sandstone, Hensingham Group, lower part of Holywell Shales (North Wales); Grits: Silsden Moor Grit Group, Pickersett Edge Beds, Shunner Fell Beds; Colsterdale Marine Band (Yorkshire); part of Edale Shales (Derbyshire); Lower part of Sabden Shales (Lancashire); Upper Limestone Group in part, Oakwood [= Lickar], Iron Scar [= Corbridge], Sugar Sands [= Thornborough], Foxton [=Felltop] & Botany Limestones (Northumberland & Durham); Upper Limestone Group, Index, Orchard, Calmy & Castlecary Limestones, lower part of Roslin Sandstone (Scotland).
		Eumorphoceras Zone E_1	Skipton Moor Grits, Pendle Grit Group, Grassington Grit and Upper Bowland Shales (Lancashire & Yorkshire); part of Edale Shales (Derbyshire); Upper Limestone Group in part: Great [=Main= Dryburn], Little [=Cushat], Crag [=Cross] & Stonesdale Limestones, Lower & Upper Coal Sill Groups (Yorkshire, Durham & Northumberland); Limestone Coal Group: from the base of the Top Hosie Limestone to the base of the Index Limestone (Scotland).

VI. Permian System

	GERMANY	ENGLAND (County Durham)	Representative beds elsewhere in England, Scotland and Northern Ireland
UPPER PERMIAN	UPPER ZECHSTEIN	UPPER MAGNESIAN LIMESTONE Red Beds with salt (in boring only); Hartlepool and Roker Dolomites on coast; 'Filograna' Beds at Seaham Harbour; Cannon-ball and Concretionary Limestone, on coast from Marsden to Sunderland; Flexible Limestone at Fulwell with fish.	Cutties Hillock Beds with reptiles, Cummingstone Beds with reptile tracks } Elgin, Scotland. Upper Permian Marls and Magnesian Limestone (Yorkshire & Nottinghamshire), Manchester Marls (Lancashire); Kirklinton and St. Bees Sandstone and Marls (Cumberland), unfossiliferous. Filograna Beds (Yorkshire, Nottinghamshire and County Tyrone, Northern Ireland).
	MIDDLE ZECHSTEIN	MIDDLE MAGNESIAN LIMESTONE Shelly limestone with Reefs A–D, dwarfed fauna in reef D at Heselden Dene; reef C at Beacon Hill with reduced fauna; reefs B & A with brachiopods, polyzoans and bivalves. Reefs A–C at Humbleton and Tunstall Hills; A at Claxheugh.	Middle Permian Marls (Yorkshire & Nottinghamshire); Magnesian Limestone (Cumberland & West Lancashire), usually unfossiliferous (correlation uncertain). Breccia (Lancashire). Permian Beds (Cultra, County Down, also County Tyrone and County Antrim, Northern Ireland. Correlation uncertain). Magnesian Limestone with reefs, marine fossils (Yorkshire & Nottinghamshire).
	LOWER ZECHSTEIN Limestone	LOWER MAGNESIAN LIMESTONE Lower Limestone at Claxheugh, Raisby, East Thickley, with marine fauna.	
	Kupferschiefer with fish	Marl Slate at East Thickley, Down Hill, with plant and fish remains.	Hilton Plant Beds (Westmorland); Lower Permian Marl (Yorkshire & Nottinghamshire) with plant and fish remains.
	Conglomerate	Yellow Sands (also in Yorkshire and Derbyshire, breccia in Nottinghamshire).	
LOWER PERMIAN	UPPER ROTLIEGENDE Terrestrial beds with reptiles and plants.	Probably not represented.	Penrith Sandstones & Brockram (Cumberland); Collyhurst Sandstone (Lancashire); Dumfries & Mauchline Sandstones (South Scotland). Some beds with reptile tracks may be Lower Permian in part.
	LOWER ROTLIEGENDE		

In Midlands, Somerset and Devon, Permian may be represented by unfossiliferous marls, red sandstones, breccias and conglomerates, and by Watcombe Clay and Sandstone (Devon only). Correlation uncertain.

Geological Distribution of the Species Illustrated

The numbers appended to the name of each species refer to the plate and figure which illustrate it.

CAMBRIAN SYSTEM

LOWER CAMBRIAN

Brachiopoda	*Obolella comleyensis* Cobbold	**1,** 10, 11
Trilobita	*Olenelloides armatus* Peach	**1,** 5
	Olenellus lapworthi Peach	**1,** 6
	Protolenus latouchei Cobbold	**1,** 4
Gastropoda	*Helcionella subrugosa* (Orbigny)	**1,** 2

MIDDLE CAMBRIAN

Porifera	*Protospongia fenestrata* Salter	**1,** 1
Trilobita	*Centropleura henrici* (Salter)	**1,** 3
	Paradoxides davidis Salter	**2,** 7

UPPER CAMBRIAN

Porifera	*Protospongia fenestrata* Salter	**1,** 1
Brachiopoda	*Lingulella davisi* (M'Coy)	**1,** 7, 8
	Orusia lenticularis (Wahlenberg)	**1,** 9
Trilobita	*Eodiscus punctatus* (Salter)	**2,** 4
	Lotagnostus trisectus (Salter)	**2,** 2
	Olenus gibbosus (Wahlenberg)	**2,** 5
	Parabolina spinulosa (Wahlenberg)	**2,** 6
	Peltura scarabaeoides (Wahlenberg)	**2,** 3
Crustacea	*Hymenocaris vermicauda* Salter	**2,** 1

ORDOVICIAN SYSTEM

TREMADOC SERIES

Hyolithida	*Hyolithes magnificus* Stubblefield & Bulman	**6**, 11
Eocrinoidea	*Macrocystella mariae* Callaway	**3**, 6
Trilobita	*Angelina sedgwicki* Salter	**8**, 6
	Asaphellus homfrayi (Salter)	**7**, 6
	Euloma monile (Salter)	**7**, 7
	Geragnostus callavei (Lake)	**7**, 4
	Parabolinella triarthra (Callaway)	**7**, 8
	Shumardia pusilla (Sars)	**7**, 5
Crustacea	*Hymenocaris vermicauda* Salter	**2**, 1
Graptolithina	*Clonograptus tenellus* (Linnarsson)	**13**, 9
	Dictyonema flabelliforme (Eichwald)	**13**, 8

ARENIG SERIES

Brachiopoda	*Monobolina plumbea* (Salter)	**4**, 4
Trilobita	*Neseuretus murchisoni* (Salter)	**8**, 8
	Ogygiocaris selwyni (Salter)	**8**, 7
Graptolithina	*Callograptus* cf. *salteri* Hall	**13**, 1
	Dichograptus octobrachiatus (Hall)	**13**, 10
	Didymograptus hirundo (Salter)	**13**, 2
	Phyllograptus angustifolius Hall	**13**, 6
	Ptilograptus acutus (Hopkinson)	**13**, 7
	Tetragraptus serra (Brongniart)	**13**, 5

LLANVIRN SERIES

Trilobita	*Ampyx linleyensis* Whittard	**8**, 4
	Placoparia zippei (Boeck)	**8**, 5
	Placoparina sedgwicki (M'Coy)	**8**, 2, 3
	Selenopeltis inermis (Beyrich)	**9**, 8
	Stapeleyella inconstans Whittard	**8**, 1

Graptolithina	*Didymograptus bifidus* Hall	**14**, 5
	Didymograptus murchisoni (Beck)	**14**, 4

LLANDEILO SERIES

Porifera	*Ischadites koenigi* Murchison	**15**, 7
Trilobita	*Basilicus tyrannus* (Murchison)	**10**, 7
	Cnemidopyge nuda (Murchison)	**10**, 3
	Flexicalymene cambrensis (Salter)	**9**, 1, 2
	Marrolithus favus (Salter)	**9**, 5
	Ogygiocarella debuchi (Brongniart)	**10**, 6
	Platycalymene duplicata (Murchison)	**9**, 3, 4
	Selenopeltis inermis (Beyrich)	**9**, 8
	Trinucleus fimbriatus Murchison	**10**, 1
Graptolithina	*Glyptograptus teretiusculus* (Hisinger)	**13**, 4
	Nemagraptus gracilis (Hall)	**14**, 6
Conodonta	*Trichonodella flexa* Rhodes	**14**, 13

CARADOC SERIES

Porifera	*Ischadites koenigi* Murchison	**15**, 7
Anthozoa	*Lyopora favosa* (M'Coy)	**3**, 4
Cystoidea	*Heliocrinites* sp.	**3**, 9
Crinoidea	*Diabolocrinus globularis* (Nicholson & Etheridge)	**4**, 2
	Rhaphanocrinus basalis (M'Coy)	**4**, 3
Edrioasteroidea	*Cyclocystoides* sp.	**3**, 8
Polyzoa	*Prasopora grayae* Nicholson & Etheridge	**3**, 1–3

Brachiopoda	*Christiania perrugata* (Reed)	**5,** 1
	Dalmanella horderleyensis (Whittington)	**4,** 11–13
	Dinorthis flabellulum (J. de C. Sowerby)	**4,** 9, 10
	Harknessella vespertilio (J. de C. Sowerby)	**6,** 7–9
	Heterorthis alternata (J. de C. Sowerby)	**4,** 6–8
	Heterorthis retrorsistria (M'Coy)	**4,** 5
	Macrocoelia expansa (J. de C. Sowerby)	**5,** 7, 8
	Nicolella actoniae (J. de C. Sowerby)	**5,** 3, 4
	Onniella broeggeri Bancroft	**5,** 2
	Reuschella horderleyensis Bancroft	**6,** 3, 4
	Sowerbyella sericea (J. de C. Sowerby)	**5,** 5, 6
	Strophomena grandis (J. de C. Sowerby)	**5,** 9, 10
Bivalvia	*Byssonychia radiata* (Hall)	**6,** 13
	Modiolopsis orbicularis (J. de C. Sowerby)	**6,** 12
Gastropoda	*Cyrtolites nodosus* (Salter)	**7,** 2
Trilobita	*Broeggerolithus broeggeri* (Bancroft)	**11,** 3–5
	Brongniartella bisulcata (M'Coy)	**11,** 6, 7
	Chasmops extensa (Boeck)	**11,** 1, 2
	Flexicalymene caractaci (Salter)	**9,** 9
	Kloucekia apiculata (M'Coy)	**11,** 8, 9
	Ogygiocarella debuchi (Brongniart)	**10,** 6
	Onnia gracilis (Bancroft)	**10,** 5
	Platycalymene duplicata (Murchison)	**9,** 3, 4
	Remopleurides girvanensis Reed	**10,** 2
	Salterolithus caractaci (Murchison)	**10,** 4
	Trinucleus fimbriatus Murchison	**10,** 1
Ostracoda	*Tallinnella scripta* (Harper)	**12,** 11
Other Arthropoda	*Pinnocaris lapworthi* Etheridge	**12,** 13
Graptolithina	*Climacograptus bicornis* (Hall)	**14,** 8
	Climacograptus wilsoni Lapworth	**14,** 11
	Dicranograptus clingani Carruthers	**14,** 3
	Diplograptus multidens (Elles)	**14,** 7
	Leptograptus flaccidus (Hall)	**14,** 1
	Nemagraptus gracilis (Hall)	**14,** 6
	Orthograptus calcaratus (Lapworth)	**14,** 10
	Orthograptus truncatus (Lapworth)	**14,** 9
	Pleurograptus linearis (Carruthers)	**14,** 2

ASHGILL SERIES

Porifera	*Ischadites koenigi* Murchison	**15**, 7
Carpoidea	*Cothurnocystis elizae* Bather	**3**, 7
Cystoidea	*Heliocrinites* sp.	**3**, 9
Crinoidea	*Cupulocrinus heterobrachialis* Ramsbottom	**3**, 5
	Protaxocrinus girvanensis Ramsbottom	**4**, 1
Edrioasteroidea	*Cyclocystoides* sp.	**3**, 8
Echinoidea	*Aulechinus grayae* Bather & Spencer	**3**, 10
Ophiuroidea	*Lapworthura miltoni* (Salter)	**22**, 3
Brachiopoda	*Hirnantia sagittifera* (M'Coy)	**6**, 5, 6
	Sampo ruralis (Reed)	**6**, 1, 2
Bivalvia	*Byssonychia radiata* (Hall)	**6**, 13
Gastropoda	*Cyclonema longstaffae* Lamont	**6**, 10
	Sinuites subrectangularis Reed	**7**, 1
Cephalopoda	'*Orthoceras*' *vagans* Salter	**7**, 3
Trilobita	*Corrugatagnostus sol* Whittard	**12**, 9, 10
	Dalmanitina robertsi (Reed)	**12**, 7, 8
	Diacalymene drummuckensis (Reed)	**11**,10,11
	Encrinuroides sexcostatus (Salter)	**9**, 6, 7
	Flexicalymene quadrata (King)	**12**, 2
	Paracybeloides girvanensis (Reed)	**11**, 12
	Phillipsinella parabola (Barrande)	**12**, 5
	'*Proetus*' *girvanensis* Nicholson & Etheridge	**12**, 1
	Pseudosphaerexochus octolobatus (M'Coy)	**12**, 4
	Sphaerocoryphe thomsoni (Reed)	**12**, 6
	Tretaspis ceriodes (Angelin) subsp. *sortita* (Reed)	**12**, 3
Ostracoda	*Primitia maccoyi* Salter	**12**, 12
Class uncertain	*Serpulites longissimus* Murchison	**17**, 1
Graptolithina	*Callograptus* cf. *salteri* Hall	**13**, 1
	Dicellograptus anceps Nicholson	**14**, 12

SILURIAN SYSTEM

LLANDOVERY SERIES

Plantae	*Mastopora favus* (Salter)	**15,** 9
Porifera	*Ischadites koenigi* Murchison	**15,** 7
Edrioasteroidea	*Cyclocystoides* sp.	**3,** 8
Ophiuroidea	*Lapworthura miltoni* (Salter)	**22,** 3
Brachiopoda	*Atrypa reticularis* (Linné)	**20,** 1
	Camarotoechia nucula (J. de C. Sowerby)	**21,** 6, 7
	Cyrtia exporrecta (Wahlenberg)	**20,** 4
	Leptaena rhomboidalis (Wahlenberg)	**19,** 3, 4
	Lingula lewisi J. Sowerby	**21,** 3
	Pentamerus oblongus J. de C. Sowerby	**17,** 10, 11
	Plectatrypa imbricata (J. de C. Sowerby)	**20,** 3
	Plectodonta transversalis (Wahlenberg)	**19,** 9
	Resserella elegantula (Dalman)	**17,** 8, 9
	Skenidioides lewisi (Davidson)	**17,** 7
	Stricklandia lirata (J. de C. Sowerby)	**17,** 12
	Strophonella euglypha (Dalman)	**19,** 5, 6
	Strophonella funiculata (M'Coy)	**19,** 7, 8
Bivalvia	*Pteronitella retroflexa* (Wahlenberg)	**24,** 3
Gastropoda	*Loxoplocus cancellatulus* (M'Coy)	**26,** 2, 3
Trilobita	*Calymene replicata* Shirley	**27,** 6, 7
	Cheirurus bimucronatus Murchison	**28,** 6
	Dalmanites myops (König)	**28,** 5
	Encrinurus onniensis Whittard	**27,** 5
	Encrinurus punctatus (Wahlenberg)	**29,** 6
Class uncertain	*Serpulites longissimus* Murchison	**17,** 1
	Tentaculites scalaris Schlotheim	**17,** 3
Graptolithina	*Diplograptus modestus* (Lapworth)	**30,** 8
	Monograptus lobiferus (M'Coy)	**30,** 3
	Monograptus priodon (Bronn)	**30,** 2
	Monograptus sedgwicki (Portlock)	**30,** 1

Graptolithina (contd,)	*Monograptus turriculatus* (Barrande)	**30,** 7
	Petalograptus minor Elles	**30,** 6
Agnatha	Thelodont scale	**37,** 1

WENLOCK SERIES

Porifera	*Ischadites koenigi* Murchison	**15,** 7
Hydrozoa	*Labechia conferta* (Lonsdale)	**16,** 10
Anthozoa	*Acervularia ananas* (Linné)	**15,** 2
	Arachnophyllum murchisoni (Edwards & Haime)	**15,** 4
	Favosites gothlandicus forma *forbesi* (Edwards & Haime)	**15,** 1
	Goniophyllum pyramidale (Hisinger)	**16,** 2
	Halysites catenularius (Linné)	**15,** 3
	Heliolites interstinctus (Linné)	**16,** 5
	Ketophyllum subturbinatum (Orbigny)	**16,** 3
	Kodonophyllum truncatum (Linné)	**16,** 7, 8
	Rhabdocyclus fletcheri (Edwards & Haime)	**16,** 4
	Syringopora bifurcata Lonsdale	**16,** 6
	Thamnopora cristata (Blumenbach)	**15,** 5
	Thecia swinderniana (Goldfuss)	**16,** 9
	Tryplasma loveni (Edwards & Haime)	**15,** 6
Carpoidea	*Placocystites forbesianus* Koninck	**23,** 4, 5
Cystoidea	*Lepocrinites quadrifasciatus* (Pearce)	**24,** 1
Crinoidea	*Crotalocrinites rugosus* (Miller)	**22,** 1, 2
	Eucalyptocrinites decorus (Phillips)	**23,** 1
	Gissocrinus goniodactylus (Phillips)	**24,** 2
	Periechocrinites moniliformis (Miller)	**23,** 2
	Sagenocrinites expansus (Phillips)	**23,** 3
Ophiuroidea	*Lapworthura miltoni* (Salter)	**22,** 3
Vermes	*Keilorites squamosus* (Phillips)	**17,** 6
	Spirorbis tenuis J. de C. Sowerby	**17,** 2
Polyzoa	*Favositella interpuncta* (Quenstedt)	**16,** 1

Brachiopoda	*Anastrophia deflexa* (J. de C. Sowerby)	**18,** 3
	Atrypa reticularis (Linné)	**20,** 1
	Camarotoechia nucula (J. de C. Sowerby)	**21,** 6, 7
	Cyrtia exporrecta (Wahlenberg)	**20,** 4
	Dayia navicula (J. de C. Sowerby)	**21,** 5
	Dicoelosia biloba (Linné)	**18,** 4
	Dolerorthis rustica (J. de C. Sowerby)	**18,** 5–7
	Eospirifer radiatus (J. de C. Sowerby)	**20,** 2
	Gypidula dudleyensis Schuchert	**18,** 2
	Howellella elegans (Muir-Wood)	**20,** 5
	Leptaena rhomboidalis (Wahlenberg)	**19,** 3, 4
	Lingula lewisi J. de C. Sowerby	**21,** 3
	Meristina obtusa (J. Sowerby)	**20,** 6
	Plectatrypa imbricata (J. de C. Sowerby)	**20,** 3
	Plectodonta transversalis (Wahlenberg)	**19,** 9
	Resserella elegantula (Dalman)	**17,** 8, 9
	Rhynchotreta cuneata (Dalman)	**18,** 1
	Skenidioides lewisi (Davidson)	**17,** 7
	Sphaerirhynchia wilsoni (J. Sowerby)	**19,** 2
	Strophonella euglypha (Dalman)	**19,** 5, 6
	Strophonella funiculata (M'Coy)	**19,** 7, 8
	Trigonirhynchia stricklandi (J. de C. Sowerby)	**19,** 1
Bivalvia	*Gotodonta ludensis* (Reed)	**24,** 7
	Grammysia cingulata (Hisinger)	**25,** 3
	Palaeopecten danbyi (M'Coy)	**25,** 4
	Pteronitella retroflexa (Wahlenberg)	**24,** 3
	Slava interrupta (Broderip)	**24,** 4
Gastropoda	'*Bembexia*' *lloydi* (J. de C. Sowerby)	**25,** 1
	Euomphalopterus alatus (Wahlenberg)	**27,** 1
	Platyceras haliotis (J. de C. Sowerby)	**26,** 6
	Poleumita discors (J. Sowerby)	**26,** 1
	Tremanotus dilatatus (J. de C. Sowerby)	**25,** 2
Cephalopoda	*Dawsonoceras annulatum* (J. Sowerby)	**27,** 2
Trilobita	*Acaste downingiae* (Murchison)	**29,** 8
	Acidaspis deflexa Lake	**29,** 4
	Bumastus barriensis (Murchison)	**28,** 7
	Calymene blumenbachi Brongniart	**28,** 1, 2
	Cheirurus bimucronatus (Murchison)	**28,** 6

Trilobita (contd.)	*Dalmanites myops* (Kӧnig)	**28,** 5
	Deiphon forbesi Barrande	**29,** 5
	Encrinurus punctatus (Wahlenberg)	**29,** 6
	Encrinurus variolaris (Brongniart)	**29,** 7
	Phacops stokesi Edwards	**27,** 4
	Sphaerexochus mirus Beyrich	**28,** 4
	Trimerus delphinocephalus (Green)	**28,** 3
Ostracoda	*Beyrichia* cf. *kloedeni* M'Coy	**29,** 1, 2
	Leperditia balthica (Hisinger)	**29,** 3
Class uncertain	*Cornulites serpularius* Schlotheim	**17,** 5
	Serpulites longissimus Murchison	**17,** 1
	Tentaculites ornatus J. de C. Sowerby	**17,** 4
	Tentaculites scalaris Schlotheim	**17,** 3
Graptolithina	*Cyrtograptus murchisoni* Carruthers.	**30,** 9
	Monograptus priodon (Bronn)	**30,** 2
	Monograptus turriculatus (Barrande)	**30,** 7
Agnatha	Thelodont scale	**37,** 1

LUDLOW SERIES

Porifera	*Amphispongia oblonga* Salter	**15**, 8
	Ischadites koenigi Murchison	**15,** 7
Anthozoa	*Favosites gothlandicus* forma *forbesi* (Edwards & Haime)	**15,** 1
Echinoidea	*Palaeodiscus ferox* Salter	**21,** 1
Ophiuroidea	*Lapworthura miltoni* (Salter)	**22,** 3
Vermes	*Keilorites squamosus* (Phillips)	**17,** 6
Brachiopoda	*Atrypa reticularis* (Linné)	**20,** 1
	Camarotoechia nucula (J. de C. Sowerby)	**21,** 6, 7
	Conchidium knighti (J. Sowerby)	**21,** 11, 12
	Cyrtia exporrecta (Wahlenberg)	**20,** 4
	Dayia navicula (J. de C. Sowerby)	**21,** 5

Brachiopoda (contd.)	*Dicoelosia biloba* (Linné)	**18,** 4
	Eospirifer radiatus (J. de C. Sowerby)	**20,** 2
	Howellella elegans (Muir-Wood)	**20,** 5
	Leptaena rhomboidalis (Wahlenberg)	**19,** 3, 4
	Lingula lewisi J. de C. Sowerby	**21,** 3
	Meristina obtusa (J. Sowerby)	**20,** 6
	Protochonetes ludloviensis Muir-Wood	**21,** 4
	Resserella elegantula (Dalman)	**17,** 8, 9
	Salopina lunata (J. de C. Sowerby)	**21,** 8–10
	Shaleria ornatella (Davidson)	**21,** 2
	Sphaerirhynchia wilsoni (J. Sowerby)	**19,** 2
	Strophonella euglypha (Dalman)	**19,** 5, 6
Bivalvia	*Fuchsella amygdalina* (J. de C. Sowerby)	**24,** 6
	Goniophora cymbaeformis (J. de C. Sowerby)	**24,** 5
	Gotodonta ludensis (Reed)	**24,** 7
	Grammysia cingulata (Hisinger)	**25,** 3
	Palaeopecten danbyi (M'Coy)	**25,** 4
	Pteronitella retroflexa (Wahlenberg)	**24,** 3
	Slava interrupta (Broderip)	**24,** 4
Gastropoda	'*Bembexia*' *lloydi* (J. de C. Sowerby)	**25,** 1
	Euomphalopterus alatus (Wahlenberg)	**27,** 1
	Loxonema gregaria (J. de C. Sowerby)	**26,** 4
	Platyceras haliotis (J. de C. Sowerby)	**26,** 6
	'*Platyschisma*' *helicites* (J. Sowerby)	**26,** 5
	Poleumita discors (J. Sowerby)	**26,** 1
	Tremanotus dilatus (J. de C. Sowerby)	**25,** 2
Cephalopoda	*Dawsonoceras annulatum* (J. Sowerby)	**27,** 2
	Gomphoceras ellipticum M'Coy	**27,** 3
Trilobita	*Dalmanites myops* (König)	**28,** 5
	'*Dalmanites*' *obtusicaudatus* (Salter)	**29,** 9, 10
Ostracoda	*Leperditia balthica* (Hisinger)	**29,** 3
Other Arthropoda	*Ceratiocaris stygia* Salter	**30,** 13
	Pterygotus bilobus Salter	**30,** 14
Class uncertain	*Cornulites serpularius* Schlotheim	**17,** 5
	Serpulites longissimus Murchison	**17,** 1
	Tentaculites scalaris Schlotheim	**17,** 3

Graptolithina	*Monograptus colonus* (Barrande)	**30,** 4
	Monograptus leintwardinensis Hopkinson	**30,** 5
Conodonta	*Ozarkodina typica* Branson & Mehl	**30,** 11
	Panderodus unicostatus (Branson & Mehl)	**30,** 10
	Spathognathodus typicus (Branson & Mehl)	**30,** 12
Agnatha	Thelodont scale	**37,** 1

DEVONIAN SYSTEM

(a) MARINE DEVONIAN

Anthozoa	*Digonophyllum bilaterale* (Champernowne)	**32,** 6
	Disphyllum goldfussi (Geinitz)	**32,** 5
	Favosites goldfussi Orbigny	**31,** 5
	Heliolites porosus (Goldfuss)	**31,** 6
	Hexagonaria goldfussi (de Verneuil & Haime)	**31,** 7
	Pachyphyllum devoniense Edwards & Haime	**32,** 7
	Phillipsastraea hennahi (Lonsdale)	**31,** 9
	Stromatopora huepschii (Bargatsky)	**31,** 4
	Thamnopora cervicornis (Blainville)	**31,** 8
Crinoidea	*Hexacrinites interscapularis* (Phillips)	**32,** 8
Brachiopoda	*Camarotoechia laticosta* (Phillips)	**34,** 7
	Cyrtina heteroclita Defrance	**33,** 2
	Cyrtospirifer extensus (J. de C. Sowerby)	**33,** 1
	Hypothyridina cuboides (J. de C. Sowerby)	**34,** 5
	Ladogia triloba (J. de C. Sowerby)	**34,** 6
	Mesoplica praelonga (J. de C. Sowerby)	**32,** 2
	Plectatrypa aspera (Schlotheim)	**34,** 4
	Pyramidalia simplex (Phillips)	**33,** 3
	Productella fragaria (J. de C. Sowerby)	**32,** 1
	Rhenorensselaeria strigiceps (Roemer)	**33,** 8
	Sieberella brevirostris (Phillips)	**33,** 5, 6
	Spirifer undiferus Roemer	**33,** 4
	Stringocephalus burtini Defrance	**34,** 3
	Stropheodonta nobilis (M'Coy)	**33,** 7
	Uncites gryphus Schlotheim	**34,** 1, 2

Bivalvia	*Actinopteria placida* (Whidborne)	**35,** 3
	Buchiola retrostriata (Buch)	**35,** 2
	'*Cucullaea*' *unilateralis* J. de C. Sowerby	**35,** 1
Gastropoda	*Euryzone delphinuloides* (Schlotheim)	**35,** 6
	Murchisonia bilineata (Dechen)	**35,** 5
	'*Platyschisma*' *helicites* (J. Sowerby)	**26,** 5
	Serpulospira militaris (Whidborne)	**35,** 4
Cephalopoda	*Manticoceras intumescens* (Beyrich)	**35,** 7
	Tornoceras psittacinum (Whidborne)	**36,** 9
Trilobita	*Cheirurus pengellii* (Whidborne)	**36,** 7
	Dechenella setosa (Whidborne)	**36,** 4, 5
	Phacops accipitrinus (Phillips)	**36,** 6
	Scutellum granulatum (Goldfuss)	**36,** 3
	Trimerocephalus mastophthalmus (Richter)	**36,** 1, 2
Conodonta	*Icriodus* sp.	**36,** 8

(b) OLD RED SANDSTONE

Plantae	*Psilophyton princeps* Dawson	**31,** 1
	Zosterophyllum llanoveranum Croft & Lang	**31,** 2, 3
Brachiopoda	*Lingula cornea* J. de C. Sowerby	**32,** 3
	Lingula minima J. de C. Sowerby	**32,** 4
Bivalvia	*Archanodon jukesi* (Baily)	**35,** 8
Agnatha	*Pteraspis rostrata* (Agassiz) subsp. *trimpleyensis* White	**37,** 3
	Cephalaspis lyelli Agassiz	**37,** 2
	Thelodont scale	**37,** 1
Pisces	*Asterolepis maxima* (Agassiz)	**37,** 5
	Coccosteus cuspidatus Miller	**36,** 10
	Holoptychius giganteus Agassiz	**37,** 4

CARBONIFEROUS SYSTEM

LOWER CARBONIFEROUS

Plantae	*Rhacopteris petiolata* Goeppert	**41**, 2
	Rhodea tenuis Gothan	**40**, 4
	Telangium affine (Lindley & Hutton)	**39**, 1
Foraminifera	*Archaediscus karreri* Brady	**42**, 1, 2
	Climacammina antiqua Brady	**42**,12,13
	Endothyranopsis crassus (Brady)	**42**, 5
	Howchinia bradyana (Howchin)	**42**,10,11
	Lugtonia concinna (Brady)	**42**, 14
	Plectogyra bradyi (Mikhailov)	**42**, 6
	Stacheia pupoides Brady	**42**, 8, 9
	Stacheoides polytremoides (Brady)	**42**, 7
	Tetrataxis conica Ehrenberg	**42**, 3, 4
Porifera	*Hyalostelia smithi* Young & Young	**41**, 1
Anthozoa	*Amplexizaphrentis enniskilleni* (Edwards & Haime) var. *derbiensis* Lewis	**44**, 3
	Amplexus coralloides J. Sowerby	**44**, 1
	Aulophyllum fungites (Fleming)	**44**, 2
	Dibunophyllum bipartitum (M'Coy)	**43**, 1
	Lithostrotion junceum (Fleming)	**43**, 2, 3
	Lithostrotion vorticale (Parkinson)	**43**, 4, 5
	Lonsdaleia floriformis (Fleming)	**44**, 4
	Michelinia tenuisepta (Phillips)	**45**, 4
	Palaeosmilia murchisoni Edwards & Haime	**44**, 6, 7
	Palaeosmilia regium (Phillips)	**44**, 5
	Siphonophyllia gigantea (Michelin)	**45**, 2
	Syringopora geniculata Phillips	**45**, 3
Blastoidea	*Codaster acutus* M'Coy	**59**, 3, 4
	Orbitremites ellipticus (G. B. Sowerby)	**59**, 5, 6
	Orophocrinus verus (Cumberland)	**59**, 7
Crinoidea	*Actinocrinites triacontadactylus* Miller	**61**, 1
	Amphoracrinus gigas Wright	**60**, 3
	Gilbertsocrinus konincki Grenfell	**61**, 2
	Platycrinites gigas Phillips	**60**, 4

Echinoidea	*Archaeocidaris urii* (Fleming)	**59**, 9
	Archaeocidaris sp.	**59**, 8
	Lovenechinus lacazei (Julien)	**59**, 10
	Melonechinus etheridgei (Keeping)	**60**, 1
Vermes	*Spirorbis pusillus* (Martin)	**46**, 11
Polyzoa	*Fenestella plebeia* M'Coy	**45**, 1
Brachiopoda	*Actinoconchus lamellosus* (Léveillé)	**52**, 4
	Antiquatonia hindi (Muir-Wood)	**47**, 4
	Brachythyris pinguis (J. Sowerby)	**49**, 3
	Composita ambigua (J. Sowerby)	**50**, 1
	Daviesiella llangollensis (Davidson)	**49**, 4
	Dictyoclostus semireticulatus (Martin)	**47**, 5
	Dielasma hastatum (J. de C. Sowerby)	**52**, 5
	Eomarginifera setosa (Phillips)	**46**, 5, 6
	Gigantoproductus giganteus (J. Sowerby)	**47**, 6
	Krotovia spinulosa (J. Sowerby)	**47**, 3
	Leptagonia analoga (Phillips)	**48**, 1, 2
	Lingula mytiloides J. Sowerby	**46**, 8
	Lingula squamiformis Phillips	**46**, 9
	Linoproductus corrugatus (M'Coy)	**46**, 10
	Martinia glabra (Martin)	**50**, 2
	Orbiculoidea nitida (Phillips)	**46**, 7
	Overtonia fimbriata (J. de C. Sowerby)	**46**, 1
	Phricodothyris lineata (J. Sowerby)	**48**, 7, 8
	Productus productus (Martin)	**46**, 2–4
	Pugnax acuminatus (J. Sowerby)	**52**, 3
	Pugnoides pleurodon (Phillips)	**51**, 2
	Punctospirifer scabricostus ashfellensis North	**52**, 1
	Pustula pustulosa (Phillips)	**48**, 3, 4
	Rhipidomella michelini (Léveillé)	**48**, 5, 6
	Rugosochonetes hardrensis (Phillips)	**47**, 1
	Schellwienella crenistria (Phillips)	**49**, 2
	Schizophoria resupinata (Martin)	**49**, 1
	Spirifer attenuatus J. de C. Sowerby	**52**, 2
	Spirifer striatus (Martin)	**50**, 3
	Syringothyris cuspidata (J. Sowerby)	**51**, 3
Bivalvia	*Aviculopecten plicatus* (J. de C. Sowerby)	**54**, 7
	Conocardium hibernicum J. Sowerby	**53**, 5, 6

Bivalvia (contd.)	*Edmondia sulcata* (Phillips)	**54**, 2
	Lithophaga lingualis (Phillips)	**53**, 2
	Polidevcia attenuata (Fleming)	**53**, 1
	Posidonia becheri Bronn	**53**, 3
	Posidoniella vetusta (J. de C. Sowerby)	**53**, 4
	Pterinopectinella granosa (J. de C. Sowerby)	**54**, 5
	Sanguinolites costellatus M'Coy	**54**, 4
	Wilkingia elliptica (Phillips)	**54**, 3
Gastropoda	*Euconospira conica* (Phillips)	**56**, 2
	Euphemites urei (Fleming)	**56**, 1
	Glabrocingulum armstrongi Thomas	**56**, 9
	Glabrocingulum atomarium (Phillips)	**56**, 4
	Mourlonia carinata (J. Sowerby)	**56**, 7
	Naticopsis elliptica (Phillips)	**57**, 1
	Palaeostylus rugiferus (Phillips)	**57**, 2
	Platyceras vetustum (J. de C. Sowerby)	**56**, 5
	Soleniscus acutus (J. de C. Sowerby)	**56**, 6
	Straparollus dionysii de Montfort	**56**, 3
	Straparollus pentangulatus (J. Sowerby)	**56**, 8
Cephalopoda	*Beyrichoceras obtusum* (Phillips)	**58**, 4, 5
	Goniatites crenistria Phillips	**59**, 1
	Muensteroceras truncatum (Phillips)	**58**, 2, 3
	Neoglyphioceras spirale (Phillips)	**59**, 2
Trilobita	*Brachymetopus ouralicus* (Verneuil)	**62**, 3, 4
	Cummingella jonesi (Portlock)	**62**, 2
	Griffithides seminiferus (Phillips)	**62**, 1
	Phillipsia gemmulifera (Phillips)	**62**, 5
	'*Phillipsia*' *laticaudata* Woodward	**62**, 8, 9
	Spatulina spatulata (Woodward)	**62**, 6, 7
Ostracoda	*Amphissites bipartitus* (Vine)	**63**, 3
	Entomoconchus scouleri M'Coy	**63**, 1
	Richteria biconcentrica (Jones)	**63**, 2
Other Crustacea	*Perimecturus parki* (Peach)	**62**, 10
Class uncertain	*Conularia quadrisulcata* J. de C. Sowerby	**45**, 5

Pisces	*Cladodus mirabilis* Agassiz	**63,** 9
	Gyracanthus formosus Agassiz	**64,** 5
	Helodus turgidus (Agassiz)	**64,** 3
	Orodus ramosus Agassiz	**64,** 4
	Psammodus rugosus Agassiz	**64,** 2
	Psephodus magnus (Portlock)	**64,** 1
	Rhizodus hibberti (Agassiz)	**65,** 4

UPPER CARBONIFEROUS

Plantae	*Alethopteris serli* Brongniart	**40,** 5
	Annularia stellata (Schlotheim)	**38,** 1
	Asterophyllites equisetiformis (Schlotheim)	**38,** 4
	Calamites suckowi Brongniart	**38,** 5
	Cyclopteris trichomanoides Brongniart	**41,** 4
	Cordaites angulosostriatus Grand' Eury	**41,** 5
	Lepidodendron aculeatum Sternberg	**39,** 5
	Lepidodendron sternbergi Brongniart	**39,** 6
	Mariopteris nervosa (Brongniart)	**40,** 2, 3
	Neuropteris gigantea Sternberg	**41,** 3
	Pecopteris polymorpha Brongniart	**40,** 1
	Sigillaria mamillaris Brongniart	**39,** 4
	Sphenophyllum emarginatum Brongniart	**38,** 2
	Sphenopteris alata Brongniart	**39,** 2
	Stigmaria ficoides Brongniart	**38,** 3
	Trigonocarpus sp.	**39,** 3
Foraminifera	*Lugtonia concinna* (Brady)	**42,** 14
	Stacheoides polytremoides (Brady)	**42,** 7
	Tetrataxis conica Ehrenberg	**42,** 3, 4
Anthozoa	*Dibunophyllum bipartitum* (M'Coy)	**43,** 1
	Lithostrotion junceum (Fleming)	**43,** 2, 3
	Lonsdaleia floriformis (Fleming)	**44,** 4
	Palaeosmilia regium (Phillips)	**44,** 5
Brachiopoda	*Brachythyris pennystonensis* (George)	**51,** 1
	Composita ambigua (J. Sowerby)	**50,** 1
	Dictyoclostus semireticulatus (Martin)	**47,** 5
	Dielasma hastatum (J. de C. Sowerby)	**52,** 5

Brachiopoda (contd.)	*Eomarginifera setosa* (Phillips)	**46**, 5, 6
	Krotovia spinulosa (J. Sowerby)	**47**, 3
	Leptagonia analoga (Phillips)	**48**, 1, 2
	Lingula mytiloides J. Sowerby	**46**, 8
	Lingula squamiformis Phillips	**46**, 9
	Martinia glabra (Martin)	**50**, 2
	Orbiculoidea nitida (Phillips)	**46**, 7
	Overtonia fimbriata (J. de C. Sowerby)	**46**, 1
	Phricodothyris lineata (J. Sowerby)	**48**, 7, 8
	'*Productus*' *craigmarkensis* (Muir-Wood)	**47**, 2
	Productus productus (Martin)	**46**, 2–4
	Pugnoides pleurodon (Phillips)	**51**, 2
	Rhipidomella michelini (Léveillé)	**48**, 5–6
	Schellwienella crenistria (Phillips)	**49**, 2
	Schizophoria resupinata (Martin)	**49**, 1
Bivalvia	*Anthraconaia adamsi* (Salter)	**55**, 7
	Anthracosia atra (Trueman)	**55**, 3
	Anthracosia planitumida (Trueman)	**55**, 4
	Anthracosphaerium exiguum (Davies & Trueman)	**55**, 2
	Carbonicola communis Davies & Trueman	**55**, 5
	Carbonicola pseudorobusta Trueman	**55**, 6
	Dunbarella papyracea (J. de C. Sowerby)	**54**, 6
	Naiadites modiolaris J. de C. Sowerby	**55**, 1
	Polidevcia attenuata (Fleming)	**53**, 1
	Sanguinolites costellatus M'Coy	**54**, 4
	Schizodus carbonarius (J. de C. Sowerby)	**54**, 1
	Wilkingia elliptica (Phillips)	**54**, 3
Gastropoda	*Glabrocingulum armstrongi* Thomas	**56**, 9, 10
	Palaeostylus rugiferus (Phillips)	**57**, 2
Cephalopoda	*Gastrioceras carbonarium* (Buch)	**58**, 6
	Homoceras diadema (Beyrich)	**58**, 1
	Reticuloceras bilingue (Salter)	**57**, 4
	Reticuloceras reticulatum (Phillips)	**57**, 3
Arthropoda	*Eophrynus prestvici* (Buckland)	**63**, 6
	Euphoberia ferox (Salter)	**63**, 5
	Euproops rotundatus (Prestwich)	**63**, 4

Class uncertain	*Conularia quadrisulcata* J. Sowerby	**45,** 5
Conodonta	*Gnathodus bilineatus* (Roundy)	**63,** 8
	Idiognathoides corrugata (Harris & Hollingsworth)	**63,** 7
Pisces	*Gyracanthus formosus* Agassiz	**64,** 5
	Megalichthys hibberti Agassiz	**65,** 1, 2
	Xenacanthus laevissimus (Agassiz)	**64,** 6
	Rhabdoderma tingleyense (Davis)	**65,** 3
	Sagenodus inaequalis Owen	**66,** 1
Amphibia	Anthracosaurian vertebra	**66,** 2
	Keraterpeton galvani Huxley	**66,** 3
	Megalocephalus cf. *macromma* Barkas	**66,** 4

PERMIAN SYSTEM

Foraminifera	*Nodosinella digitata* Brady	**67,** 5, 6
Polyzoa	*Fenestella retiformis* (Schlotheim)	**67,** 7, 8
Brachiopoda	*Dielasma elongatum* (Schlotheim)	**68,** 2
	Horridonia horrida (J. Sowerby)	**68,** 4, 5
	Orthothrix excavata (Geinitz)	**67,** 1, 2
	Pterospirifer alatus (Schlotheim)	**68,** 1
	Spiriferellina cristata (Schlotheim)	**68,** 3
	Stenoscisma humbletonensis (Howse)	**67,** 3, 4
Bivalvia	*Bakevellia binneyi* (Brown)	**69,** 3, 4
	Parallelodon striatus (Schlotheim)	**69,** 1
	Permophorus costatus (Brown)	**69,** 2
	Pseudomonotis speluncularia (Schlotheim)	**69,** 6
	Schizodus obscurus (J. Sowerby)	**69,** 5
Pisces	*Palaeoniscus freieslebenensis* Blainville	**69,** 7

Scientific Names of Fossils

The scientific name of a species is established by its publication with a description of the distinctive characters and preferably also with an illustration of the species. The worker describing the latter is alluded to as its author. The name of each species consists essentially of two words which are either Latin or treated as Latin. The first word is the name of the genus to which the species is assigned, and the second (the specific name) denotes the species. Sometimes the species of a genus are grouped in subgenera which also have Latin names. The subgeneric name is then placed between the generic and specific names, but in round brackets. The name of the author of a species is usually placed after the specific name; this gives a clue to where the description of a species is to be found. If the species has been transferred to a different genus from that under which it was originally described, its author's name is placed in round brackets. If the specific name is an adjective, it must agree in gender with the generic name. Some specific names, however, are nouns in apposition to the generic name and are not liable to change according to the gender of the latter.

Sometimes it is desired to indicate that a specimen belongs to a definite subspecies, that is, a group in which, perhaps, geographical isolation or evolutionary changes have resulted in slight differences from typical specimens of the species. In such cases a Latin subspecific name is used, and this and its author's name follow the names already mentioned.

The same genus or species has sometimes been described by different workers under different names, and in such cases, except in certain circumstances, the name first used must be accepted. The discovery of earlier names has thus been one reason for changes in nomenclature. A more important cause of changes in the name of organisms lies in the fact that nomenclature is dependent upon classification. Increased knowledge of a species may show that it was referred by its author to a genus with which it has no affinity, as in the case of the species from the Coal Measures which was originally called *Unio acutus* but is now known not to belong even to the same family as *Unio* and is placed in the genus *Carbonicola*. Moreover, one worker will treat a group of species as a distinct genus, whereas another will include the same group in a genus described earlier. Similarly, one worker will unite in a single species a series of specimens which another will consider to belong to two or more distinct species. While many goniatites were formerly included in a single genus *Goniatites* and many Palaeozoic brachiopods in *Dalmanella*, *Orthis*, *Productus* or *Spirifer*, species of these groups are now classified in a great number of different genera. The views of modern authorities have been the main criterion in deciding what names should be used for any species illustrated in the present handbook. Other names which have been used from time to time (and which may differ in either the generic or the specific name, or in both) are, if thought important enough, cited as synonyms (abbreviation 'syn'.).

L.R.C.

Explanation of Plates

The geological range given for each species is that at present known and applies only to Great Britain.

Two or more drawings bearing the same number and linked by a broken line are views of the same specimen.

The names quoted in square brackets after the abbreviation Syn. (=Synonym) are other names that have been used, sometimes incorrectly, for the species (see p. 51).

An asterisk by the name of a species indicates that it may be found exhibited in the second bay of the Fossil Mammal Gallery at the British Museum (Natural History).

Plate 1

Cambrian Sponge (Fig. 1), Gastropod (Fig. 2), Trilobites (Figs. 3–6) and Brachiopods (Figs. 7–11)

1.* **Protospongia fenestrata** Salter. Group of spicules ($\times 2\frac{1}{2}$). Middle Cambrian; St. David's, Pembrokeshire. RANGE: Middle-Upper Cambrian.

2. **Helcionella subrugosa** (d'Orbigny). ($\times 1\frac{1}{2}$). Lower Cambrian; near Church Stretton, Shropshire. RANGE: Lower Cambrian. [Syn., *Helcion rugosa* (Hall).]

3. **Centropleura henrici** (Salter). Cranidium ($\times \frac{3}{4}$). Middle Cambrian; St. David's, Pembrokeshire. RANGE: Middle Cambrian. [Syn., *Anopolenus henrici.*]

4. **Protolenus latouchei** Cobbold. Cephalon ($\times 2$). Lower Cambrian; Comley, near Church Stretton, Shropshire. RANGE: Lower Cambrian.

5.* **Olenelloides armatus** Peach. ($\times 1\frac{1}{2}$). Lower Cambrian; Meall a' Ghiubhais, near Kinlochewe, Ross-shire. RANGE: Lower Cambrian.

6.* **Olenellus lapworthi** Peach. ($\times 1\frac{1}{2}$). Lower Cambrian; Meall a' Ghiubhais, near Kinlochewe, Ross-shire. RANGE: Lower Cambrian.

7, 8.* **Lingulella davisi** (M'Coy). Upper Cambrian. 7 ($\times 2$). Tremadoc, Carnarvonshire. 8, interior of ventral valve ($\times 1\frac{1}{2}$). Dolgelly, Merionethshire. RANGE: Genus, Upper Cambrian–Ordovician; Species, Upper Cambrian.

9. **Orusia lenticularis** (Wahlenberg). Dorsal valve ($\times 4$). Upper Cambrian; near Tremadoc, Carnarvonshire. RANGE: Upper Cambrian.

10, 11.* **Obolella comleyensis** Cobbold. 10, ventral valve ($\times 5$). 11, internal mould of dorsal valve ($\times 8$). Lower Cambrian; Comley, near Church Stretton, Shropshire. RANGE: Lower Cambrian.

Plate 1

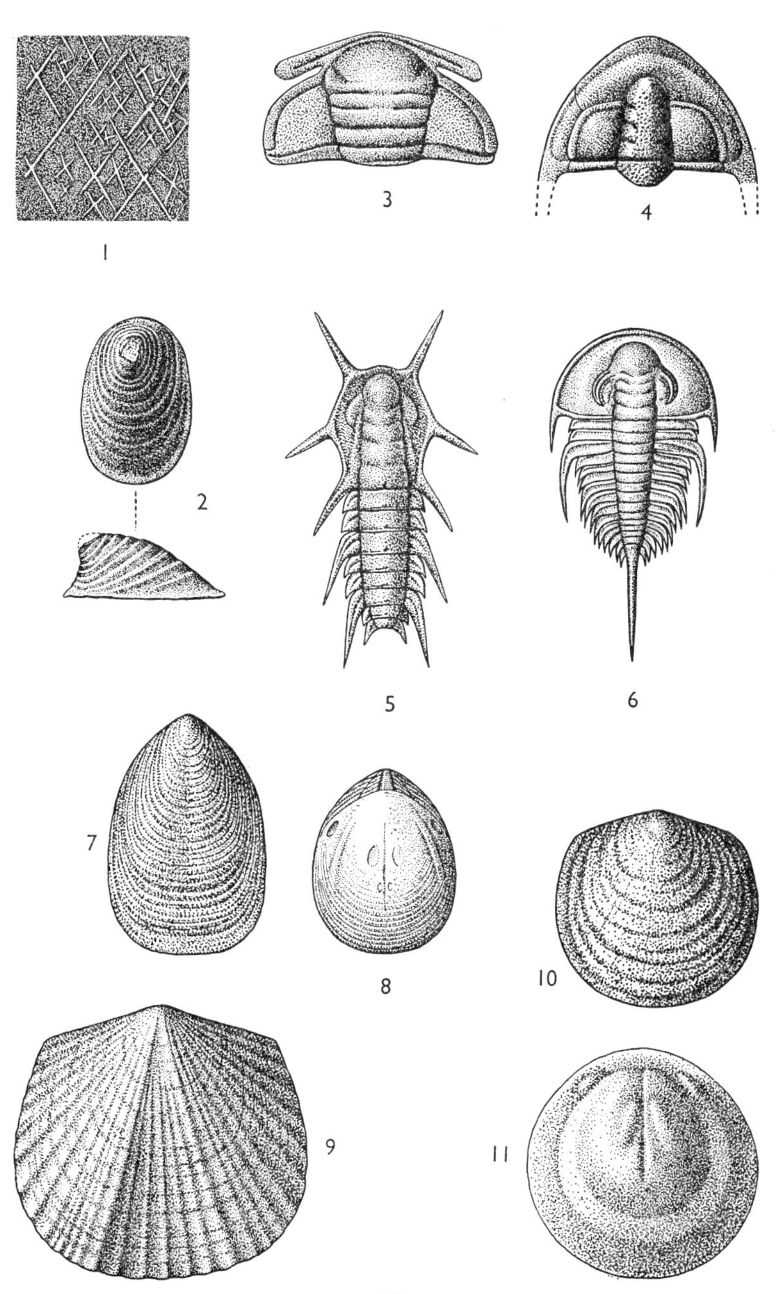

Plate 2

Cambrian Malacostracan Crustacean (Fig. 1) and Trilobites (Figs. 2–7)

1. **Hymenocaris vermicauda** Salter. (×1.) Upper Cambrian; Borth-y-Gest, Portmadoc, Carnarvonshire. RANGE: Upper Cambrian–Ordovician, Tremadoc Series.

2. **Lotagnostus trisectus** (Salter). (×3.) Upper Cambrian; south-western end of Malvern Hills, Herefordshire. RANGE: Upper Cambrian. [Syn., *Agnostus trisectus.*]

3.* **Peltura scarabaeoides** (Wahlenberg). (×4.) Upper Cambrian; Dolgelly, Merionethshire. RANGE: Upper Cambrian.

4. **Eodiscus punctatus** (Salter). (×3.) Middle Cambrian; St. David's, Pembrokeshire. RANGE: Upper Cambrian. [Syn., *Microdiscus punctatus.*]

5. **Olenus gibbosus** (Wahlenberg). (×1¼.) Upper Cambrian; Dolgelly, Merionethshire. RANGE: Upper Cambrian.

6.* **Parabolina spinulosa** (Wahlenberg). (×2.) Upper Cambrian; Dolgelly, Merionethshire. RANGE: Upper Cambrian.

7.* **Paradoxides davidis** Salter. (×½.) Middle Cambrian; St. David's, Pembrokeshire. RANGE: Middle Cambrian.

Plate 2

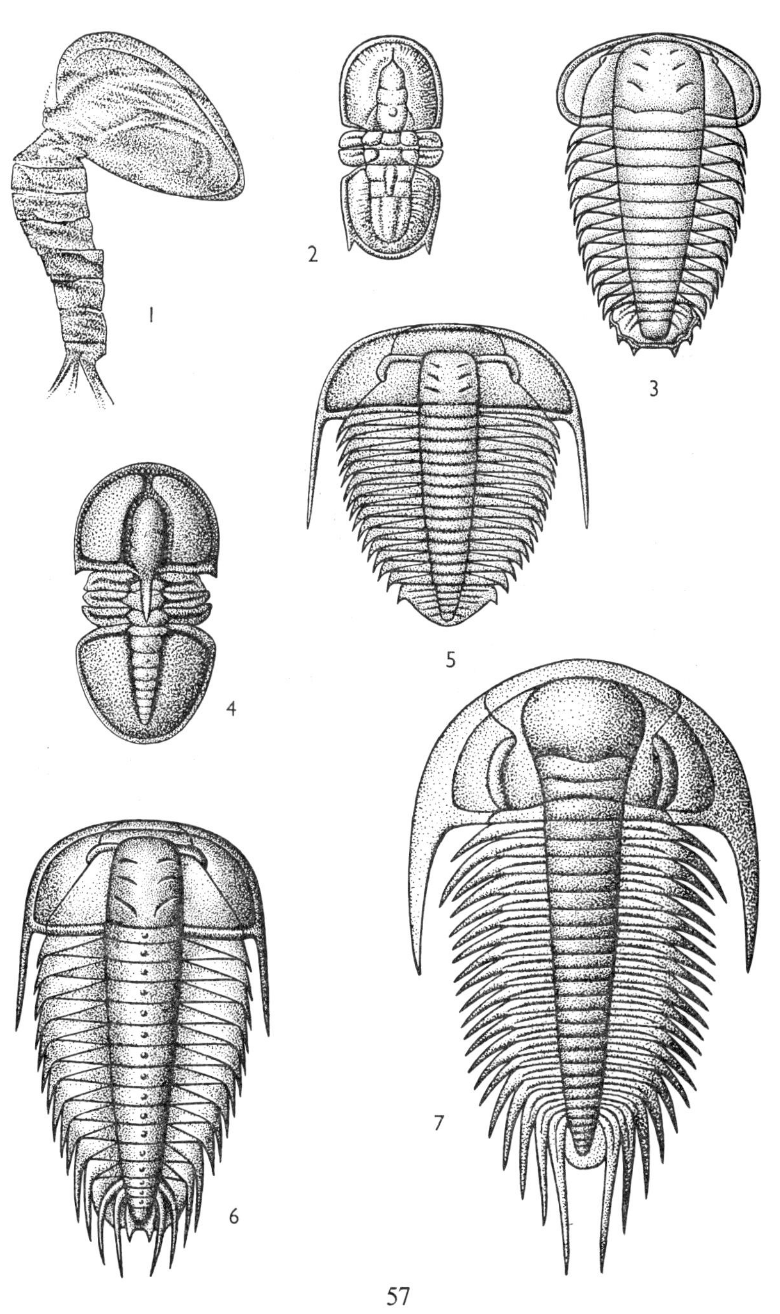

Plate 3

Ordovician Polyzoan (Figs. 1–3), Coral (Fig. 4) and Echinoderms (Figs. 5–10)

1–3.* **Prasopora grayae** Nicholson & Etheridge. 1 (×1). 2,3, transverse and longitudinal sections (×15). Caradoc Series; Craighead, Girvan, Ayrshire. RANGE: Caradoc Series.

4.* **Lyopora favosa** (M'Coy). (×3½.) Caradoc Series; Craighead, Girvan, Ayrshire. RANGE: Caradoc Series.

5.* **Cupulocrinus heterobrachialis** Ramsbottom. Artificial cast (×1). Ashgill Series; Thraive Glen, Girvan, Ayrshire. RANGE: Ashgill Series.

6. **Macrocystella mariae** Callaway. Artificial cast (×1). Tremadoc Series; Sheinton, Shropshire. RANGE: Tremadoc Series.

7.* **Cothurnocystis elizae** Bather. (×1½.) Ashgill Series; Thraive Glen, Girvan, Ayrshire. RANGE: Ashgill Series.

8. **Cyclocystoides** sp. Artificial cast. (×3½.) Ashgill Series; Thraive Glen, Girvan, Ayrshire. RANGE: Caradoc Series–Silurian, Llandovery Series.

9,* **Heliocrinites** sp. (× 1.) Probably Ashgill Series; Nant Fawr Waterfall, Bwlch-y-Gaseg, near Cynwyd, Merionethshire. RANGE: Caradoc–Ashgill Series.

10.* **Aulechinus grayae** Bather & Spencer. (×1¼.) Ashgill Series; Thraive Glen, Girvan, Ayrshire. RANGE: Ashgill Series.

Plate 3

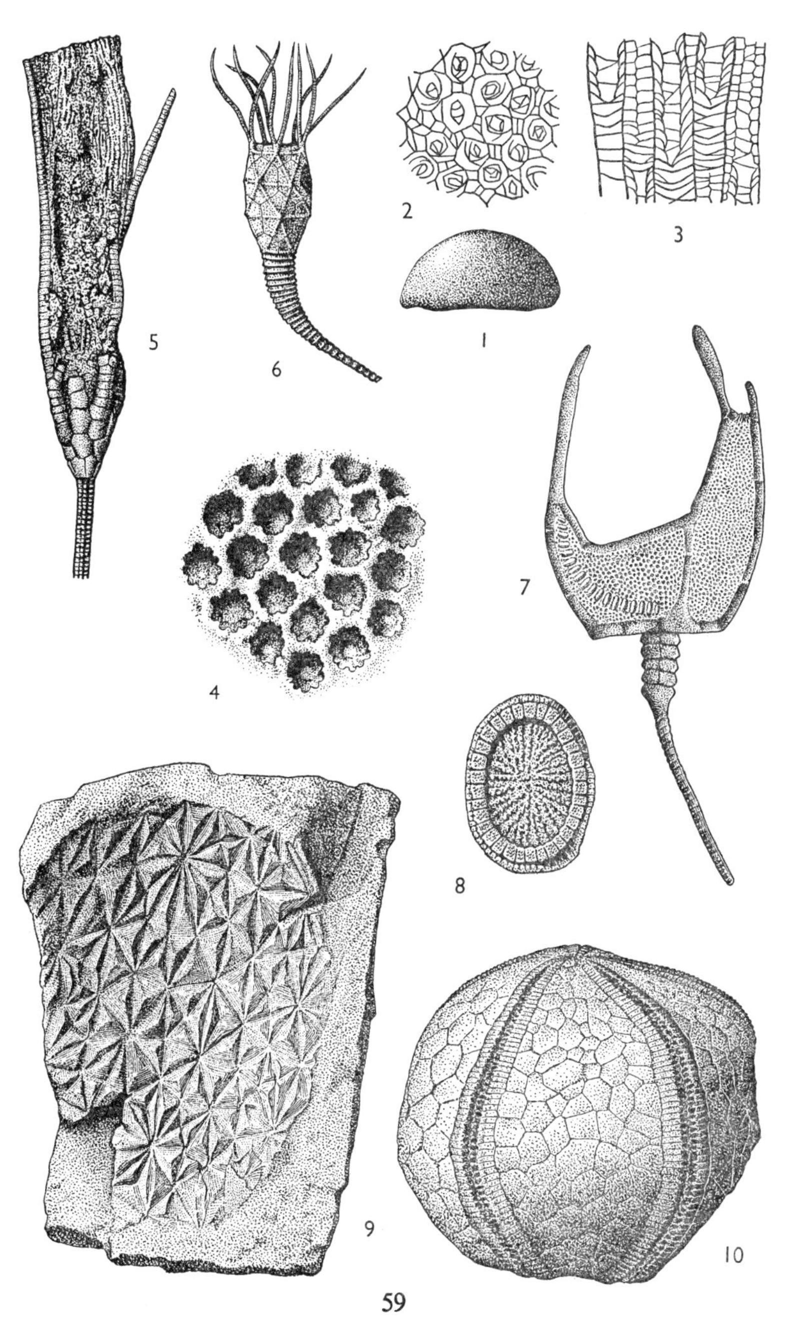

Plate 4
Ordovician Crinoids (Figs. 1–3) and Brachiopods (Figs. 4–13)

1.* **Protaxocrinus girvanensis** Ramsbottom. Artificial cast (×1½). Ashgill Series; Thraive Glen, Girvan, Ayrshire. RANGE: Ashgill Series.

2. **Diabolocrinus globularis** (Nicholson & Etheridge). (×2.) Caradoc Series; Craighead, Girvan, Ayrshire. RANGE: Caradoc Series.

3. **Rhaphanocrinus basalis** (M'Coy). (×1.) Caradoc Series; near Church Stretton, Shropshire. RANGE: Caradoc Series. [Syn., *Glyptocrinus basalis, Balacrinus basalis.*]

4.* **Monobolina plumbea** (Salter). (×1½.) Arenig Series; near Shelve, west Shropshire. RANGE: Arenig Series. [Syn., *Lingula plumbea, Obolella plumbea.*]

5. **Heterorthis retrorsistria** (M'Coy). (×1.) Caradoc Series; near Moelfre, Carmarthenshire. RANGE: Caradoc Series. [Syn., *Orthis retrorsistria.*]

6–8.* **Heterorthis alternata** (J. de C. Sowerby). (×1.) 6, dorsal valve, internal mould. 7,8, ventral valve, artificial cast and internal mould. Caradoc Series; Soudley, near Church Stretton, Shropshire. RANGE: Caradoc Series. [Syn., *Orthis alternata.*]

9, 10. **Dinorthis flabellulum** (J. de C. Sowerby). Internal moulds of ventral and dorsal valves (×1¼). Caradoc Series; Coston, near Clunbury, Shropshire. RANGE: Caradoc Series. [Syn., *Orthis flabellulum.*]

11–13. **Dalmanella horderleyensis** (Whittington). (×1½.) 11, artificial cast of ventral valve. 12,13, internal moulds of ventral and dorsal valves. Caradoc Series; Horderley, Shropshire. RANGE: Genus, Ordovician, Llanvirn Series–Silurian; Species, Caradoc Series. [Syn., *Wattsella horderleyensis.*]

Plate 4

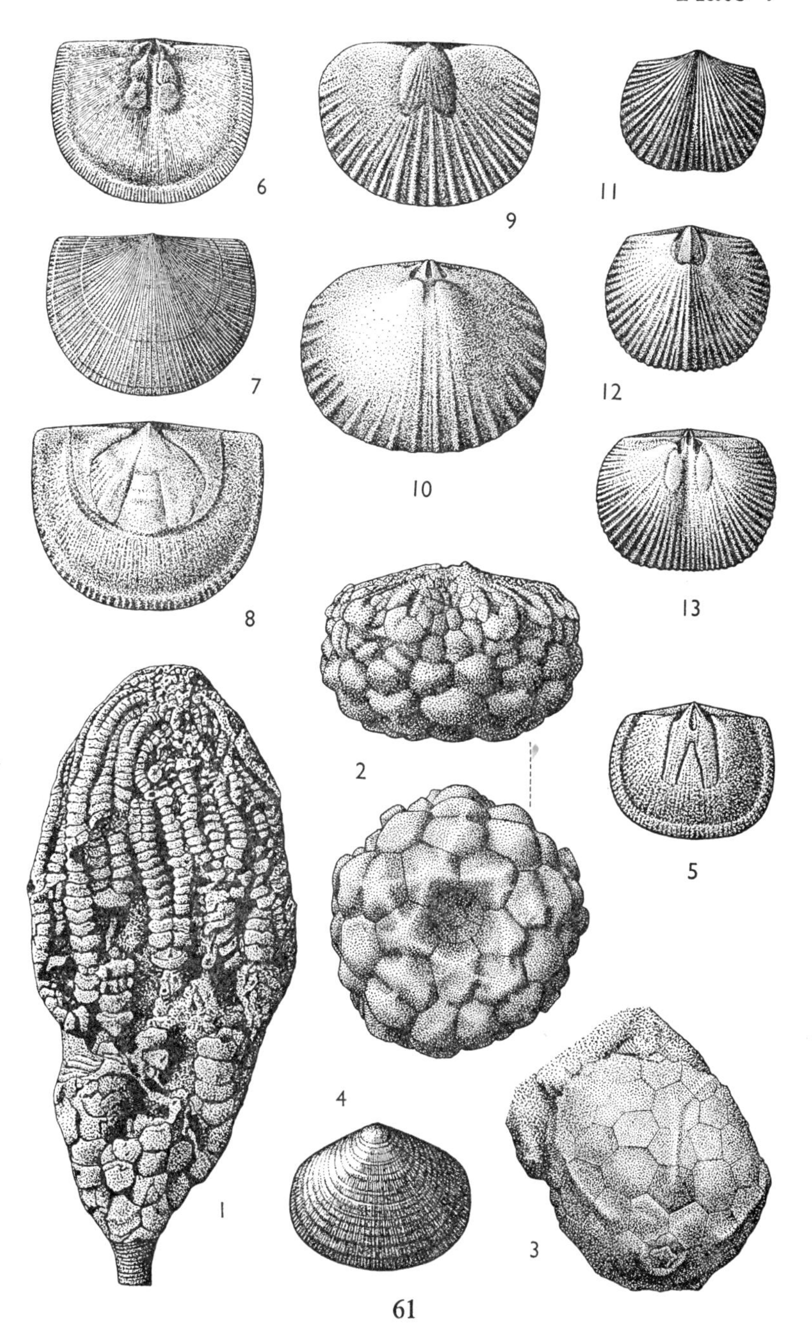

Plate 5
Ordovician Brachiopods

1. **Christiania perrugata** (Reed). Interior of dorsal valve ($\times 1\frac{1}{2}$). Caradoc Series; Ardmillan, Girvan, Ayrshire. RANGE: Genus, Caradoc-Ashgill Series; Species, Caradoc Series.

2.* **Onniella broeggeri** Bancroft. ($\times 2\frac{1}{2}$.) Caradoc Series; River Onny Valley, near Wistanstow, Shropshire. RANGE: Genus, Caradoc-Ashgill Series; Species, Caradoc Series.

3, 4. **Nicolella actoniae** (J. de C. Sowerby). ($\times 1\frac{1}{2}$.) 3, internal mould of ventral valve; 4, exterior of dorsal valve. Caradoc Series; near Acton Scott, Shropshire. RANGE: Genus, Caradoc-Ashgill Series; Species, Caradoc Series. [Syn., *Orthis actoniae*.]

5, 6.* **Sowerbyella sericea** (J. de C. Sowerby). Internal mould and exterior of ventral valve ($\times 2$). Caradoc Series; 5, near Horderley, Shropshire. 6, Soudley, Shropshire. RANGE: Genus, Ordovician, Llanvirn Series–Silurian; Species, Caradoc Series.

7, 8.* **Macrocoelia expansa** (J. de C. Sowerby). 7, ventral valve ($\times 1\frac{1}{4}$). 8, internal mould of ventral valve ($\times \frac{3}{4}$). Caradoc Series; near Welshpool, Montgomeryshire. RANGE: Genus, Llandeilo-Caradoc Series; Species, Caradoc Series. [Syn., *Rafinesquina expansa*, *Strophomena expansa*.]

9, 10.* **Strophomena grandis** (J. de C. Sowerby). 9, Internal mould of ventral valve, and 10, of dorsal valve ($\times 1$). Caradoc Series; near Cheney Longville, Shropshire. RANGE: Caradoc Series. [Syn., *Longvillia grandis*, *Orthis grandis*.]

Plate 5

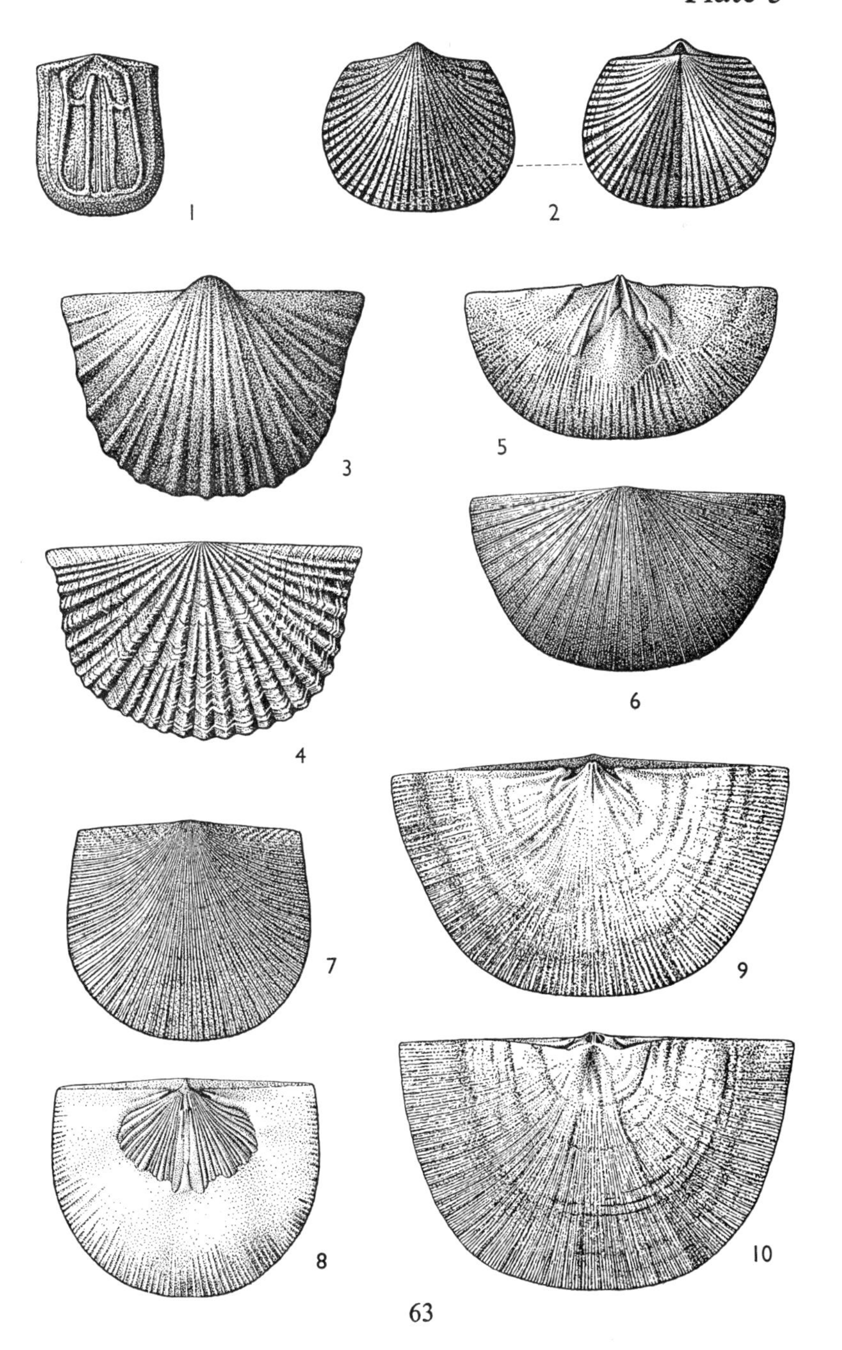

Plate 6

Ordovician Brachiopods (Figs. 1–9), Gastropod (Fig. 10), Hyolithid (Fig. 11) and Bivalves (Figs. 12, 13)

1, 2. **Sampo ruralis** (Reed). (×1½.) Ashgill Series; Thraive Glen, Girvan, Ayrshire. RANGE: Genus, Caradoc–Ashgill Series; Species, Ashgill Series. [Syn., *Plectambonites ruralis.*]

3, 4. **Reuschella horderleyensis** Bancroft. Internal moulds of ventral and dorsal valves. (×1.) Caradoc Series; Horderley, Shropshire. RANGE: Caradoc Series.

5, 6. **Hirnantia sagittifera** (M'Coy). Dorsal valve and internal mould of ventral valve. (×1.) Ashgill Series; near Knock, Westmorland. RANGE: Ashgill Series. [Syn., *Orthis sagittifera.*]

7–9.* **Harknessella vespertilio** (J. de C. Sowerby). (×1¼.) 7,8. Internal moulds of dorsal and ventral valves. 9, dorsal valve. Caradoc Series; Coston, near Clunbury, Shropshire. RANGE: Genus, Llandeilo–Caradoc Series; Species, Caradoc Series. [Syn., *Orthis vespertilio.*]

10.* **Cyclonema longstaffae** Lamont. (×1.) Ashgill Series; Shalloch Mill, Girvan, Ayrshire. RANGE: Genus, Caradoc Series–Upper Silurian; Species, Ashgill Series.

11. **Hyolithes magnificus** Stubblefield & Bulman. (×1.) Tremadoc Series; Cherme's Dingle, near the Wrekin, Shropshire. RANGE: Genus, Lower Cambrian–Upper Silurian; Species, Tremadoc Series.

12.* **Modiolopsis orbicularis** (J. de C. Sowerby). (×¾.) Caradoc Series; Hatton, Shropshire. RANGE: Genus, Ordovician, Llandeilo Series–Lower Devonian (Downton Series); Species, Caradoc Series, [Syn., *Ambonychia orbicularis.*]

13.* **Byssonychia radiata** (Hall). (×1.) Ashgill Series; Girvan, Ayrshire. RANGE: Genus, Ordovician, Caradoc Series–Silurian; Species, Caradoc–Ashgill Series.

Plate 6

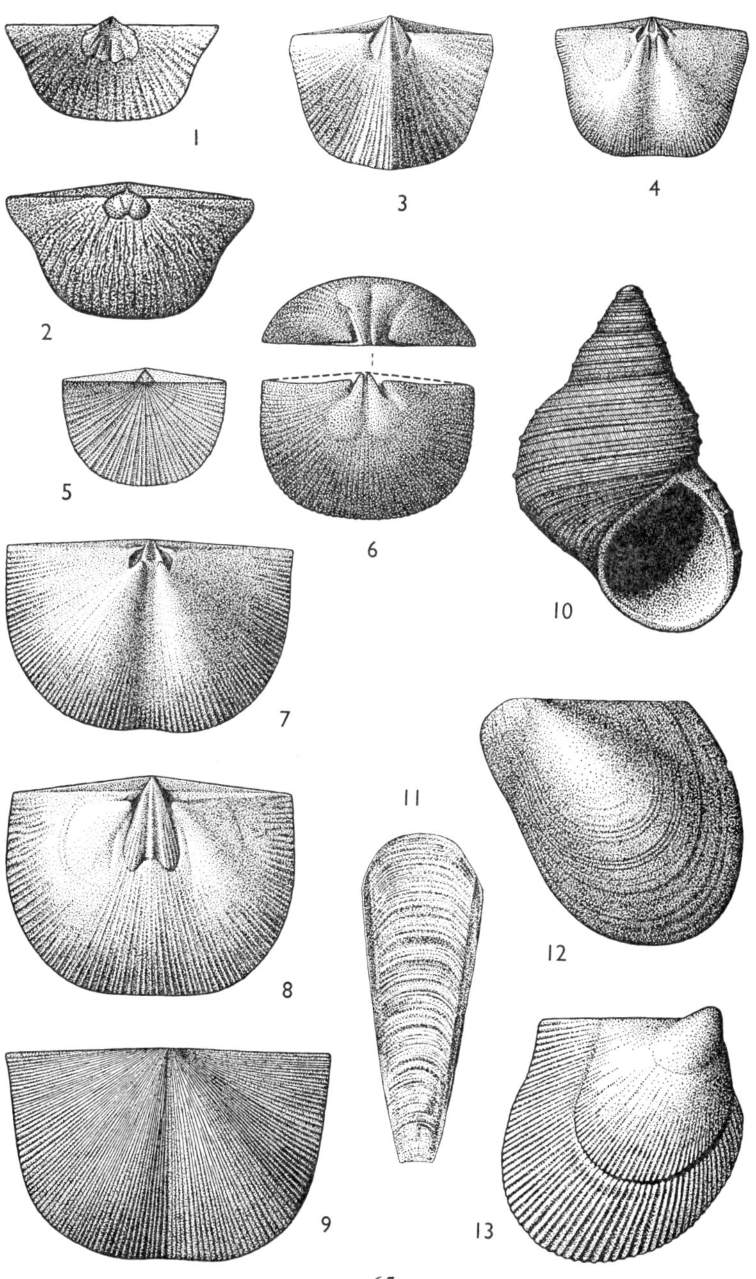

Plate 7
Ordovician Gastropods (Figs. 1, 2), Cephalopod (Fig. 3) and Trilobites (Figs. 4–8)

1.* **Sinuites subrectangularis** Reed. (×1.) Ashgill Series; Girvan, Ayrshire. RANGE: Genus, Ordovician, Caradoc Series–Upper Silurian; Species, Ashgill Series.

2.* **Cyrtolites nodosus** (Salter). (×2.) Caradoc Series; Cheney Longville, Shropshire. RANGE: Genus, Ordovician, Llandeilo Series–Lower Silurian; Species, Caradoc Series. [Syn., *Bellerophon nodosus.*]

3.* **'Orthoceras' vagans** Salter. (×1½.) Ashgill Series; near Bala, Merionethshire. RANGE: Ashgill Series.

4. **Geragnostus callavei** (Lake). (×3.) Tremadoc Series; Sheinton, Shropshire. RANGE: Genus, Tremadoc–Caradoc Series; Species, Tremadoc Series. [Syn., *Agnostus callavei.*]

5. **Shumardia pusilla** (Sars). (×6.) Tremadoc Series; Sheinton, Shropshire. RANGE: Genus, Tremadoc–Ashgill Series; Species, Tremadoc Series.

6.* **Asaphellus homfrayi** (Salter). (×¾.) Tremadoc Series; Sheinton, Shropshire. RANGE: Tremadoc Series. [Syn., *Asaphus homfrayi.*]

7. **Euloma monile** Salter. Cephalon (×6). Tremadoc Series; Sheinton, Shropshire. RANGE: Tremadoc Series.

8.* **Parabolinella triarthra** (Callaway). (×1.) Tremadoc Series; Sheinton, Shropshire. RANGE: Tremadoc Series. [Syn., *Olenus triarthrus.*]

Plate 7

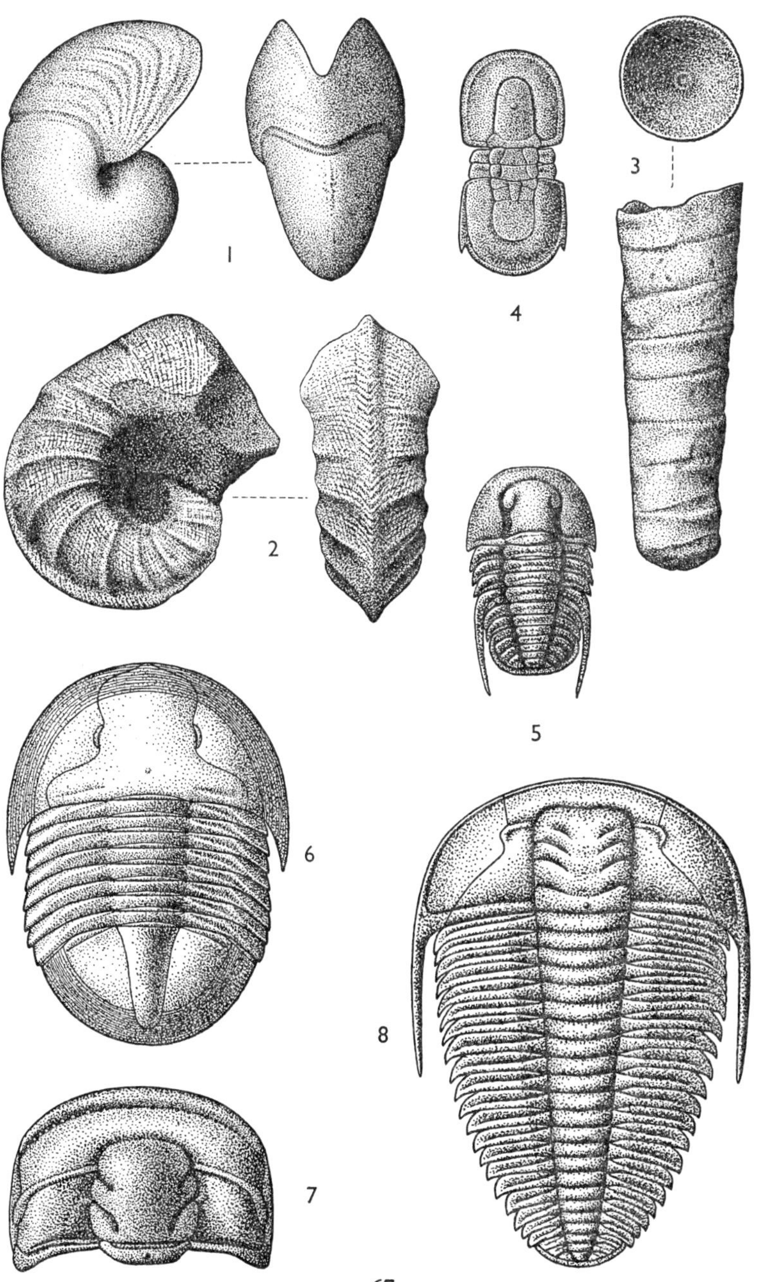

Plate 8
Ordovician Trilobites

1. **Stapeleyella inconstans** Whittard. (×3.) Llanvirn Series; Linley, Shropshire. RANGE: Llanvirn Series. [Syn., *Trinucleus murchisoni* of authors, in part.]

2, 3. **Placoparina sedgwicki** (M'Coy). Cephalon and pygidium (×1½.) Llanvirn Series; Linley, Shropshire. RANGE: Llanvirn Series. [Syn., *Cheirurus sedgwicki*, *Eccoptochile sedgwicki*.]

4. **Ampyx linleyensis** Whittard. (×1½.) Llanvirn Series; Linley, Shropshire. RANGE: Genus, Llanvirn–Caradoc Series; Species, Llanvirn Series. [Syn., *Ampyx mammillatus* subsp. *austini* of authors.]

5. **Placoparia zippei** (Boeck). (×4.) Llanvirn Series; Ritton Castle, Shropshire. RANGE: Llanvirn Series.

6.* **Angelina sedgwicki** Salter. (×1.) Tremadoc Series; Tremadoc, Carnarvonshire. RANGE: Tremadoc Series.

7. **Ogygiocaris selwyni** (Salter). (×1.) Arenig Series; Shelve, Shropshire. RANGE: Genus, Tremadoc–Arenig Series; Species, Arenig Series. [Syn., **Niobella selwyni,** *Ogygia selwyni*.]

8. **Neseuretus murchisoni** (Salter). Cranidium (×1.) Arenig Series; near Shelve, Shropshire. RANGE: Genus, Arenig–Llanvirn Series; Species, Arenig Series. [Syn., *Calymene murchisoni*, *Neseuretus ramseyensis* Hicks, *Synhomalonotus murchisoni*.]

Plate 8

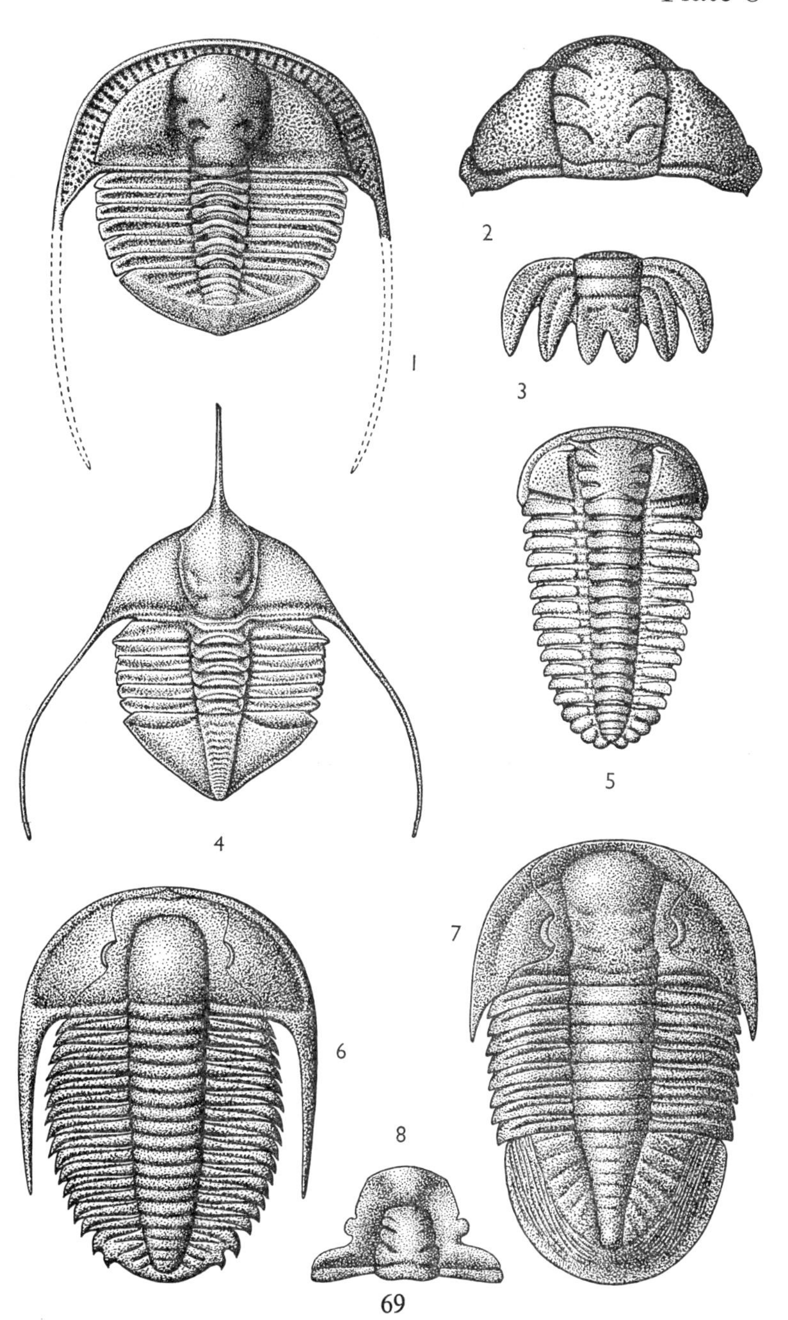

Plate 9
Ordovician Trilobites

1, 2.* **Flexicalymene cambrensis** (Salter). Llandeilo Series; 1, cephalon (×1½), Llandilo, Carmarthenshire. 2, pygidium (×1), Meadowtown, Shropshire. RANGE: Genus, Ordovician, Llandeilo Series–Lower Silurian; Species, Llandeilo Series. [Syn., *Calymene cambrensis.*]

3, 4.* **Platycalymene duplicata** (Murchison). Llandeilo Series. 3, cephalon (×1½), Gwernyffyd, Radnorshire; 4, pygidium (×1¼), Llandrindod Wells, Radnorshire. RANGE: Llandeilo–Caradoc Series. (Syn., *Calymene duplicata.*]

5. **Marrolithus favus** (Salter). Cephalon (×3). Llandeilo Series; Llandilo, Carmarthenshire. RANGE: Genus, Llanvirn–Caradoc Series; Species, Llandeilo Series. [Syn., *Trinucleus favus.*]

6, 7. **Encrinuroides sexcostatus** (Salter). Cephalon and pygidium (×1). Ashgill Series; near Haverfordwest, Pembrokeshire. RANGE: Ashgill Series. [Syn., *Encrinurus sexcostatus.*]

8. **Selenopeltis inermis** (Beyrich). (×1½.) Llanvirn Series; Llanvirn, Pembrokeshire. RANGE: Llanvirn–Llandeilo Series. [Syn., *Acidaspis buchi* (Barrande), *Selenopeltis buchi.*]

9. **Flexicalymene caractaci** (Salter). (×1.) Caradoc Series; Marshbrook, Shropshire. RANGE: Genus, Ordovician, Llandeilo Series–Lower Silurian; Species, Caradoc Series. [Syn., *Calymene caractaci.*]

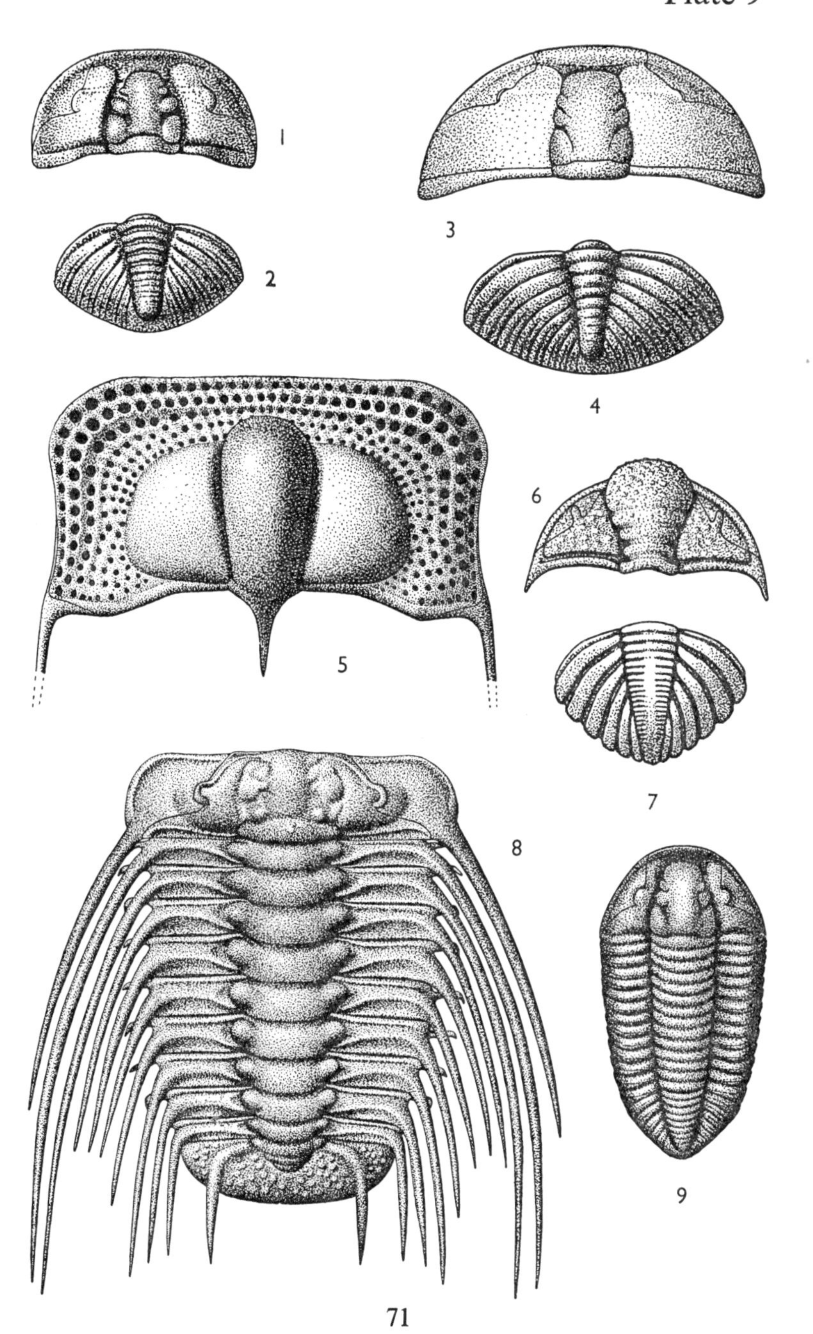
1
2
3
4
5
6
7
8
9

Plate 10
Ordovician Trilobites

1.* **Trinucleus fimbriatus** Murchison. ($\times 2$.) Llandeilo Series; Builth Wells, Radnorshire. RANGE: Genus, Llanvirn–Caradoc Series; Species, Llandeilo–Caradoc Series.

2. **Remopleurides girvanensis** Reed. ($\times 1\frac{1}{2}$.) Caradoc Series; Girvan, Ayrshire. RANGE: Genus, Caradoc–Ashgill Series; Species, Caradoc Series.

3.* **Cnemidopyge nuda** (Murchison). ($\times 1\frac{1}{2}$.) Llandeilo Series; Builth Wells, Radnorshire. RANGE: Llandeilo Series. [Syn., *Ampyx nudus*.]

4. **Salterolithus caractaci** (Murchison). ($\times 1\frac{1}{4}$.) Caradoc Series; Welshpool, Montgomeryshire. RANGE: Caradoc Series. [Syn., *Trinucleus caractaci*, *Trinucleus concentricus* of authors in part, *Trinucleus intermedius* Wade.]

5.* **Onnia gracilis** (Bancroft). ($\times 1\frac{1}{4}$.) Caradoc Series; River Onny Valley, near Wistanstow, Shropshire. RANGE: Caradoc Series. [Syn., *Trinucleus concentricus* of authors in part, *Cryptolithus gracilis*.]

6.* **Ogygiocarella debuchi** (Brongniart). ($\times \frac{3}{4}$.) Llandeilo Series; Gwernyffyd, Radnorshire. RANGE: Llandeilo–Caradoc Series. [Syn., *Ogygia buchi* of authors, *Ogygiocaris buchi*.]

7.* **Basilicus tyrannus** (Murchison). ($\times \frac{1}{2}$.) Llandeilo Series; Llandilo, Carmarthenshire. RANGE: Llandeilo Series. [Syn. *Asaphus tyrannus*.]

Plate 10

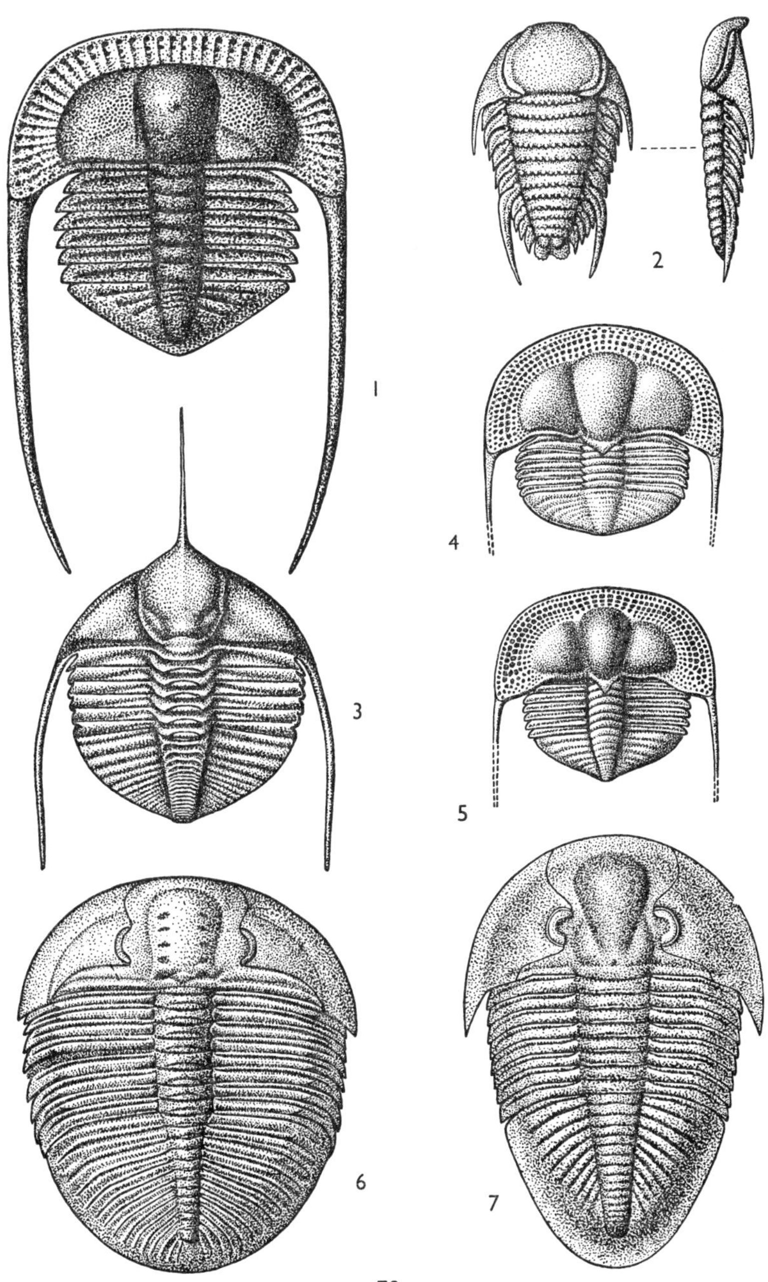

Plate 11
Ordovician Trilobites

1, 2. **Chasmops extensa** (Boeck). ($\times\frac{3}{4}$.) 1, cephalon. 2, pygidium. Caradoc Series; River Onny Valley, near Wistanstow, Shropshire. RANGE: Genus, Caradoc–Ashgill Series; Species, Caradoc Series.

3–5. **Broeggerolithus broeggeri** (Bancroft). ($\times$2.) 3, 4, ventral and dorsal views of cephalon. 5, pygidium. Caradoc Series; near Horderley, Shropshire. RANGE: Caradoc Series.

6, 7. **Brongniartella bisulcata** (M'Coy). 6, cephalon ($\times\frac{1}{2}$). 7, pygidium ($\times\frac{3}{4}$). Caradoc Series; Marshbrook, Shropshire. RANGE: Caradoc Series. [Syn., *Homalonotus bisulcatus.*]

8, 9. **Kloucekia apiculata** (M'Coy). ($\times 1\frac{1}{2}$.) 8, cephalon. 9, pygidium. Caradoc Series; Horderley, Shropshire. RANGE: Caradoc Series. [Syn., *Acaste apiculata, Phacopidina apiculata, Phacops apiculatus.*]

10, 11.* **Diacalymene drummuckensis** (Reed). 10, cephalon ($\times 1\frac{1}{2}$). 11, pygidium ($\times$2). Ashgill Series; Girvan, Ayrshire. RANGE: Genus, Ordovician, Caradoc Series–Silurian; Species, Ashgill Series. [Syn., *Calymene blumenbachi* var. *drummuckensis.*]

12. **Paracybeloides girvanensis** (Reed). ($\times$1.) Ashgill Series; Girvan, Ayrshire. RANGE: Genus, Caradoc–Ashgill Series; Species, Ashgill Series. [Syn., *Cybeloides loveni* var. *girvanensis.*]

Plate 11

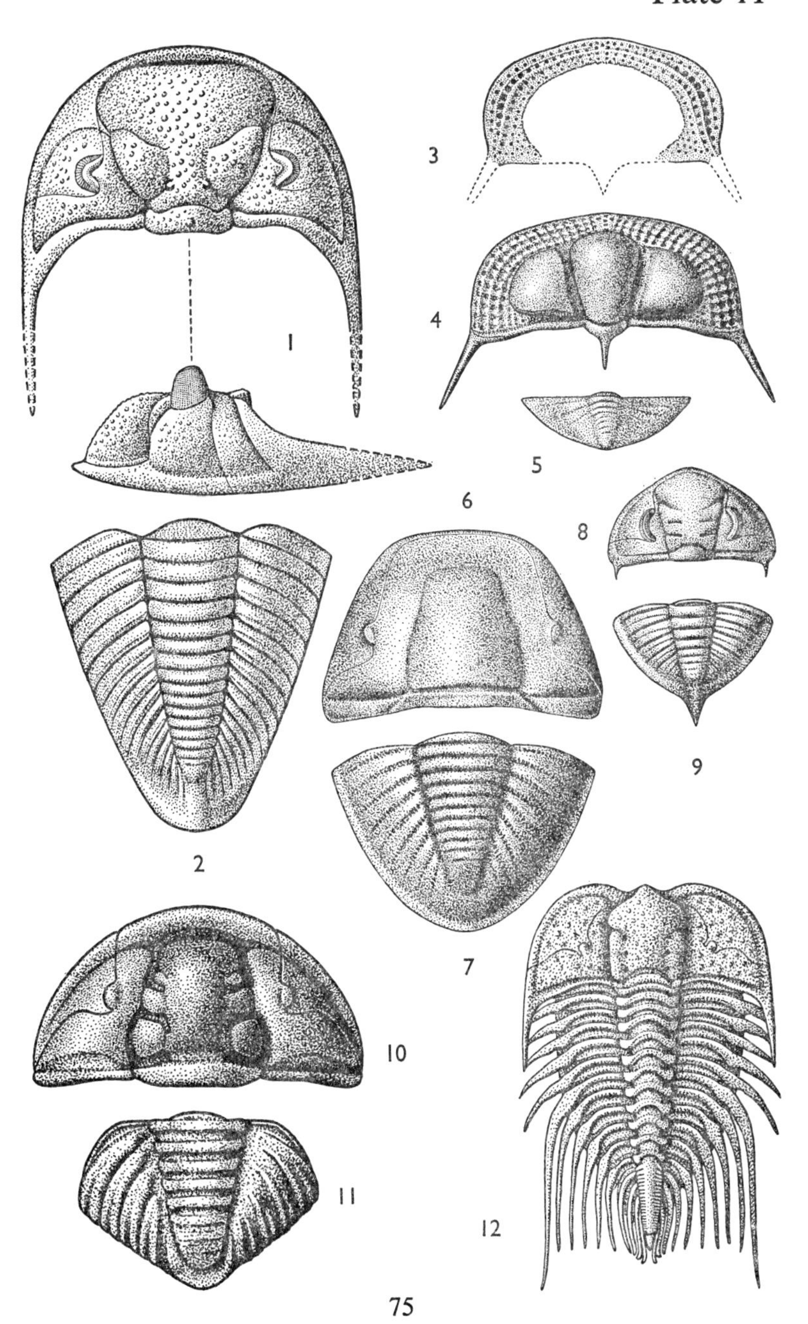

Plate 12

Ordovician Trilobites (Figs. 1–10), Ostracods (Figs. 11, 12) and Crustacean (Fig. 13)

1.* **'Proetus' girvanensis** Nicholson & Etheridge. (×1½.) Ashgill Series; Girvan, Ayrshire. RANGE: Genus, Ordovician–Devonian; Species, Ashgill Series.

2. **Flexicalymene quadrata** (King). (×1½.) Ashgill Series; Blaen-y-Cwm Valley, Berwyn Hills, Montgomeryshire. RANGE: Genus Llandeilo Series–Lower Silurian; Species, Ashgill Series. [Syn., *Calymene quadrata.*]

3. **Tretaspis ceriodes** (Angelin) subsp. **sortita** (Reed). (×2.) Ashgill Series; near Girvan, Ayrshire. RANGE: Genus, Caradoc–Ashgill Series; Species, Ashgill Series. [Syn., *Trinucleus ceriodes* var. *sortita.*]

4.* **Pseudosphaerexochus octolobatus** (M'Coy). (×¾.) Ashgill Series; Girvan, Ayrshire. RANGE: Genus, Caradoc–Ashgill Series; Species, Ashgill Series. [Syn., *Cheirurus octolobatus.*]

5. **Phillipsinella parabola** (Barrande). (×2.) Ashgill Series; Girvan, Ayrshire. RANGE: Ashgill Series.

6. **Sphaerocoryphe thomsoni** (Reed). (×2.) Ashgill Series; Girvan, Ayrshire. RANGE: Ashgill Series. [Syn., *Cheirurus thomsoni.*]

7, 8. **Dalmanitina robertsi** (Reed). 7, cephalon (×1½). 8, pygidium (×1¼). Ashgill Series; Haverfordwest, Pembrokeshire. RANGE: Genus, Caradoc Series–Lower Silurian; Species, Ashgill Series. [Syn., *Phacops robertsi.*]

9, 10. **Corrugatagnostus sol** Whittard. (×3.) 9, cephalon. 10, pygidium. Ashgill Series; near Girvan, Ayrshire. RANGE: Genus, Llanvirn–Ashgill Series; Species, Ashgill Series. [Syn., *Agnostus perrugatus* of authors, in part.]

11. **Tallinnella scripta** (Harper). (×10.) Caradoc Series; near Cressage, Shropshire. RANGE: Genus, Llandeilo–Caradoc Series; Species, Caradoc Series. [Syn., *Tetradella scripta.*]

12. **Primitia maccoyi** Salter. (×10.) Ashgill Series; Chair of Kildare, Kildare, Eire. RANGE: Genus, Llandeilo–Ashgill Series; Species, Ashgill Series.

13.* **Pinnocaris lapworthi** Etheridge (×2.) Caradoc Series; Girvan, Ayrshire. RANGE: Caradoc Series.

Plate 12

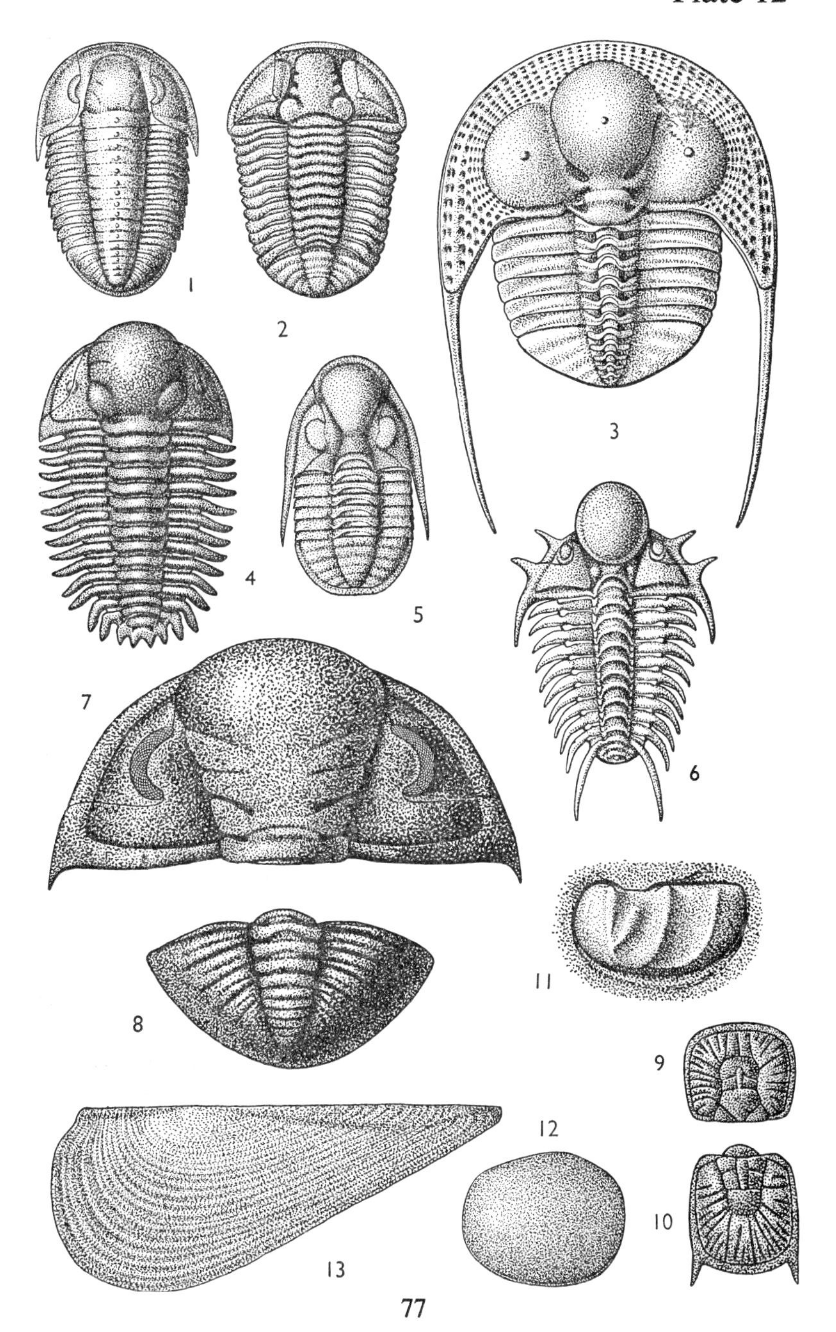

Plate 13
Ordovician Graptolites

1.* **Callograptus** cf. **salteri** Hall. (×1.) Ashgill Series; near Girvan, Ayrshire. RANGE: Genus, Upper Cambrian–Lower Carboniferous; Species, Ashgill Series.

2.* **Didymograptus hirundo** Salter. (×2.) Arenig Series; Skiddaw, Keswick, Cumberland. RANGE: Genus, Arenig–Llandeilo Series; Species, Arenig Series.

3. **Didymograptus extensus** (Hall). (×2.) Arenig Series; Lleyn, Carnarvonshire. RANGE: Genus, Arenig–Llandeilo Series; Species, Arenig Series.

4. **Glyptograptus teretiusculus** (Hisinger). (×2.) Llandeilo Series; near Pwllheli, Carnarvonshire. RANGE: Genus, Ordovician, Arenig Series–Silurian, Llandovery Series; Species, Llandeilo Series.

5. **Tetragraptus serra** (Brongniart). (×2.) Arenig Series; near Keswick, Cumberland. RANGE: Genus, Arenig–Llanvirn Series; Species, Arenig Series.

6. **Phyllograptus angustifolius** Hall. (×2.) Arenig Series; near Keswick, Cumberland. RANGE: Arenig Series.

7. **Ptilograptus acutus** (Hopkinson). (× 1½.) Arenig Series; Shelve, Shropshire. RANGE: Genus, Lower Ordovician–Upper Silurian; Species, Arenig Series.

8.* **Dictyonema flabelliforme** (Eichwald). (×1.) Tremadoc Series; near Ffestiniog, Carnarvonshire. RANGE: Genus, Upper Cambrian–Lower Carboniferous; Species, Tremadoc–Arenig Series.

9.* **Clonograptus tenellus** (Linnarsson). (×2.) Tremadoc Series; Cherme's Dingle, near The Wrekin, Shropshire. RANGE: Tremadoc–Arenig Series.

10. **Dichograptus octobrachiatus** (Hall). (×2.) Arenig Series; near Keswick, Cumberland. RANGE: Genus, Arenig–Llanvirn Series; Species, Arenig Series.

Plate 13

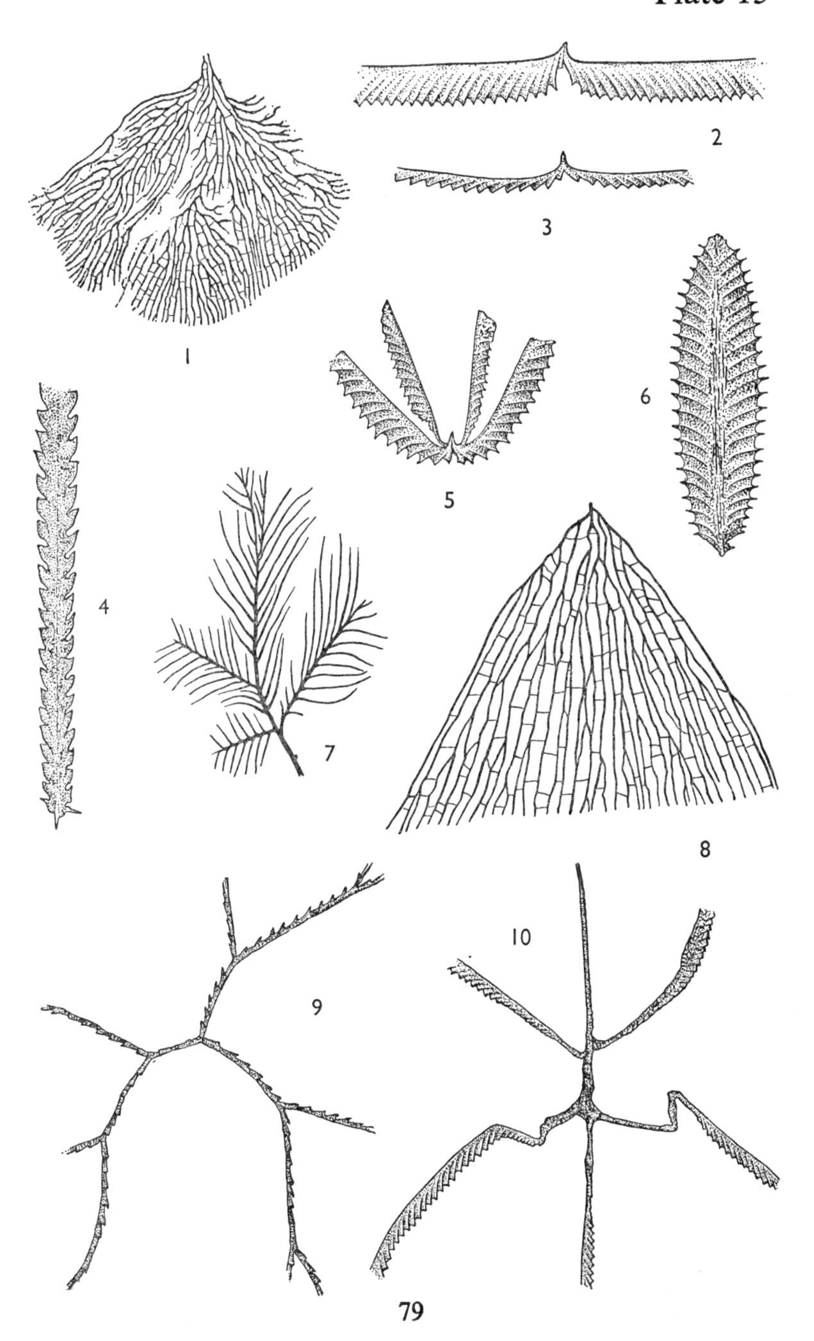

Plate 14

Ordovician Graptolites (Figs. 1–12) and Conodont (Fig. 13)

1. **Leptograptus flaccidus** (Hall). (×2.) Caradoc Series; near Moffat, Dumfriesshire. RANGE: Genus, Arenig–Caradoc Series; Species, Caradoc Series.

2. **Pleurograptus linearis** (Carruthers). (×2.) Caradoc Series; near Moffat, Dumfriesshire. RANGE: Caradoc Series.

3.* **Dicranograptus clingani** Carruthers. (×2.) Caradoc Series; near Moffat, Dumfriesshire. RANGE: Genus, Llandeilo–Caradoc Series; Species, Caradoc Series.

4.* **Didymograptus murchisoni** (Beck). (×1.) Llanvirn Series; Abereiddy Bay, Pembrokeshire. RANGE: Genus, Arenig–Llandeilo Series; Species, Llanvirn Series.

5. **Didymograptus bifidus** Hall. (×2.) Llanvirn Series; near Aberdaron, Carnarvonshire. RANGE: Genus, Arenig–Llandeilo Series; Species, Llanvirn Series.

6. **Nemagraptus gracilis** (Hall). (×2.) Caradoc Series; near Moffat, Dumfriesshire. RANGE: Llandeilo-Caradoc Series.

7.* **Diplograptus multidens** (Elles). (×2.) Caradoc Series; near Haverfordwest, Pembrokeshire. RANGE: Genus, Ordovician, Llanvirn Series–Silurian, Llandovery Series; Species, Caradoc Series. [Syn., *Mesograptus multidens*.]

8.* **Climacograptus bicornis** (Hall). (×2.) Caradoc Series; Moffat, Dumfriesshire. RANGE: Genus, Ordovician, Arenig Series–Silurian, Llandovery Series; Species, Caradoc Series.

9. **Orthograptus truncatus** (Lapworth). (×2.) Caradoc Series; near Girvan, Ayrshire. RANGE: Genus, Ordovician, Caradoc Series–Silurian, Llandovery Series; Species, Caradoc Series.

10.* **Orthograptus calcaratus** (Lapworth). (×2.) Caradoc Series; Conway, Carnarvonshire. RANGE: Genus, Ordovician, Caradoc Series–Silurian, Llandovery Series; Species, Caradoc Series.

11. **Climacograptus wilsoni** Lapworth. (×2.) Caradoc Series; near Moffat, Dumfriesshire. RANGE: Genus, Ordovician, Arenig Series–Silurian, Llandovery Series; Species, Caradoc Series.

12.* **Dicellograptus anceps** Nicholson. (×2.) Ashgill Series; near Moffat, Dumfriesshire. RANGE: Genus, Llanvirn–Ashgill Series; Species, Ashgill Series.

13. **Trichonodella flexa** Rhodes. (×40.) Llandeilo Series; near Llanfihangel Aberbythych, Carmarthenshire. RANGE: Genus, Middle Ordovician–Upper Silurian; Species, Llandeilo Series.

Plate 14

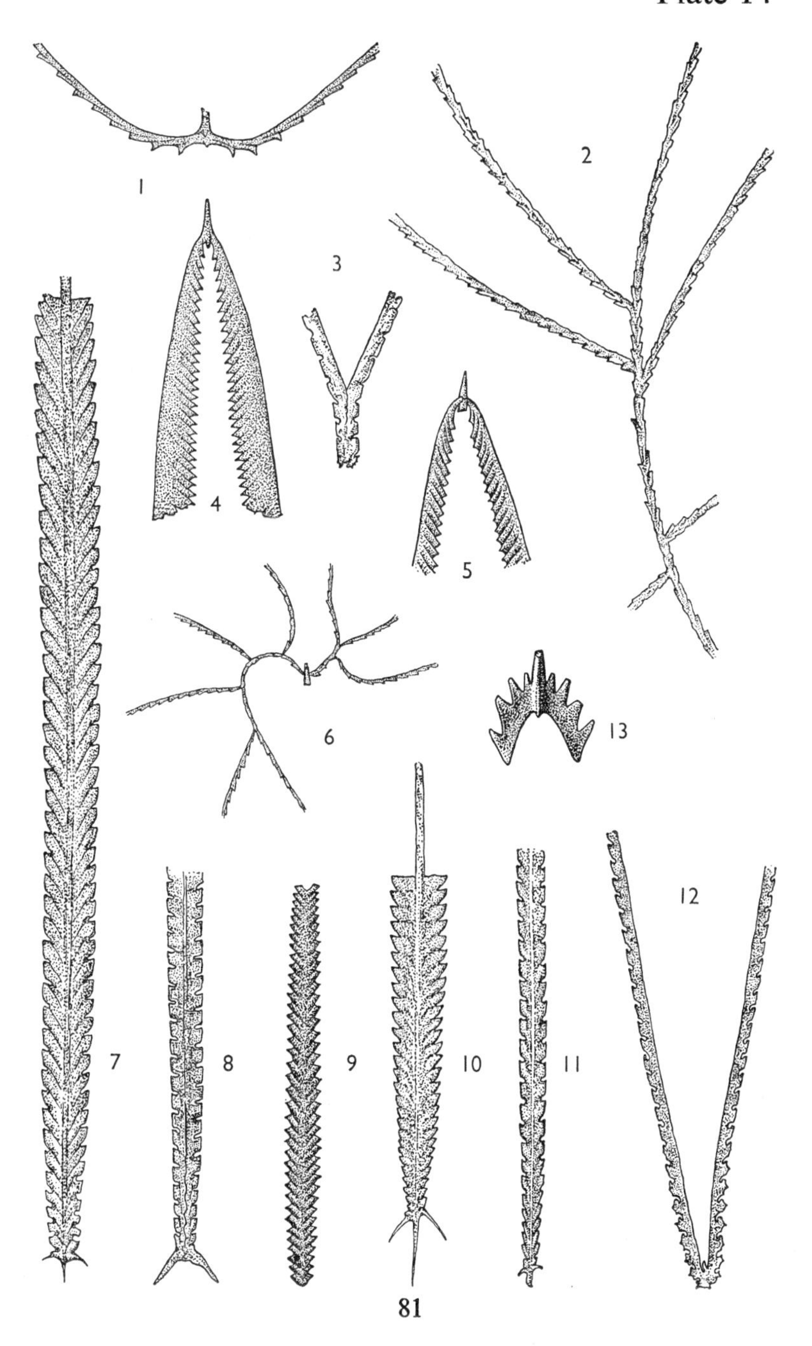

Plate 15
Silurian Corals (Figs. 1–6), Sponges (Figs. 7, 8) and Alga (Fig. 9)

1.* **Favosites gothlandicus** Lamarck forma **forbesi** (Edwards & Haime). 1 (×$\frac{3}{4}$), 1*a* (×1$\frac{1}{2}$). Wenlock Series; Dudley, Worcestershire. RANGE: Genus, Upper Ordovician–Upper Devonian (? Trias); Species, Wenlock–Ludlow Series.

2.* **Acervularia ananas** (Linné). (×2.) Wenlock Series; Dudley, Worcestershire. RANGE: Genus, Silurian; Species, Wenlock Series.

3.* **Halysites catenularius** (Linné). (×4.) Wenlock Series; Dorrington, near Hereford. RANGE: Genus, Ordovician–Silurian; Species, Wenlock Series.

4.* **Arachnophyllum murchisoni** (Edwards & Haime). 4 (×$\frac{3}{4}$), 4*a* (×1$\frac{1}{2}$). Wenlock Series; Dudley, Worcestershire. RANGE: Genus, Llandovery–Wenlock Series; Species, Wenlock Series. [Syn., *Strombodes murchisoni, Strombodes phillipsi* (Orbigny).]

5. **Thamnopora cristata** (Blumenbach). 5 (×1), 5*a* (×3). Wenlock Series; Dudley, Worcestershire. RANGE: Genus, Silurian–Permian; Species, Wenlock Series. [Syn., *Favosites cristata, Pachypora cristata.*]

6.* **Tryplasma loveni** (Edwards & Haime). 6 (×1), 6*a* (×1$\frac{1}{2}$). Wenlock Series; Dudley, Worcestershire. RANGE: Genus, Silurian–Lower Devonian; Species, Wenlock Series. [Syn., *Cyathophyllum? loveni, Pholidophyllum loveni.*]

7.* **Ischadites koenigi** Murchison. (×1$\frac{1}{2}$.) Wenlock Series; Dudley, Worcestershire. RANGE: Genus, Ordovician–Silurian; Species, Ordovician, Llandeilo Series–Silurian, Ludlow Series.

8.* **Amphispongia oblonga** Salter. (×$\frac{3}{4}$.) Ludlow Series; Pentland Hills, Midlothian. RANGE: Genus, Silurian; Species, Ludlow Series.

9. **Mastopora favus** (Salter). (×1.) Llandovery Series; Mulloch Hill, Girvan, Ayrshire. RANGE: Genus, Ordovician–Silurian; Species, Llandovery Series. [Syn., *Nidulites favus.*]

Plate 15

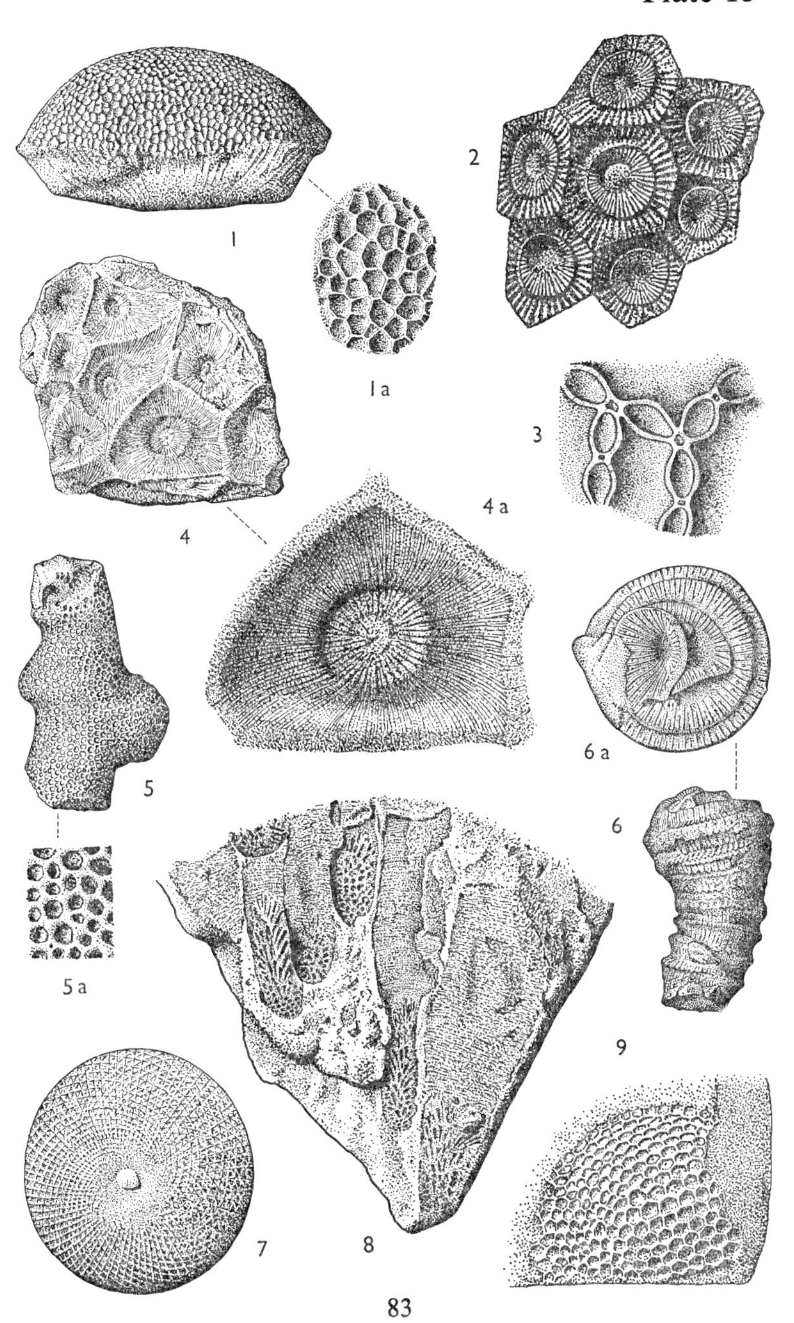

Plate 16

Silurian Polyzoan (Fig. 1), Corals (Figs. 2–9) and Hydrozoan (Fig. 10)

1. **Favositella interpuncta** (Quenstedt). 1 (×½), 1*a* (×4). Wenlock Series; Dudley, Worcestershire. RANGE: Genus, Ordovician–Silurian; Species, Wenlock Series.

2.* **Goniophyllum pyramidale** (Hisinger). (×1.) Wenlock Series; Dudley, Worcestershire. RANGE: Genus, Llandovery–Wenlock Series; Species, Wenlock Series.

3.* **Ketophyllum subturbinatum** (Orbigny). (×½.) Wenlock Series; Dudley, Worcestershire. RANGE: Genus, Llandovery–Wenlock Series; Species, Wenlock Series. [Syn., *Omphyma subturbinata.*]

4. **Rhabdocyclus fletcheri** (Edwards & Haime). (×2.) Wenlock Series; Dudley, Worcestershire. RANGE: Genus, Silurian; Species, Wenlock Series. [Syn., *Palaeocyclus fletcheri.*]

5.* **Heliolites interstinctus** (Linné). (×6.) Wenlock Series; Wenlock, Shropshire. RANGE: Genus, Silurian–Middle Devonian; Species, Wenlock Series.

6. **Syringopora bifurcata** Lonsdale. (×¾.) Wenlock Series; Wenlock, Shropshire. RANGE: Genus, Silurian–Carboniferous; Species, Wenlock Series.

7, 8.* **Kodonophyllum truncatum** (Linné). 7 (×2), 8 (×1). Wenlock Series; near Much Wenlock, Shropshire. RANGE: Genus, Middle–Upper Silurian; Species, Wenlock Series. [Syn., *Cyathophyllum truncatum.*]

9. **Thecia swinderniana** (Goldfuss). (×5.) Wenlock Series; Dudley, Worcestershire. RANGE: Genus, Silurian–Devonian; Species, Wenlock Series.

10. **Labechia conferta** (Lonsdale). (×1½.) Wenlock Series; Coalbrookdale, Shropshire. RANGE: Genus, Ordovician–Silurian; Species, Wenlock Series.

Plate 16

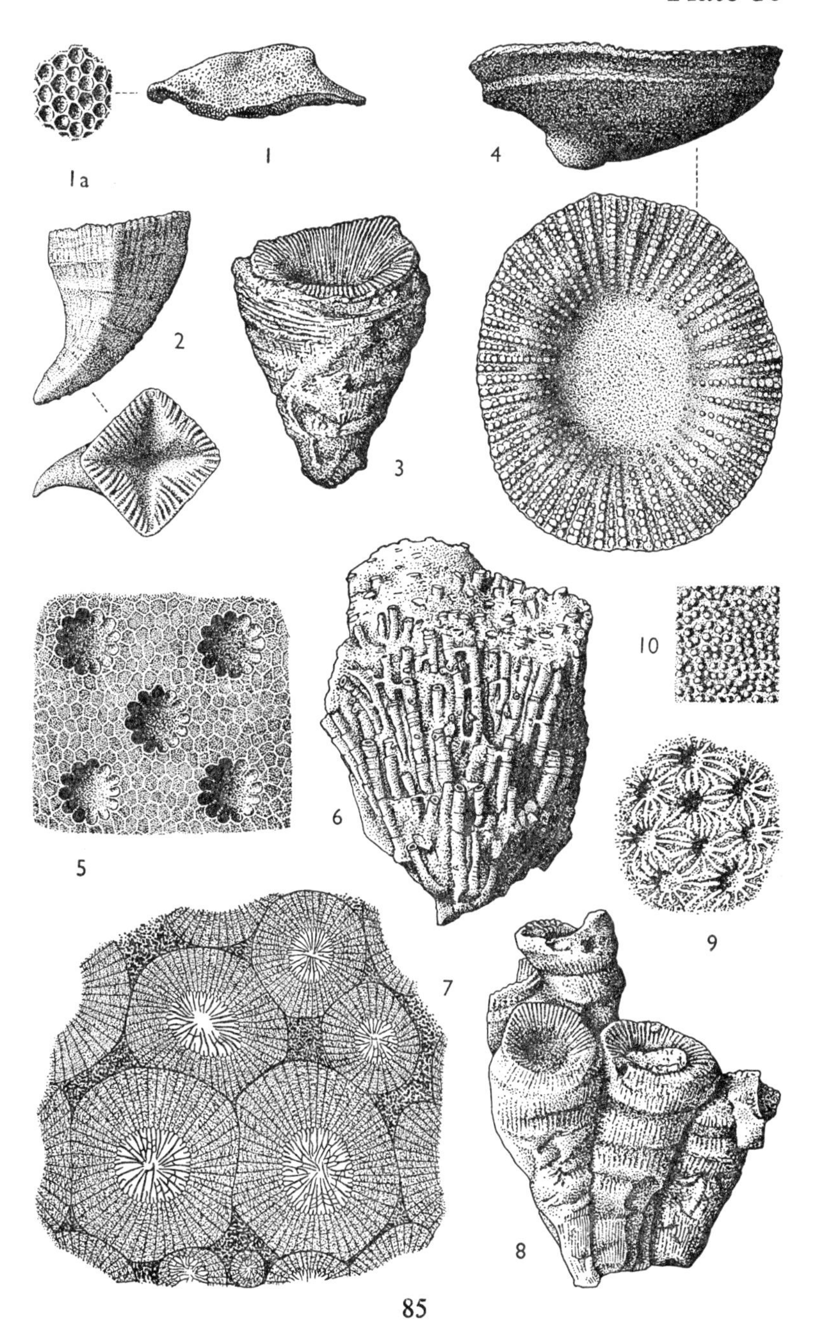

Plate 17

Silurian Class Uncertain (Figs. 1, 3–5), Worms (Figs. 2, 6), and Brachiopods (Figs. 7–12)

1.* **Serpulites longissimus** Murchison. (×¾.) Ludlow Series; Ludlow, Shropshire. RANGE: Genus, Ordovician–Carboniferous; Species, Ordovician, Ashgill Series–Silurian.

2. **Spirorbis tenuis** J. de C. Sowerby. (×6.) Wenlock Series; Dudley, Worcestershire. RANGE: Genus, Silurian–Recent; Species, Wenlock Series.

3. **Tentaculites scalaris** Schlotheim. (×2½.) Llandovery Series; Minsterley, Shropshire. RANGE: Genus, Ordovician–Devonian; Species, Silurian.

4.* **Tentaculites ornatus** J. de C. Sowerby. (×2½.) Wenlock Series; Dudley, Worcestershire. RANGE: Genus, Ordovician–Devonian; Species, Wenlock Series.

5.* **Cornulites serpularius** Schlotheim. (×1.) Wenlock Series; Dudley, Worcestershire. RANGE: Genus, Ordovician–Silurian; Species, Wenlock–Ludlow Series.

6. **Keilorites squamosus** (Phillips). (×1.) Ludlow Series; Shropshire. RANGE: Genus, Ordovician–Silurian; Species, Wenlock–Ludlow Series. [Syn., *Trachyderma squamosa*.]

7. **Skenidioides lewisi** (Davidson). (×3.) Wenlock Series; Buildwas, Shropshire. RANGE: Genus, Ordovician, Ashgill Series–Silurian; Species, Llandovery–Wenlock Series. [Syn., *Skenidium lewisi*.]

8, 9. **Resserella elegantula** (Dalman). (×2.) Wenlock Series; Dudley, Worcestershire. RANGE: Genus, Ordovician–Silurian; Species, Silurian. [Syn., *Parmorthis elegantula*.]

10, 11,* **Pentamerus oblongus** J. de C. Sowerby. (×¾.) Llandovery Series; Norbury, Shropshire. RANGE: Llandovery Series.

12. **Stricklandia lirata** (J. de C. Sowerby). (×¾.) Llandovery Series; Ledbury, Herefordshire. RANGE: Llandovery Series. [Syn., *Pentamerus liratus, Stricklandinia lirata*.]

Plate 17

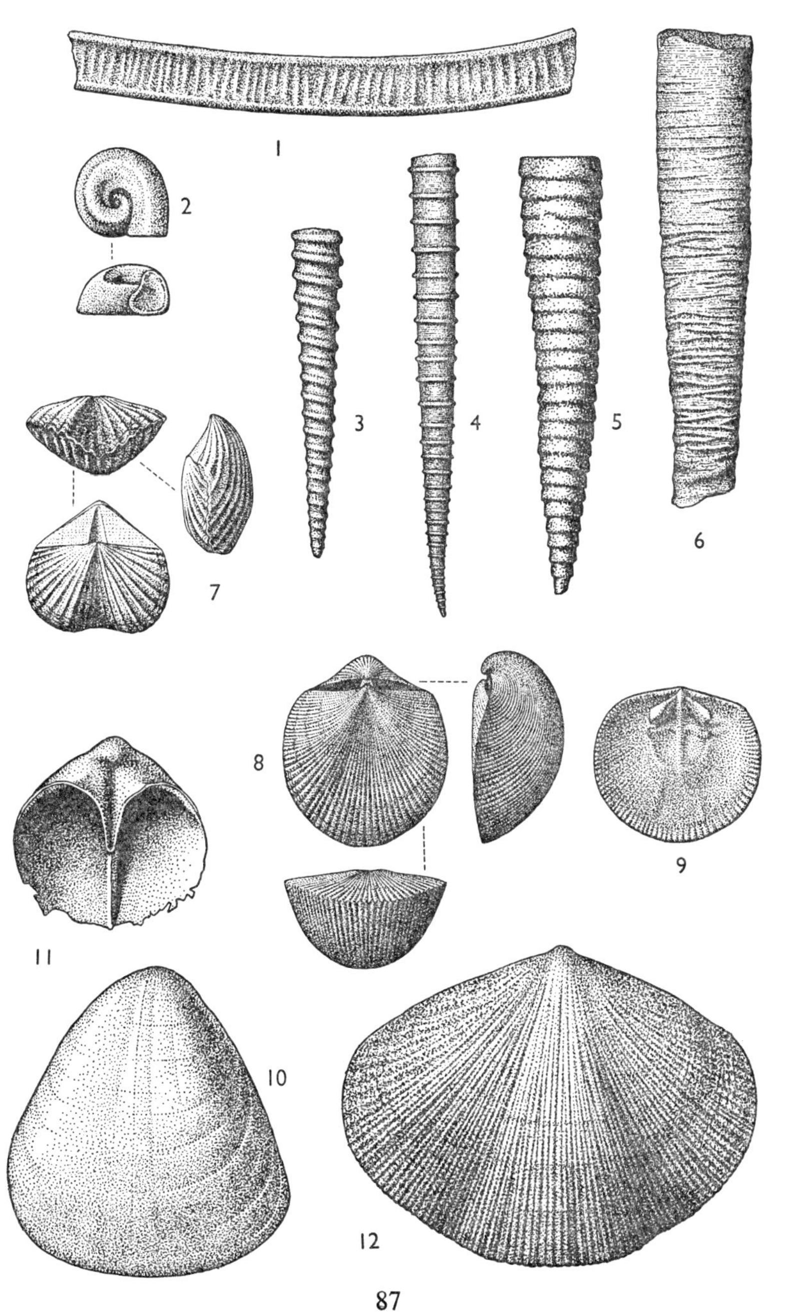

Plate 18
Silurian Brachiopods

1. **Rhynchotreta cuneata** (Dalman). (×1.) Wenlock Series; Dudley, Worcestershire. RANGE: Genus, Silurian; Species, Wenlock Series. [Syn., *Rhynchonella cuneata.*]

2. **Gypidula dudleyensis** Schuchert (×1.) Wenlock Series; near Much Wenlock, Shropshire. RANGE: Genus, Silurian–Devonian; Species, Wenlock Series. [Syn., *Pentamerus dudleyensis, Gypidula galeata* of authors.]

3. **Anastrophia deflexa** (J. de C. Sowerby). (×1½.) Wenlock Series; Dudley, Worcestershire, RANGE: Genus, Silurian–Devonian; Species, Wenlock Series. [Syn., *Rhynchonella deflexa.*]

4. **Dicoelosia biloba** (Linné). (×3½.) Wenlock Series; Dudley, Worcestershire. RANGE: Genus, Ordovician, Ashgill Series–Lower Devonian; Species, Wenlock–Ludlow Series. [Syn., *Bilobites biloba, Orthis biloba.*]

5–7. **Dolerorthis rustica** (J. de C. Sowerby). Wenlock Series. 5 (×1), Dudley, Worcestershire; 6 (×2), interior of dorsal valve, 7 (×1½), interior of ventral valve, near Coalbrookdale, Shropshire. RANGE: Genus, Ordovician–Silurian, Wenlock Series; Species, Wenlock Series. [Syn., *Hebertella rustica, Orthis rustica.*]

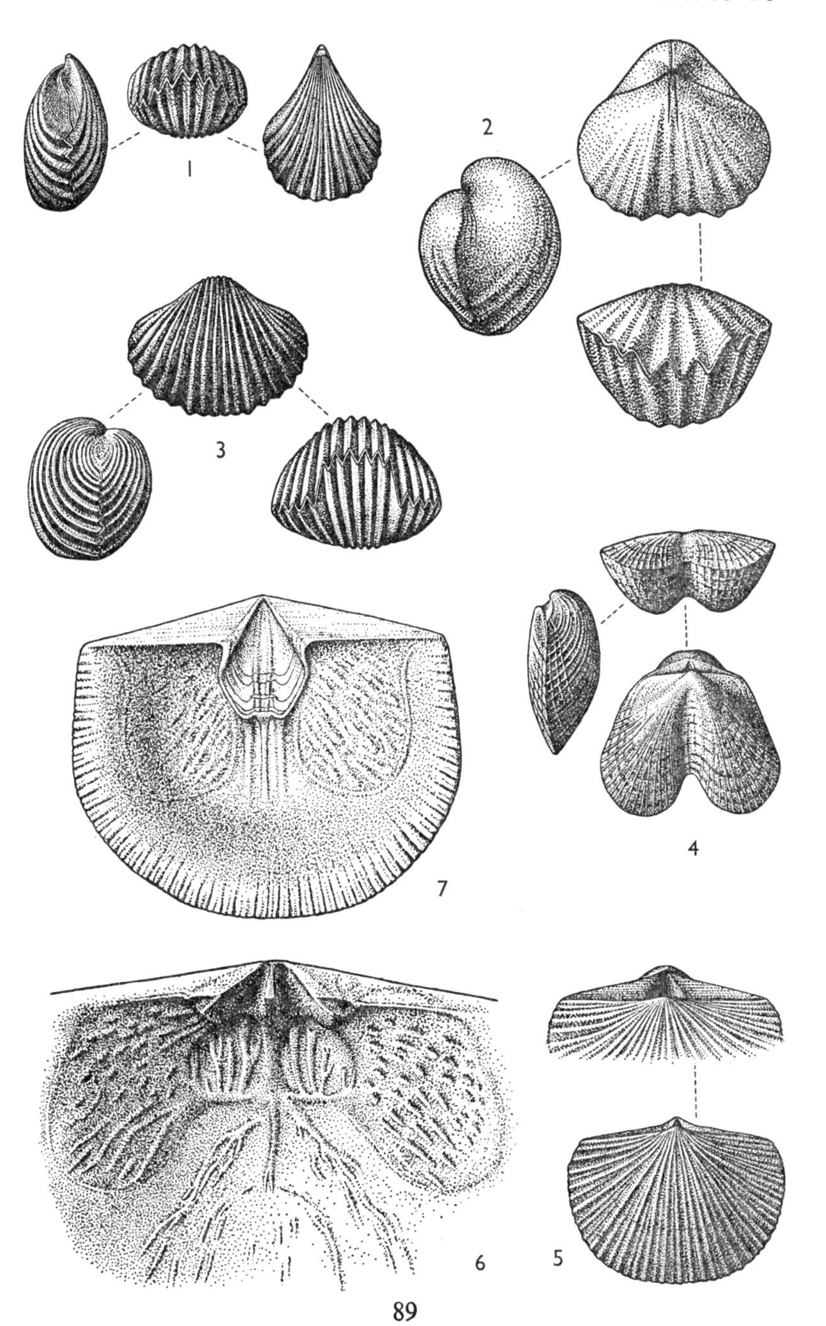
1
2
3
4
5
6
7

Plate 19
Silurian Brachiopods

1. **Trigonirhynchia stricklandi** (J. de C. Sowerby). (×1.) Wenlock Series; Malvern, Worcestershire. RANGE: Genus, Silurian; Species, Wenlock Series. [Syn., *Uncinulina stricklandi.*]

2. **Sphaerirhynchia wilsoni** (J. Sowerby). (×1½.) Wenlock Series; near Much Wenlock, Shropshire. RANGE: Genus, Silurian; Species, Wenlock–Ludlow Series. [Syn., *Rhynchonella wilsoni, Wilsonia wilsoni.*]

3, 4.* **Leptaena depressa** (J. Sowerby). (×1.) Wenlock Series. 3, Usk, Monmouthshire. 4, interior of ventral valve, Dudley, Worcestershire. RANGE: Genus, Ordovician to Silurian; Species, Silurian. [Syn., *Leptaena rhomboidalis* of authors.]

5, 6.* **Strophonella euglypha** (Dalman). (×¾.) 5, dorsal valve. 6, interior of ventral valve. Wenlock Series; near Dudley, Worcestershire. RANGE: Silurian. [Syn., *Strophomena euglypha.*]

7, 8. **Amphistrophia funiculata** (M'Coy). 7, dorsal valve (×2). 8, interior of ventral valve (×1½.) Wenlock Series; Dudley, Worcestershire. RANGE: Genus, Silurian–Devonian; Species, Wenlock–Ludlow Series. [Syn., *Strophomena funiculata, Strophonella funiculata.*]

9. **Plectodonta transversalis** (Wahlenberg). (×2.) Wenlock Series; Dudley, Worcestershire. RANGE: Genus, Ordovician–Devonian; Species, Llandovery–Wenlock Series. [Syn., *Plectambonites transversalis.*]

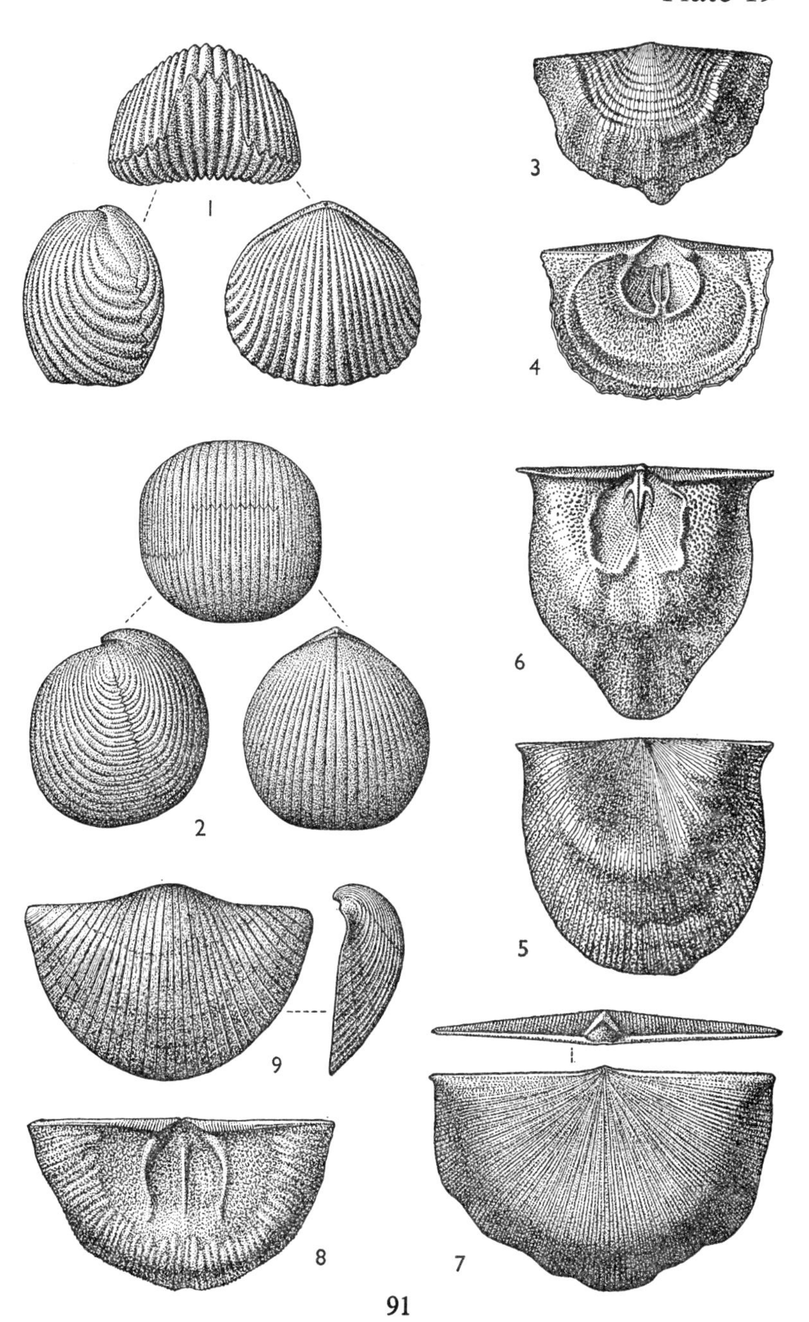
1
2
3
4
5
6
7
8
9

Plate 20
Silurian Brachiopods

1. **Atrypa reticularis** (Linné). (×1.) Wenlock Series; Dudley, Worcestershire. RANGE: Genus, Silurian–Devonian; Species, Silurian.

2. **Eospirifer radiatus** (J. de C. Sowerby). (×1.) Wenlock Series; Dudley, Worcestershire. RANGE: Genus, Silurian–Devonian; Species, Llandovery–Ludlow Series. [Syn., *Spirifer radiatus.*]

3. **Plectatrypa imbricata** (J. de C. Sowerby). (×1½.) Wenlock Series; Walsall, Staffordshire. RANGE: Genus, Silurian-Devonian; Species, Llandovery–Wenlock Series. [Syn., *Atrypa imbricata.*]

4. **Cyrtia exporrecta** (Wahlenberg). (×1.) Wenlock Series; Dudley, Worcestershire. RANGE: Silurian.

5. **Howellella elegans** (Muir-Wood). (×2.) Wenlock Series; Dudley, Worcestershire. RANGE: Genus, Silurian; Species, Llandovery–Ludlow Series. [Syn., *Delthyris elegans.*]

6. **Meristina obtusa** (J. Sowerby). (×¾.) Wenlock Series; Dudley, Worcestershire. RANGE: Wenlock–Ludlow Series. [Syn., *Meristella tumida, Meristina tumida* (Dalman).]

Plate 20

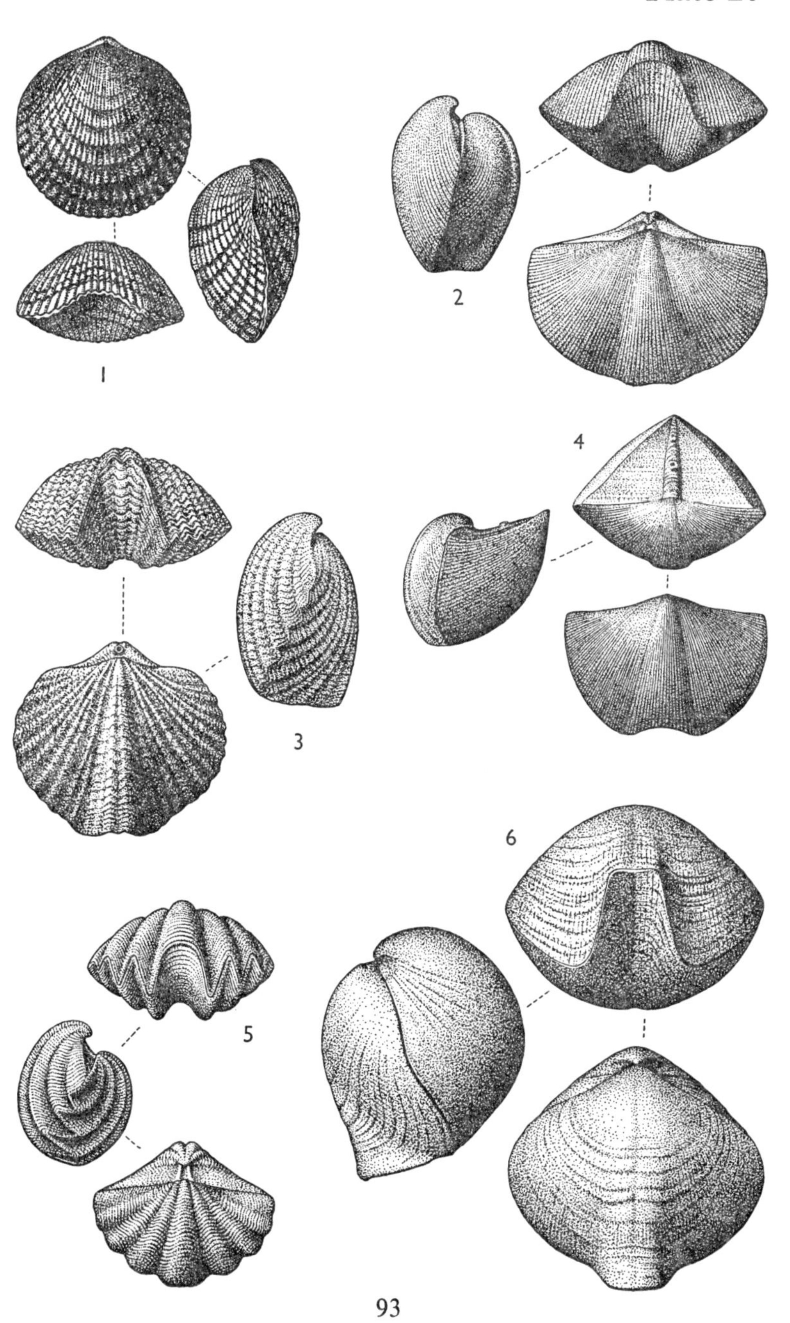

Plate 21

Silurian Echinoid (Fig. 1) and Brachiopods (Figs. 2–12)

1. **Palaeodiscus ferox** Salter. External mould of dorsal surface (×1). Ludlow Series; Church Hill, Leintwardine, Herefordshire. RANGE: Ludlow Series.

2. **Shaleria ornatella** (Davidson). Internal mould of ventral valve. 2 (×1½), 2*a* (×5). Ludlow Series; Whitcliffe, Ludlow, Shropshire. RANGE: Ludlow Series. [Syn., *Strophomena ornatella.*]

3.* **Lingula lewisi** J. de C. Sowerby. (× 1.) Ludlow Series; Ledbury, Herefordshire. RANGE: Genus, Ordovician–Recent; Species, Silurian.

4. **Protochonetes ludloviensis** Muir-Wood. (×1½.) Ludlow Series; Ludlow, Shropshire. RANGE: Genus, Wenlock–Ludlow Series; Species, Ludlow Series. [Syn., *Chonetes striatellus* of authors.]

5. **Dayia navicula** (J. de C. Sowerby). (×2½.) Ludlow Series; Ludlow, Shropshire. RANGE: Genus, Ordovician, Ashgill Series–Lower Devonian; Species, Wenlock–Ludlow Series. [Syn., *Terebratula navicula.*]

6, 7.* **'Camarotoechia' nucula** (J. de C. Sowerby). Internal moulds of dorsal and ventral valves. Ludlow Series. 6 (× 2); Ludlow, Shropshire 7 (× 1½), Llandigffyd, Monmouthshire. RANGE: Species, Silurian. [Syn., *Rhynchonella nucula.*]

8–10. **Salopina lunata** (J. de C. Sowerby). (×1½.) 8, ventral valve; 9, 10, internal moulds of ventral and dorsal valves. Ludlow Series; near Ludlow, Shropshire. RANGE: Genus, Silurian–Middle Devonian (Eifelian); Species, Ludlow Series. [Syn., *Dalmanella lunata, Orthis lunata.*]

11, 12.* **Conchidium knighti** (J. Sowerby). (×¾.) 12, transverse section. Ludlow Series; Mocktree Hill, near Leintwardine, Herefordshire. RANGE: Ludlow Series. [Syn., *Pentamerus knighti.*]

Plate 21

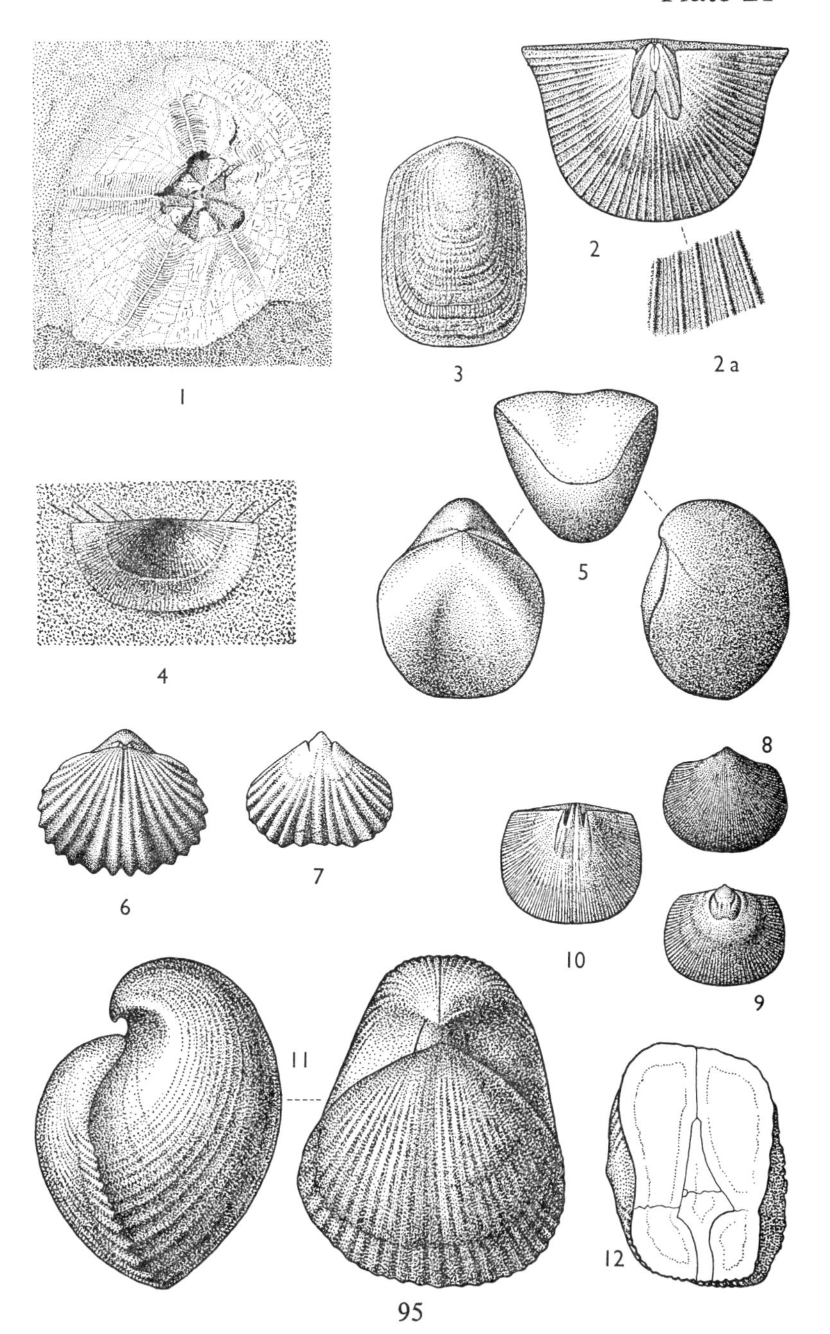

Plate 22

Silurian Crinoid (Figs. 1, 2) and Ophiuroid (Fig. 3)

1, 2.* **Crotalocrinites rugosus** (Miller). (×¾.) Wenlock Series; Dudley, Worcestershire. RANGE: Genus, Silurian; Species, Wenlock Series. [Syn., *Crotalocrinus verrucosus* (Schlotheim).]

3.* **Lapworthura miltoni** (Salter). (×¾.) Ludlow Series; Leintwardine, Herefordshire. RANGE: Ordovician, Ashgill Series–Silurian, Ludlow Series. [Syn., *Lapworthura sollasi* Spencer.]

Plate 22

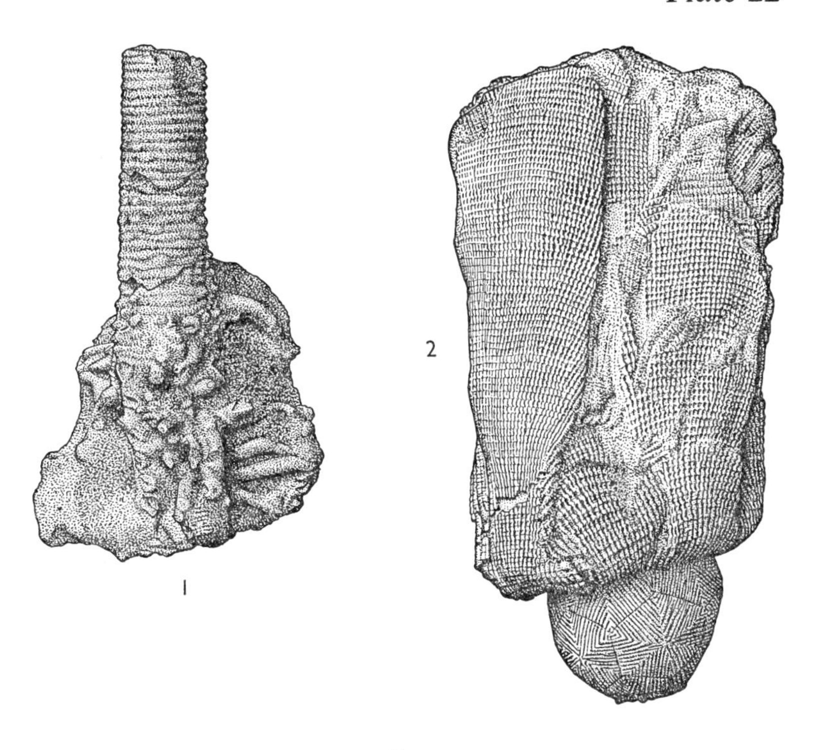

3

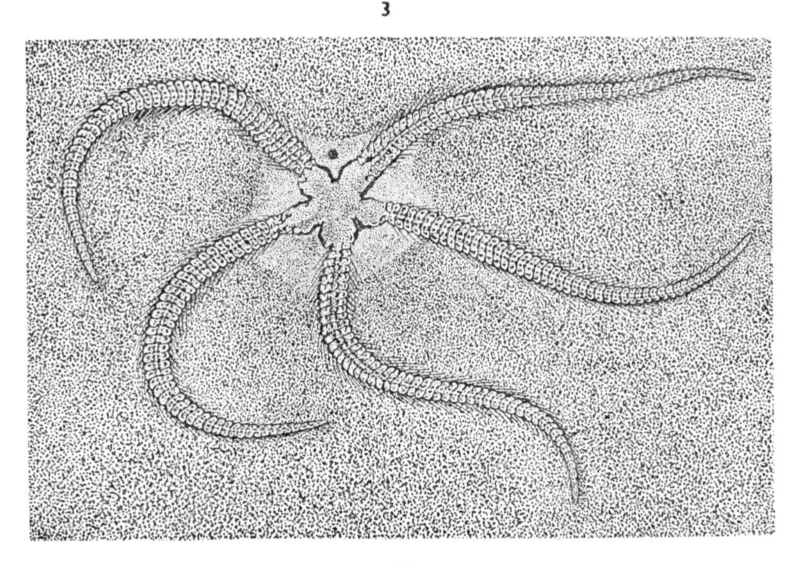

Plate 23
Silurian Crinoids (Figs. 1–3) and Carpoid (Figs. 4, 5)

1.* **Eucalyptocrinites decorus** (Phillips). (×1.) Wenlock Series; Dudley, Worcestershire. RANGE: Genus, Silurian–Devonian; Species, Wenlock Series. [Syn., *Hypanthocrinites decorus.*]

2. **Periechocrinites moniliformis** (Miller). (×¾.) Wenlock Series; Dudley, Worcestershire. RANGE: Genus, Silurian–Carboniferous; Species, Wenlock Series. [Syn., *Periechocrinites costatus* Austin & Austin.]

3.* **Sagenocrinites expansus** (Phillips). (×¾.) Wenlock Series; Dudley, Worcestershire. RANGE: Genus, Silurian; Species, Wenlock Series. [Syn., *Sagenocrinites giganteus* Austin & Austin.]

4, 5.* **Placocystites forbesianus** Koninck. (×1½.) Wenlock Series; Dudley, Worcestershire. RANGE: Genus, Silurian–? Devonian; Species, Wenlock Series.

Plate 23

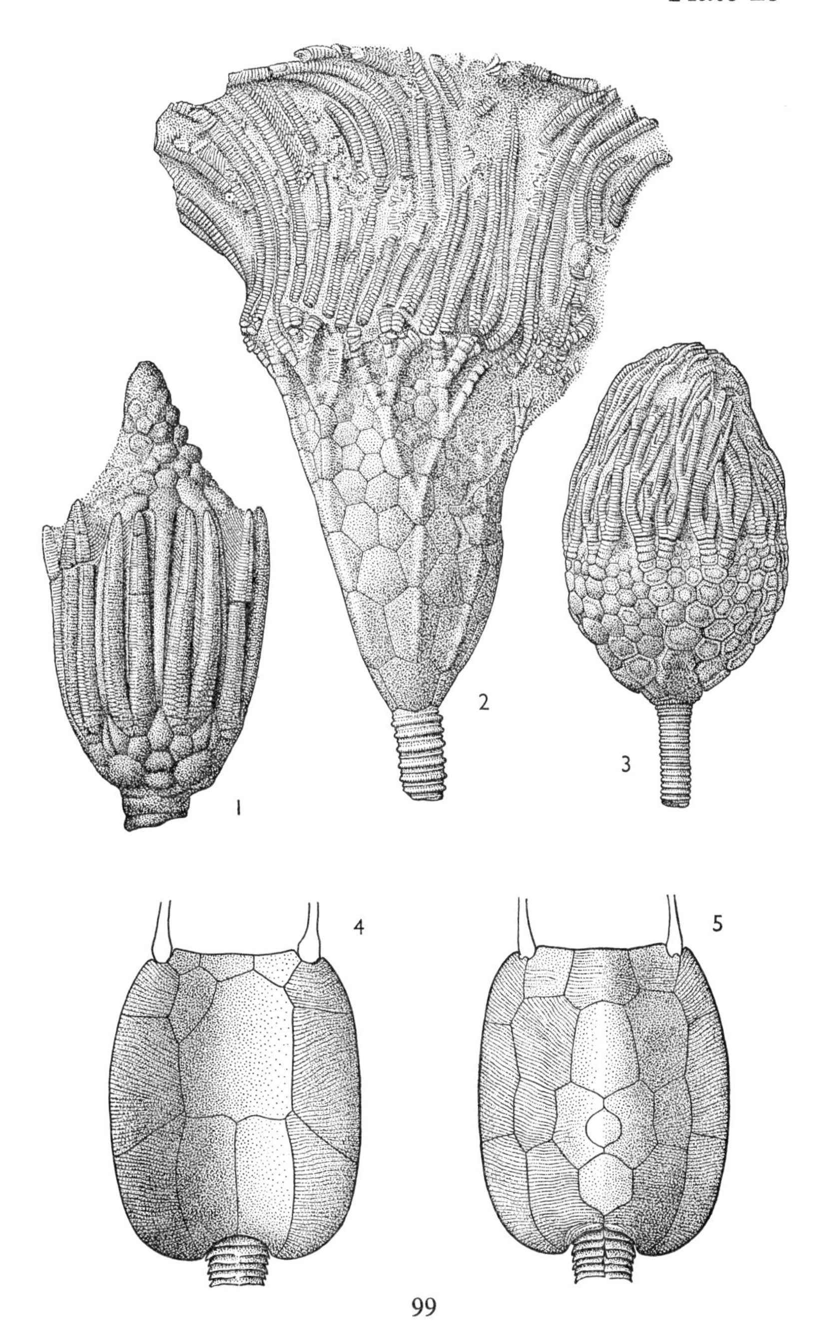

Plate 24

Silurian Cystid (Fig. 1), Crinoid (Fig. 2) and Bivalves (Figs. 3–7)

1.* **Lepocrinites quadrifasciatus** (Pearce). (×1.) Wenlock Series; Walsall, Staffordshire. RANGE: Genus, Silurian; Species, Wenlock Series. [Syn., *Lepadocrinus quadrifasciatus, Staurocystis quadrifasciata.*]

2.* **Gissocrinus goniodactylus** (Phillips). (×1.) Wenlock Series; Dudley, Worcestershire. RANGE: Genus, Silurian–? Devonian; Species, Wenlock Series.

3.* **Pteronitella retroflexa** (Wahlenberg). (×1.) Wenlock Series; Dudley, Worcestershire. RANGE: Genus, Ordovician–Silurian; Species, Silurian.

4.* **Cardiola interrupta** Broderip. (×1.) Wenlock Series; Ulverston, Lancashire. RANGE: Silurian, Wenlock–Ludlow Series.

5.* **Goniophora cymbaeformis** (J. de C. Sowerby). (×1.) Ludlow Series; Dudley, Worcestershire. RANGE: Genus, Ordovician, Llandeilo Series–Silurian, Ludlow Series; Species, Ludlow Series.

6.* **Fuchsella amygdalina** (J. de C. Sowerby). (×1.) Ludlow Series; locality not known. RANGE: Ludlow Series. [Syn., *Orthonota amygdalina.*]

7. **Gotodonta ludensis** (Reed). (×1½.) Ludlow Series; near Ludlow, Shropshire. RANGE: Genus, Silurian, Wenlock–Ludlow Series; Species, Ludlow Series. [Syn., *Tancrediopsis ludensis.*]

Plate 24

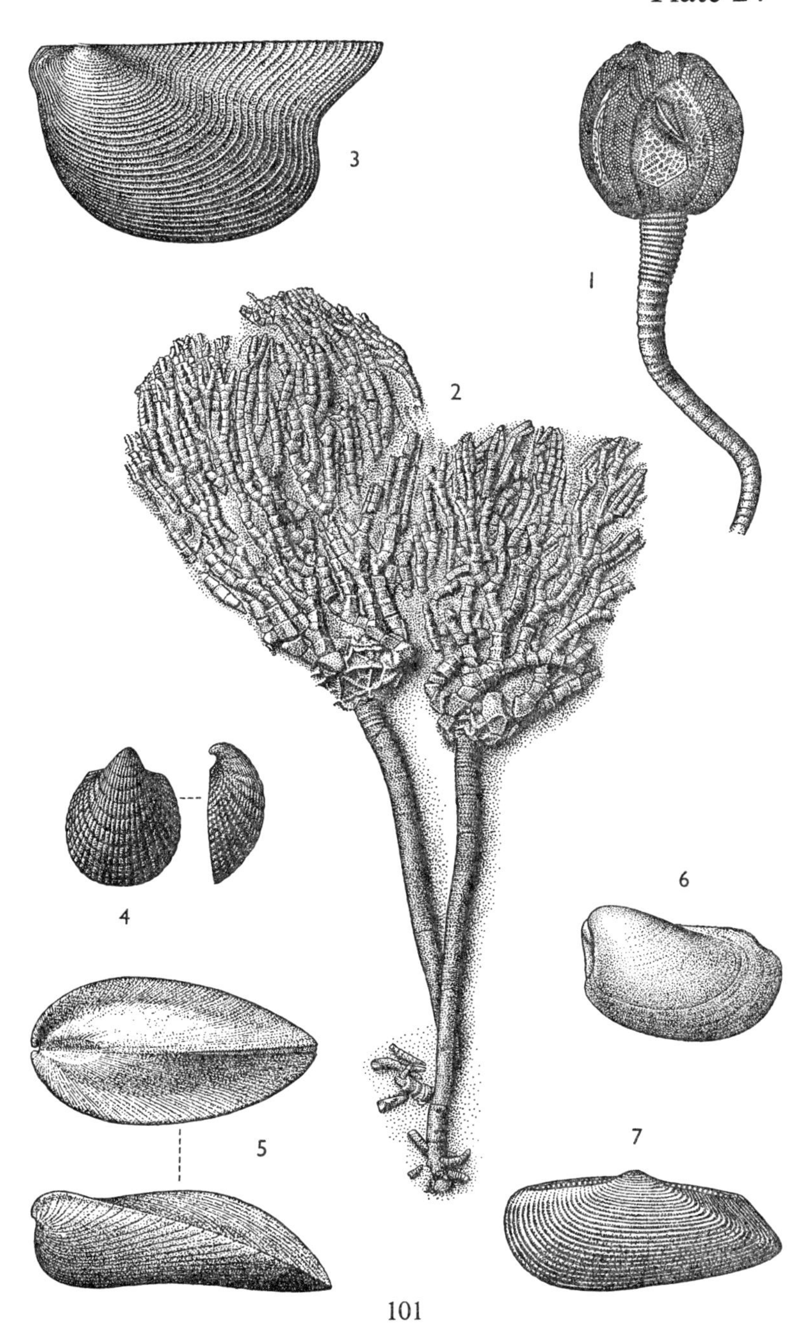

Plate 25

Silurian Gastropods (Figs. 1, 2) and Bivalves (Figs. 3, 4)

1.* **'Bembexia' lloydi** (J. de C. Sowerby). ($\times\frac{1}{2}$.) Ludlow Series; Aymestry, Herefordshire. RANGE: Silurian, Wenlock–Ludlow Series. [Syn., *'Pleurotomaria' lloydi.*]

2. **Tremanotus dilatatus** (J. de C. Sowerby). ($\times\frac{3}{4}$.) Wenlock Series; Dudley, Worcestershire. RANGE: Genus, Upper Ordovician–Silurian; Species, Wenlock–Ludlow Series. [Syn., *Tremanotus britannicus* Newton.]

3.* **Grammysia cingulata** (Hisinger). (×1.) Wenlock Series; Dudley, Worcestershire. RANGE: Genus, Ordovician, Caradoc Series–Silurian, Ludlow Series; Species, Wenlock–Ludlow Series.

4.* **Palaeopecten danbyi** (M'Coy). (×1.) Ludlow Series; Whitcliffe, near Ludlow, Shropshire. RANGE: Wenlock–Ludlow Series. [Syn., *Pterinea danbyi.*]

Plate 25

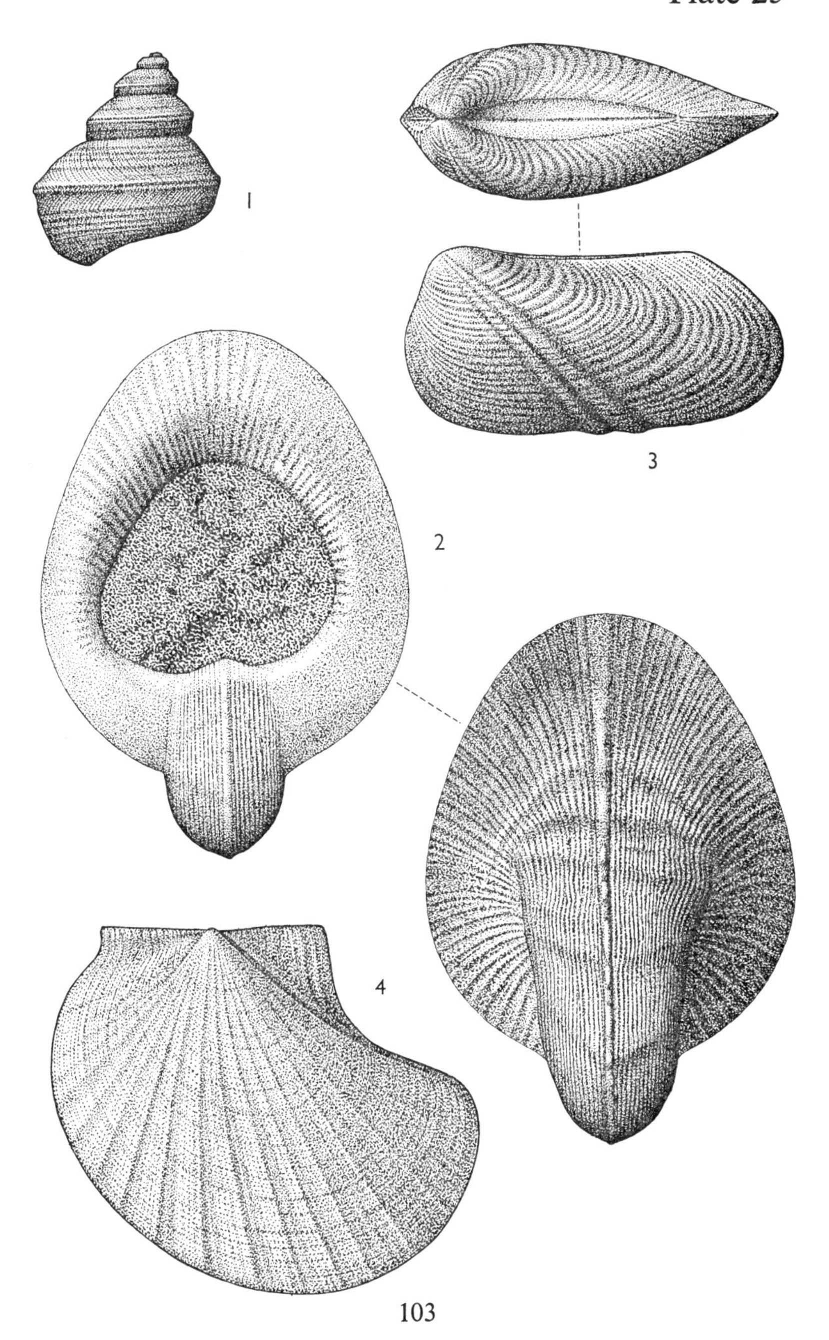

Plate 26
Silurian Gastropods

1.* **Poleumita discors** (J. Sowerby). (×1.) Wenlock Series; Benthall Edge, near Much Wenlock, Shropshire. RANGE: Genus, Silurian; Species, Wenlock–Ludlow Series. [Syn., *Horiostoma discors, Polytropina discors.*]

2, 3.* **Loxoplocus cancellatulus** (M'Coy). 2, artificial cast from external mould (×1¼), *2a*, part of same, enlarged (×5.); 3, internal mould (×1¼). Llandovery Series; Mulloch Hill, Girvan, Ayrshire. RANGE: Genus, Cambrian–Silurian; Species, Llandovery Series. [Syn., *Lophospira cancellatula.*]

4. **Loxonema gregaria** (J. de C. Sowerby). Artificial cast from external mould (×1.). Ludlow Series; Cerig y brobach, Llandovery, Carmarthenshire. RANGE: Genus, Ordovician, Caradoc Series–Devonian; Species, Silurian, Ludlow Series. [Syn., *Holopella gregaria.*]

5. **'Platyschisma' helicites** (J. Sowerby). (×1.) Ludlow Series; Ludford Lane, near Ludlow, Shropshire. RANGE: Silurian, Ludlow Series–Lower Devonian.

6. **Platyceras haliotis** (J. de C. Sowerby). (× 1.) Wenlock Series; Dudley, Worcestershire. RANGE: Genus, Silurian–Carboniferous; Species, Wenlock–Ludlow Series.

Plate 26

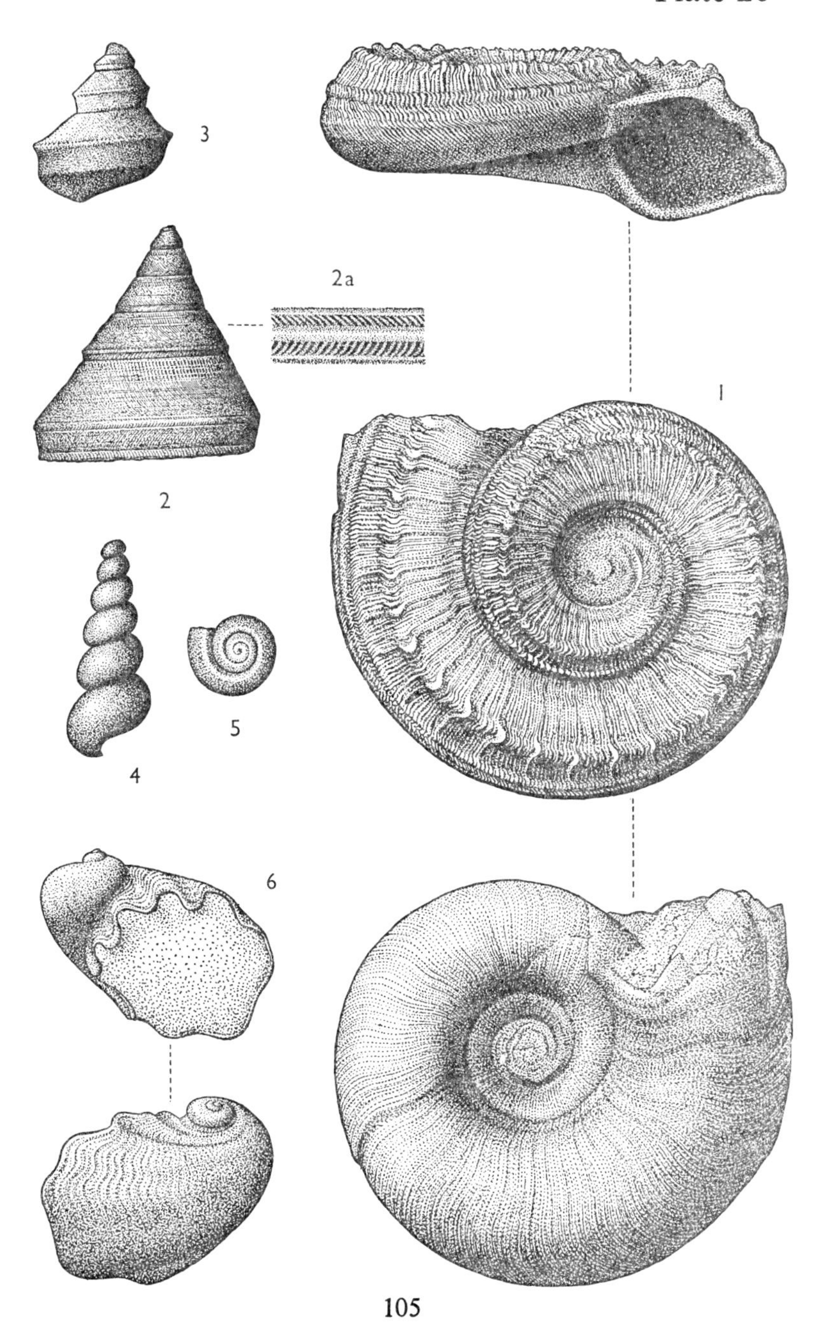

Plate 27

Silurian Gastropod (Fig. 1), Cephalopods (Figs. 2, 3) and Trilobites (Figs. 4–7)

1.* **Euomphalopterus alatus** (Wahlenberg). (×1.) Wenlock Series; near Dudley, Worcestershire. RANGE: Genus, Silurian; Species, Wenlock–Ludlow Series.

2.* **Dawsonoceras annulatum** (J. Sowerby). (×¾.) Wenlock Series; Coalbrookdale, Shropshire. RANGE: Genus, Silurian; Species, Wenlock–Ludlow Series. [Syn., *Orthoceras annulatum.*]

3.* **Gomphoceras ellipticum** M'Coy. (×¾.) Ludlow Series; Leintwardine, Herefordshire. RANGE: Genus, Silurian; Species, Ludlow Series.

4.* **Phacops stokesi** Edwards. (×1½.) Wenlock Series; Dudley, Worcestershire. RANGE: Genus, Silurian–Devonian; Species, Wenlock Series.

5. **Encrinurus onniensis** Whittard. (×3.) Llandovery Series; near Wistanstow, Shropshire. RANGE: Genus, Ordovician, Caradoc Series–Silurian; Species, Llandovery Series.

6, 7. **Calymene replicata** Shirley. (×2.) Llandovery Series; Newlands, Girvan, Ayrshire. RANGE: Genus, Silurian–Devonian; Species, Llandovery Series.

Plate 27

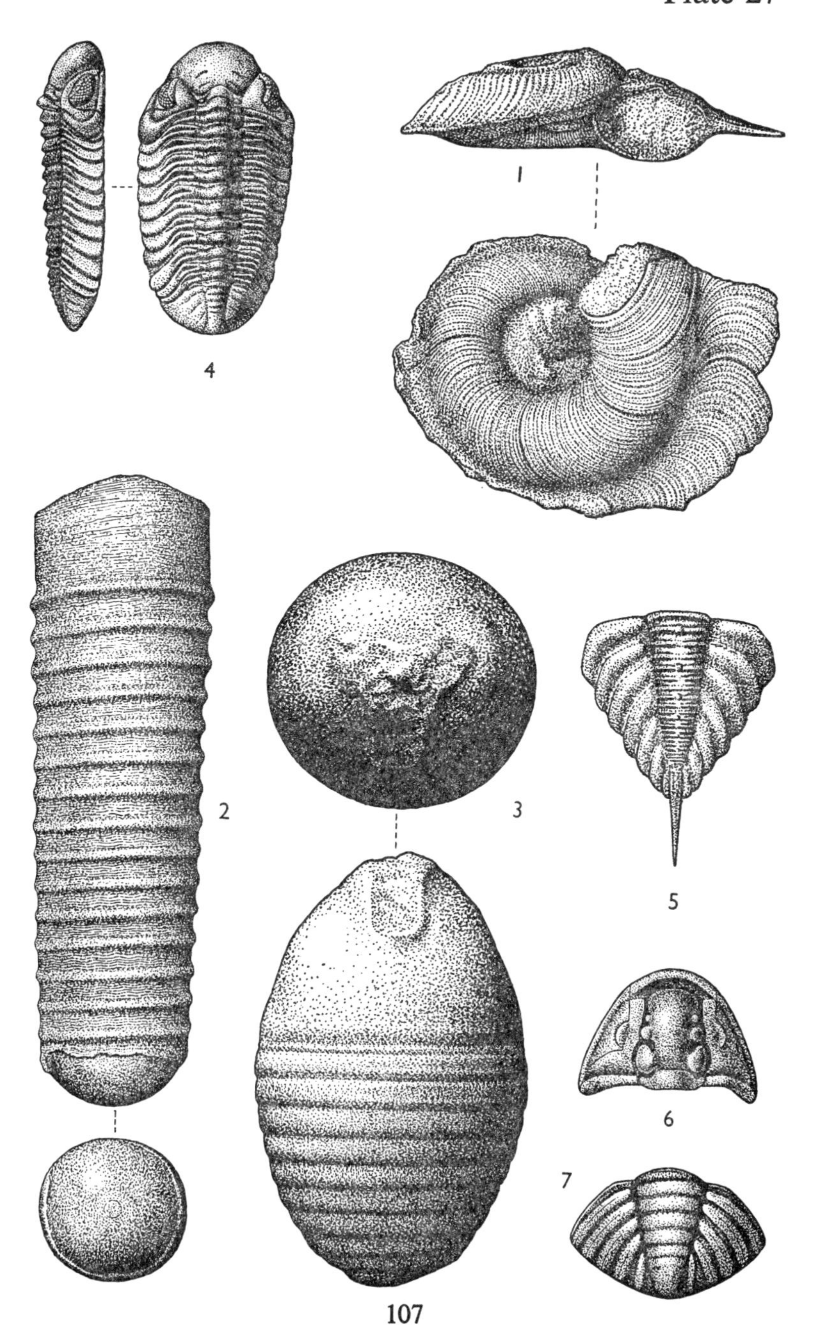

Plate 28
Silurian Trilobites

1, 2.* **Calymene blumenbachi** Brongniart. ($\times 1$.) Wenlock Series; Dudley, Worcestershire. RANGE: Genus, Silurian–Devonian; Species, Wenlock Series.

3.* **Trimerus delphinocephalus** (Green). ($\times 1$.) Wenlock Series; Dudley, Worcestershire. RANGE: Wenlock Series. [Syn., *Homalonotus delphinocephalus*.]

4.* **Sphaerexochus mirus** Beyrich. ($\times 1$.) Wenlock Series; Malvern, Worcestershire. RANGE: Genus, Ordovician, Caradoc Series–Silurian; Species, Wenlock Series.

5.* **Dalmanites myops** (König). ($\times 1\frac{1}{4}$.) Wenlock Series; Dudley, Worcestershire. RANGE: Genus, Silurian–Devonian; Species, Silurian. [Syn., *Dalmanites vulgaris* (Salter), *Phacops longicaudatus* Murchison.]

6.* **Cheirurus bimucronatus** (Murchison). ($\times 2$.) Wenlock Series; Dudley, Worcestershire. RANGE: Genus, Ordovician, Ashgill Series–Silurian; Species, Llandovery–Wenlock Series.

7.* **Bumastus barriensis** (Murchison). ($\times \frac{1}{2}$.) Wenlock Series; Dudley, Worcestershire. RANGE: Genus, Ordovician–Silurian; Species, Wenlock Series. [Syn., *Illaenus barriensis*.]

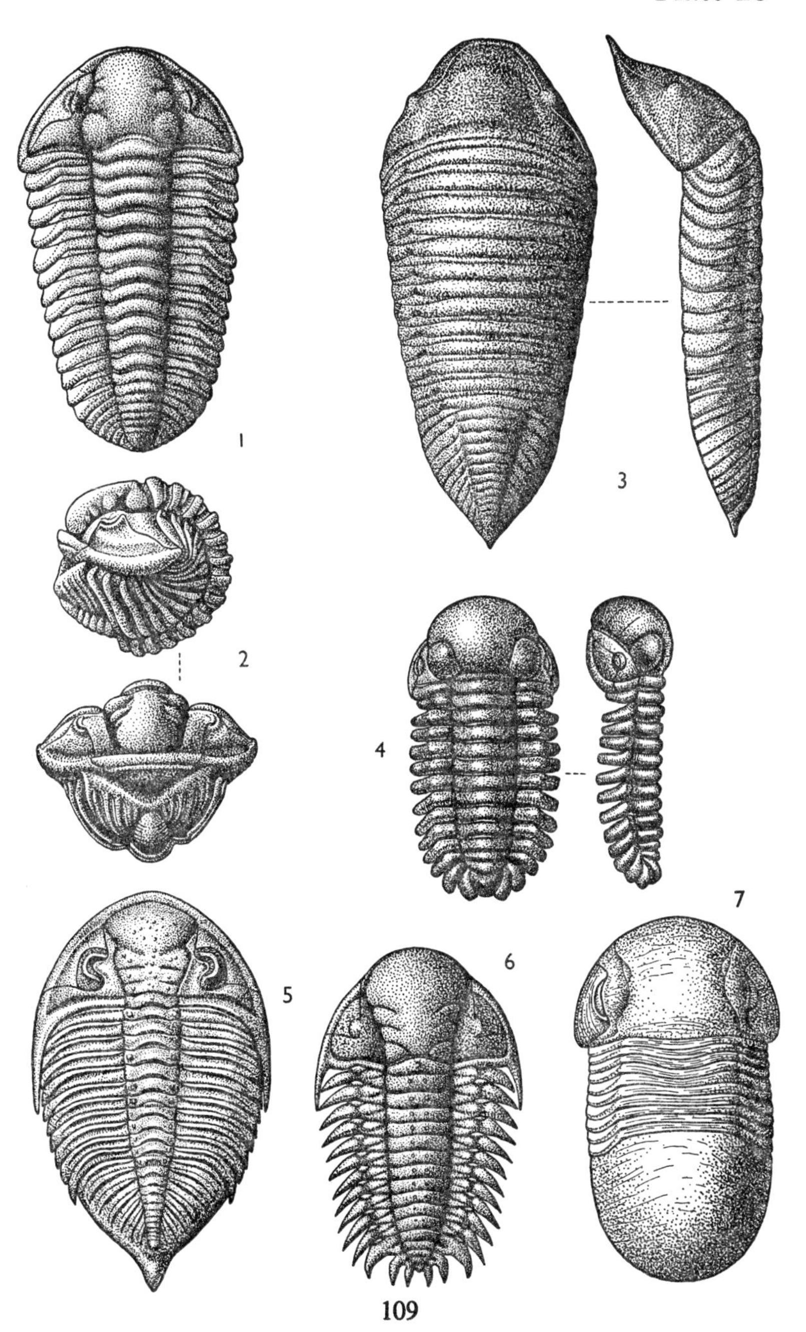
1
2
3
4
5
6
7

Plate 29
Silurian Ostracods (Figs. 1–3) and Trilobites (Figs. 4–10)

1, 2. **Beyrichia** cf. **kloedeni** M'Coy. (×10.) 1, male dimorph. 2, female dimorph. Wenlock Series; Coalbrookdale, near Ironbridge, Shropshire. RANGE: Genus, Silurian; Species, Wenlock Series.

3. **Leperditia balthica** (Hisinger). (×1.) Wenlock Series; Wren's Nest, Dudley, Worcestershire. RANGE: Genus, Silurian; Species, Wenlock–Ludlow Series.

4.* **Acidaspis deflexa** Lake. (×2.) Wenlock Series; Dudley, Worcestershire. RANGE: Genus, Ordovician, Ashgill Series–Silurian; Species, Wenlock Series.

5.* **Deiphon forbesi** Barrande. (×2.) Wenlock Series; Dudley, Worcestershire. RANGE: Genus, Silurian; Species, Wenlock Series.

6. **Encrinurus punctatus** (Wahlenberg). (×1.) Wenlock Series; Malvern, Worcestershire. RANGE: Genus, Ordovician, Caradoc Series–Silurian; Species, Llandovery–Wenlock Series.

7.* **Encrinurus variolaris** (Brongniart). (×1½.) Wenlock Series; Malvern, Worcestershire. RANGE: Genus, Ordovician, Caradoc Series–Silurian; Species, Wenlock Series.

8.* **Acaste downingiae** (Murchison). (×1½.) Wenlock Series; Dudley, Worcestershire. RANGE: Genus, Silurian; Species, Wenlock Series. [Syn., *Phacops downingiae.*]

9, 10. **Delops obtusicaudatus** (Salter). (×1.) Ludlow Series; Coldwell Quarry, Keag Castle, near Coniston, Lancashire, RANGE: Genus, Silurian, Wenlock–Ludlow Series; Species, Ludlow Series. [Syn., *Dalmanites obtusicaudatus, Phacops obtusicaudatus.*]

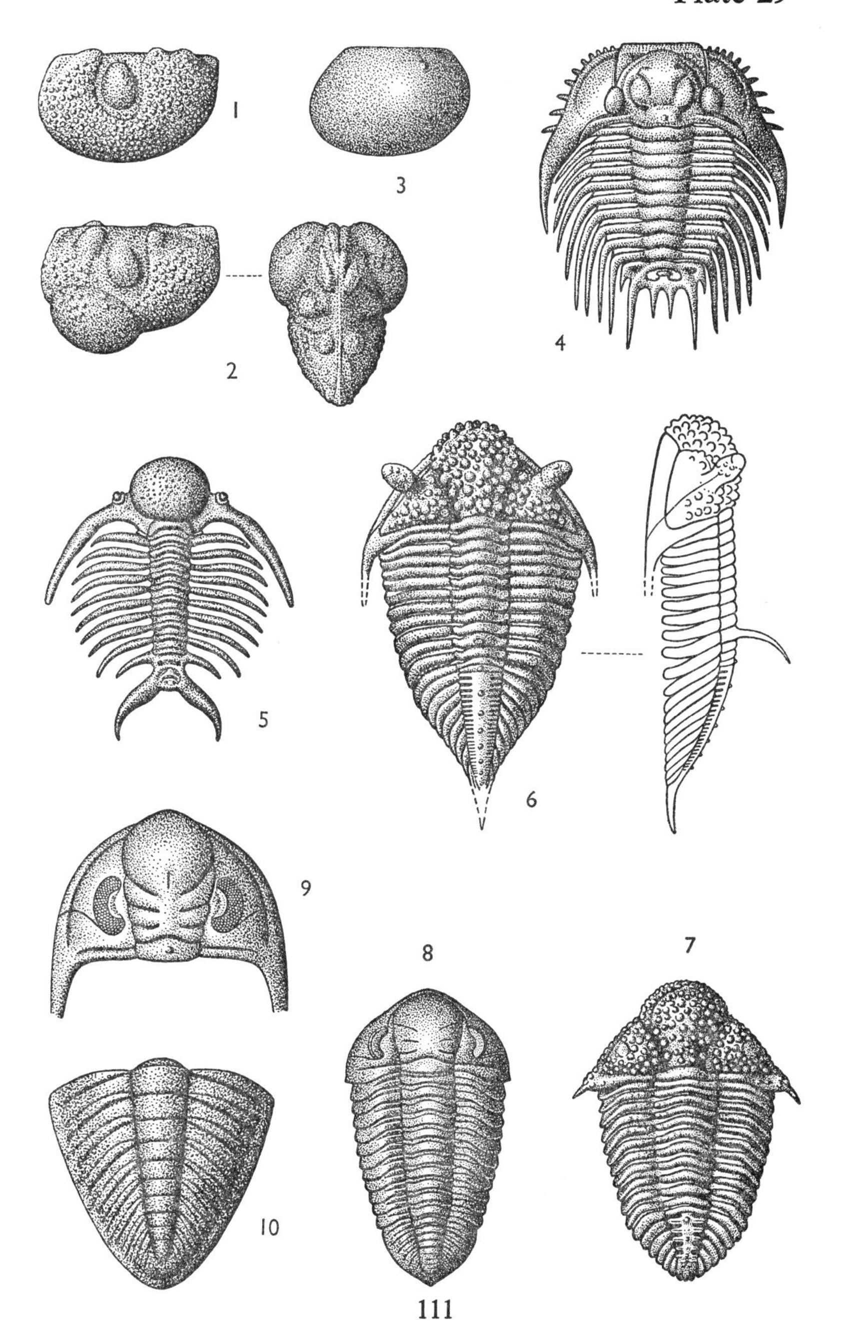
1
3
4
2
5
6
9
8
7
10

Plate 30

Silurian Graptolites (Figs. 1–9), Conodonts (Figs. 10–12), Malacostracan (Fig. 13) and Eurypterid (Fig. 14)

1.* **Monograptus sedgwicki** (Portlock). (×2.) Llandovery Series; Stockdale, near Ambleside, Westmorland. RANGE: Genus, Silurian; Species, Llandovery Series.

2.* **Monograptus priodon** (Bronn). (×2.) Llandovery Series; Grieston Quarry, south-west of Innerleithen, Peebleshire. RANGE: Genus, Silurian; Species, Llandovery–Wenlock Series.

3.* **Monograptus lobiferus** (M'Coy). (×2.) Llandovery Series; Dobbs Linn, Moffat, Dumfriesshire. RANGE: Genus, Silurian; Species, Llandovery Series.

4.* **Monograptus colonus** (Barrande). (×2.) Ludlow Series; Dudley, Worcestershire. RANGE: Genus, Silurian; Species, Ludlow Series.

5. **Monograptus leintwardinensis** Hopkinson. (×2.) Ludlow Series, Leintwardine, Herefordshire. RANGE: Genus, Silurian; Species; Ludlow Series.

6. **Petalograptus minor** Elles. (×2.) Llandovery Series; Skelgill, near Ambleside, Westmorland. RANGE: Llandovery Series.

7. **Monograptus turriculatus** (Barrande). (×2.) Llandovery Series; Stockdale, near Ambleside, Westmorland. RANGE: Genus, Silurian; Species, Llandovery Series.

8. **Diplograptus modestus** (Lapworth). (×2.) Llandovery Series; Girvan, Ayrshire. RANGE: Genus, Ordovician, Llanvirn Series –Silurian, Llandovery Series; Species, Llandovery Series. [Syn., *Mesograptus modestus*.]

9. **Cyrtograptus murchisoni** Carruthers. (×2.) Wenlock Series; near Builth Wells, Radnorshire. RANGE: Wenlock Series.

10. **Panderodus unicostatus** (Branson & Mehl). (×15.) Ludlow Series; Clungunford, Shropshire. RANGE: Genus, Silurian, Wenlock–Ludlow Series; Species, Ludlow Series.

11. **Ozarkodina typica** Branson & Mehl. (×20.) Ludlow Series; Clungunford, Shropshire. RANGE: Genus, Ordovician–Lower Carboniferous; Species, Ludlow Series.

12. **Spathognathodus typicus** (Branson & Mehl). (×20.) Ludlow Series; Clungunford, Shropshire. RANGE: Genus, Silurian –Upper Carboniferous; Species, Ludlow Series.

continued on page 114

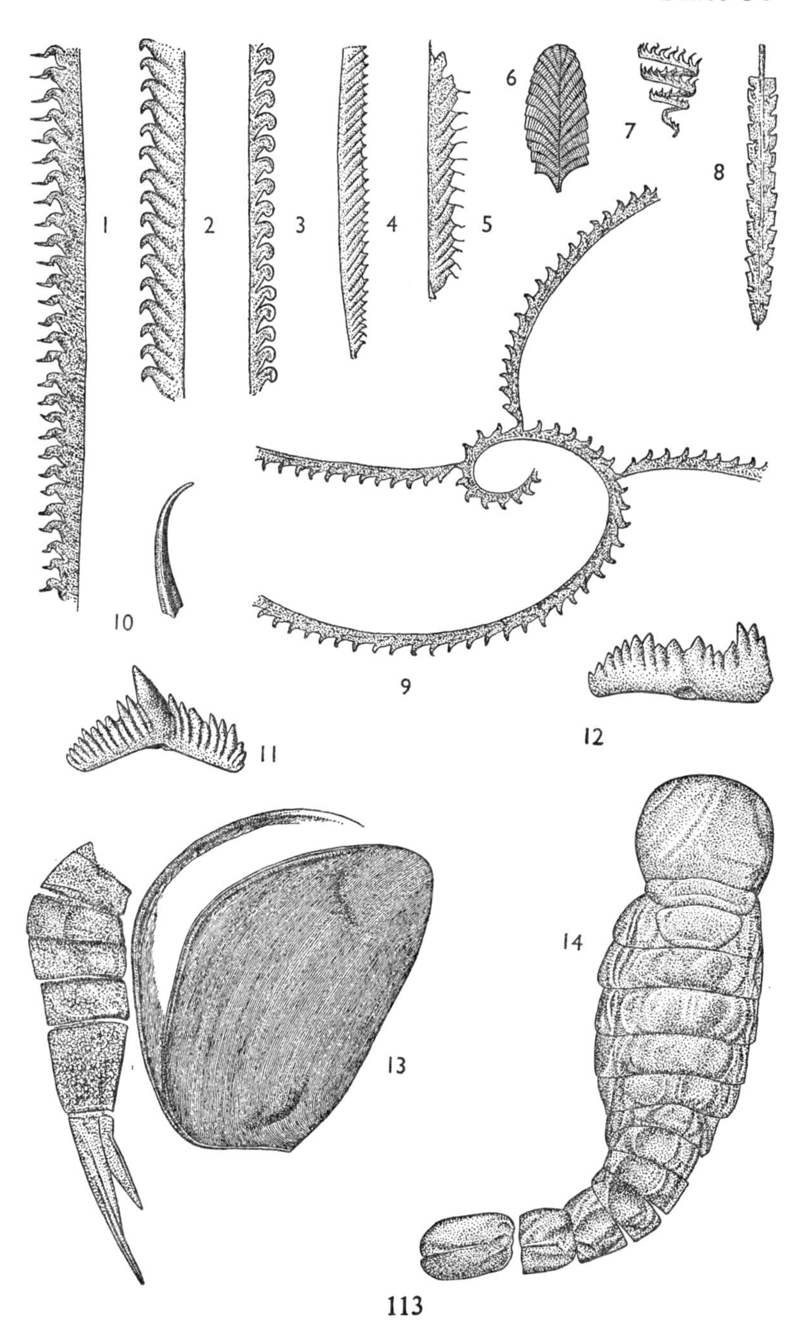
1
2
3
4
5
6
7
8
9
10
11
12
13
14

Plate 31

Devonian Plants (Figs. 1–3), Stromatoporoid (Fig.4) and Corals (Figs. 5–9)

1. **Psilophyton princeps** Dawson. Part of stem ($\times\frac{3}{4}$). Lower Old Red Sandstone, Senni Beds; Llanover, near Abergavenny, Monmouthshire RANGE: Lower Devonian.

2, 3. **Zosterophyllum llanoveranum** Croft & Lang. 2, axes; 3, sporangia ($\times 1$). Lower Old Red Sandstone, Senni Beds; Llanover, near Abergavenny, Monmouthshire. RANGE: Lower Devonian.

4. **Stromatopora huepschii** (Bargatsky). Longitudinal Section ($\times 10$). Pebble from Middle ? Devonian, Teignmouth, Devon. RANGE: Genus, Ordovician–Permian; Species, Middle–Upper Devonian.

5.* **Favosites goldfussi** Orbigny. Transverse Section ($\times 2$). Middle Devonian; South Devon. RANGE: Genus, Upper Ordovician –Upper Devonian (? Trias); Species, Middle–Upper Devonian.

6.* **Heliolites porosus** (Goldfuss). Transverse Section ($\times 5$). Middle Devonian, South Devon. RANGE: Genus, Silurian–Middle Devonian; Species, Lower–Middle Devonian.

7. **Hexagonaria goldfussi** (Verneuil & Haime). Transverse Section ($\times 3$). Upper Devonian; Babbacombe, Torquay, Devon. RANGE: Genus, Devonian; Species, Upper Devonian. [Syn., *Acervularia goldfussi.*]

8.* **Thamnopora cervicornis** (Blainville). Transverse Section ($\times 1$). Middle Devonian; Torquay, Devon. RANGE: Genus, Silurian –Permian; Species, Middle Devonian [Syn., *Pachypora cervicornis.*]

9.* **Haplothecia pengellyi** (Edwards & Haime). Transverse section ($\times 2$). Upper Devonian; pebble in Parson and Clerk Rocks, Dawlish, Devon. RANGE: Genus, Devonian; Species, probably Middle Devonian. [Syn., *Smithia pengellyi.*]

Plate 30 (*continued*)

13.* **Ceratiocaris stygia** Salter. ($\times\frac{3}{4}$.) Ludlow Series; North Cumberhead, Logan Water, Lanarkshire. RANGE: Genus, Ordovician –Lower Carboniferous; Species, Ludlow Series.

14. **Pterygotus bilobus** Salter. ($\times\frac{1}{2}$.) Ludlow Series; Lesmahagow, Lanarkshire. RANGE: Genus, Ordovician–Devonian; Species, Ludlow Series.

Plate 31

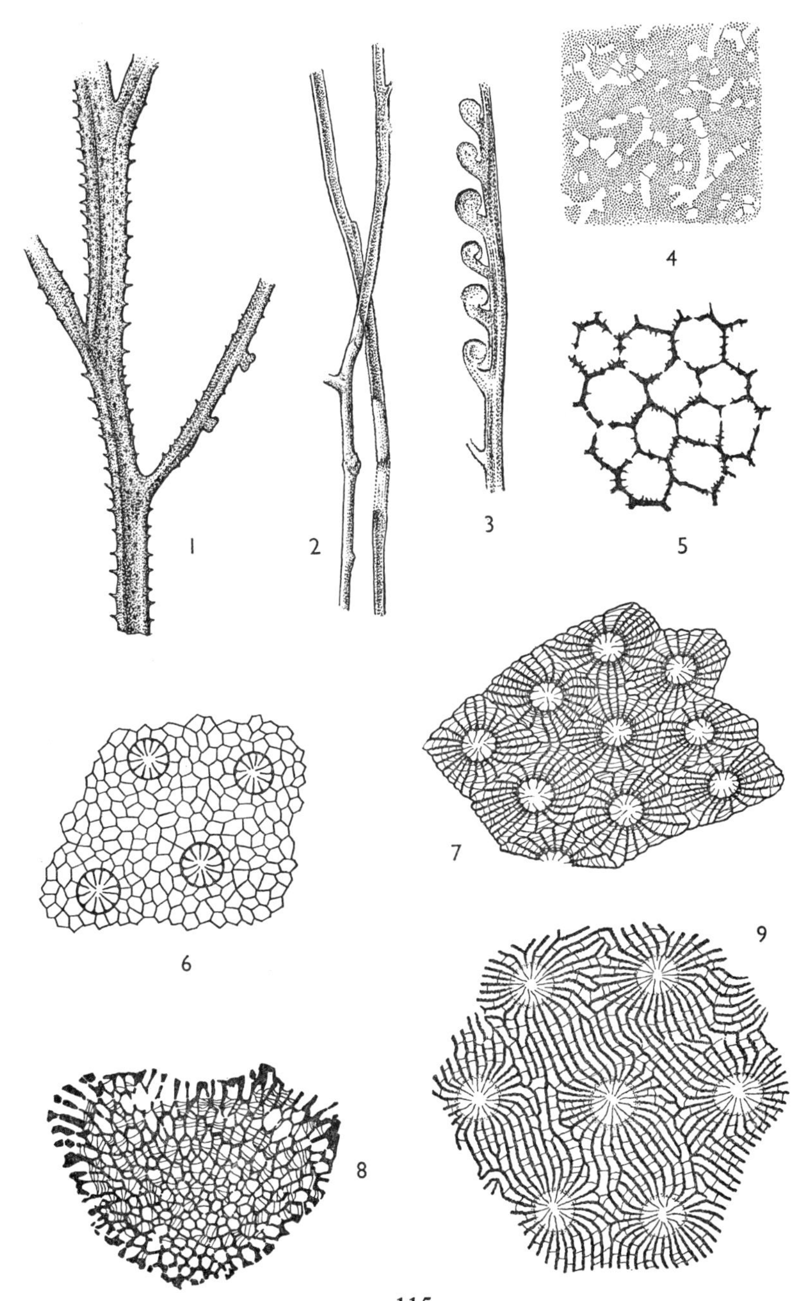

Plate 32

Devonian Brachiopods (Fig. 1–4), Corals (Figs. 5–7) and Crinoid (Fig. 8)

1.* **Productella fragaria** (J. de C. Sowerby). (×¾.) Devonian; Devon. RANGE: Genus, Lower Devonian–Lower Carboniferous; Species. Upper Devonian.

2. **Mesoplica praelonga** (J. de C. Sowerby). (×1.) Upper Devonian; near Tiverton, Devon. RANGE: Upper Devonian. [Syn., *Productella praelonga.*]

3. **Lingula cornea** J. de C. Sowerby. (×1.) Lower Old Red Sandstone, Downtonian Stage; Ludlow, Shropshire. RANGE: Genus, Ordovician–Recent; Species, Downtonian Stage.

4. **Lingula minima** J. de C. Sowerby. (×¾.) Lower Old Red Sandstone, Downtonian Stage; Ludlow, Shropshire. RANGE: Genus, Ordovician–Recent; Species, Downtonian Stage.

5.* **Disphyllum goldfussi** (Geinitz). Transverse section (×2). Pebble in Middle (?) Devonian; Teignmouth, South Devon. RANGE: Genus, Silurian, Wenlock Series–Devonian; Species, Middle –Upper Devonian. [Syn., *Cyathophyllum caespitosum* Goldfuss in part.]

6.* **Plasmophyllum (Mesophyllum) bilaterale** (Champernowne). Transverse section (×¾). Middle Devonian; Tuckenhay, northwest of Dartmouth, South Devon. RANGE: Middle Devonian. [Syn., *Cyathophyllum? bilaterale.*]

7. **Phillipsastrea devoniensis** (Edwards & Haime). Transverse section (×1½). Upper Devonian; South Devon. RANGE: Upper Devonian. [Syn., *Pachyphyllum devoniense.*]

8.* **Hexacrinites interscapularis** (Phillips). (×1.) Middle Devonian; Wolborough, near Newton Abbot, South Devon. RANGE: Genus, Devonian; Species, Middle Devonian. [Syn., *Hexacrinus melo* Austin & Austin, *Platycrinus interscapularis.*]

Plate 32

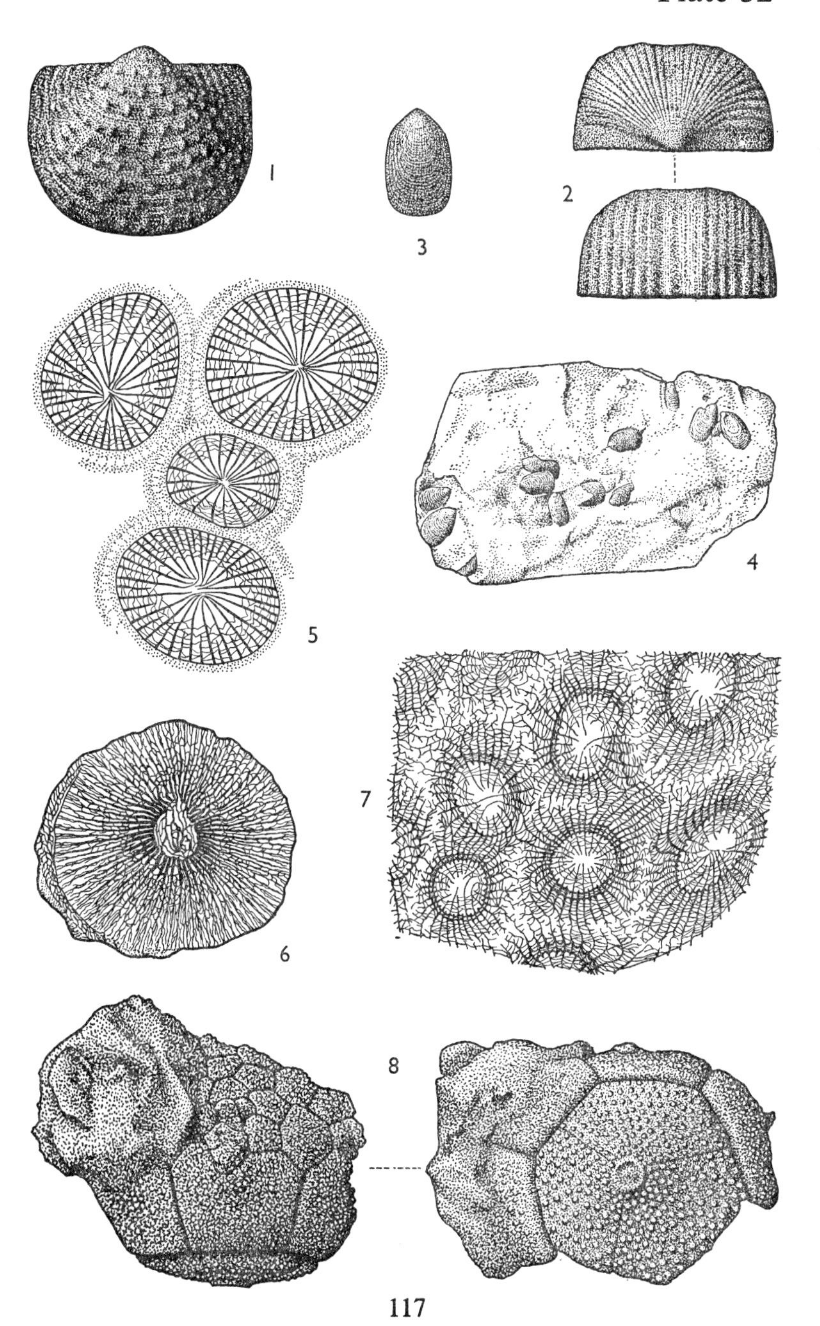

Plate 33
Devonian Brachiopods

1.* **Cyrtospirifer extensus** (J. de C. Sowerby). (×¾.) Upper Devonian; Delabole, Launceston, Cornwall. RANGE: Genus, Middle Devonian–Lower Carboniferous; Species, Upper Devonian.

2. **Cyrtina heteroclita** Defrance. (×1½.) Middle–Upper Devonian; Lummaton Hill, Barton, Torquay, South Devon. RANGE: Devonian.

3. **Pyramidalia simplex** (Phillips). (×¾.) Middle Devonian; Lummaton Hill, Barton, Torquay, South Devon. RANGE: Devonian. [Syn., *Cyrtia simplex*.]

4.* **Spirifer undiferus** Roemer. (×1.) Devonian; near Newton Abbot, South Devon. RANGE: Genus, Devonian–Permian; Species, Middle Devonian.

5, 6. **Sieberella brevirostris** (Phillips). (×1.) Middle Devonian; Lummaton Hill, Barton, Torquay, South Devon. RANGE: Genus, Silurian–Devonian; Species, Middle–Upper Devonian. [Syn., *Pentamerus brevirostris*.]

7.* **Stropheodonta nobilis** (M'Coy). (×¾.) Middle Devonian; Lummaton Hill, Barton, Torquay, South Devon. RANGE: Genus, Silurian–Devonian; Species, Middle Devonian. [Syn., *Leptaena nobilis*.]

8. **Rhenorensselaeria strigiceps** (Roemer). (×¾.) Middle Devonian, Givetian Stage; Hagginston Beach, Combe Martin Bay, North Devon. RANGE: Lower Devonian. [Syn., *Rensselaeria strigiceps*.]

Plate 33

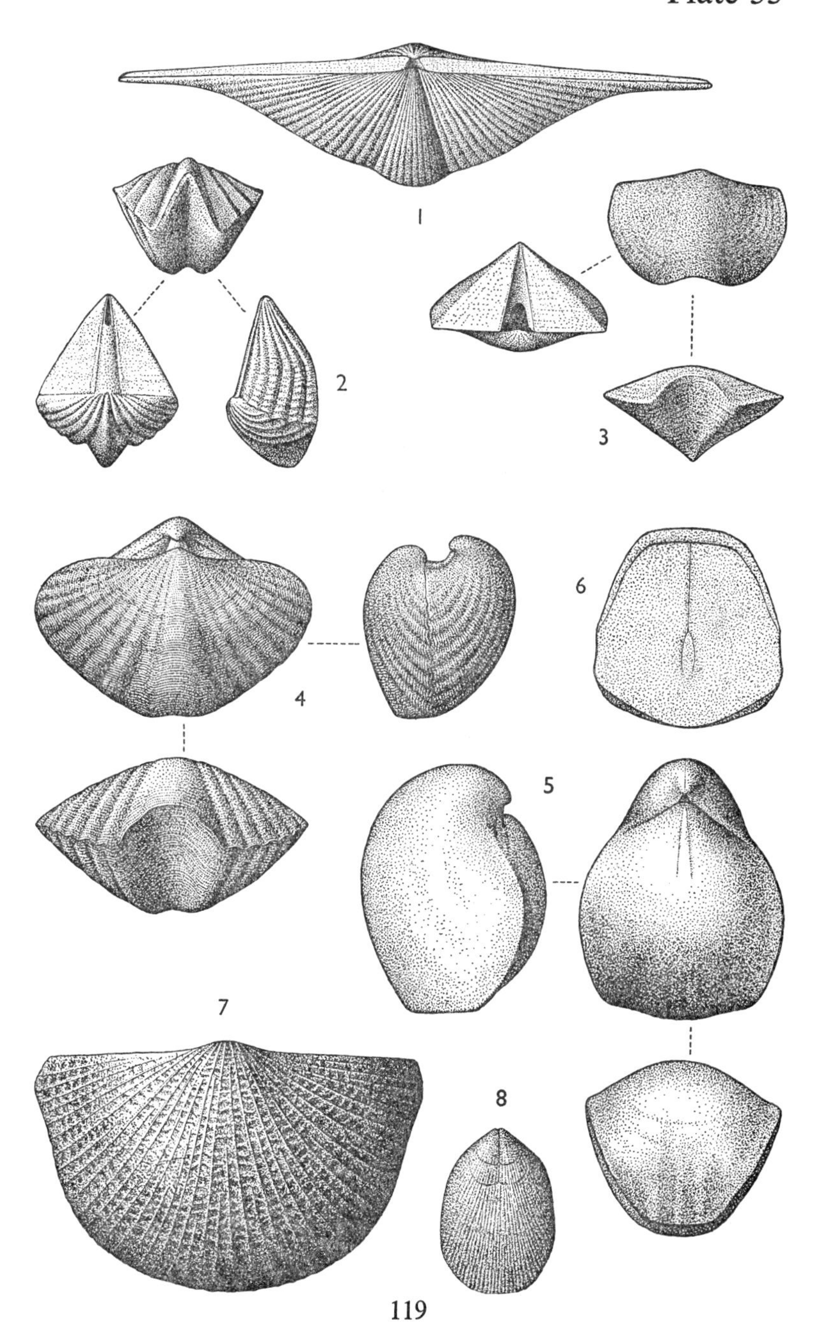

Plate 34
Devonian Brachiopods

1, 2. **Uncites gryphus** Schlotheim. (×1.) Devonian. 1, Devon (normal preservation for British specimens). 2, Paffrath near Cologne, Germany. RANGE: Devonian.

3. **Stringocephalus burtini** Defrance. (×½.) Middle Devonian; Bradley, near Newton Abbot, South Devon. RANGE: Middle Devonian.

4.* **Plectatrypa aspera** (Schlotheim). (×1.) Middle Devonian; Lummaton Hill, Barton, Torquay, South Devon. RANGE: Genus, Silurian–Devonian; Species, Middle Devonian. [Syn., *Atrypa aspera.*]

5.* **Hypothyridina cuboides** (J. de C. Sowerby). (×1.) Middle Devonian; Lummaton Hill, Barton, Torquay, South Devon. RANGE: Devonian [Syn., *Rhynchonella cuboides, Wilsonia cuboides.*]

6.* **Ladogia triloba** (J. de C. Sowerby). (×¾.) Middle Devonian; Wolborough, near Newton Abbot, South Devon. RANGE: Genus, Devonian–Lower Carboniferous; Species, Middle Devonian. [Syn., *Pugnax triloba, Rhynchonella triloba.*]

7.* **'Camarotoechia' laticosta** (Phillips). (×¾.) Upper Devonian, Famennian Stage; Baggy Point, Croyde, near Braunton, North Devon. RANGE: Species, Upper Devonian. [Syn., *Rhynchonella laticosta.*]

Plate 34

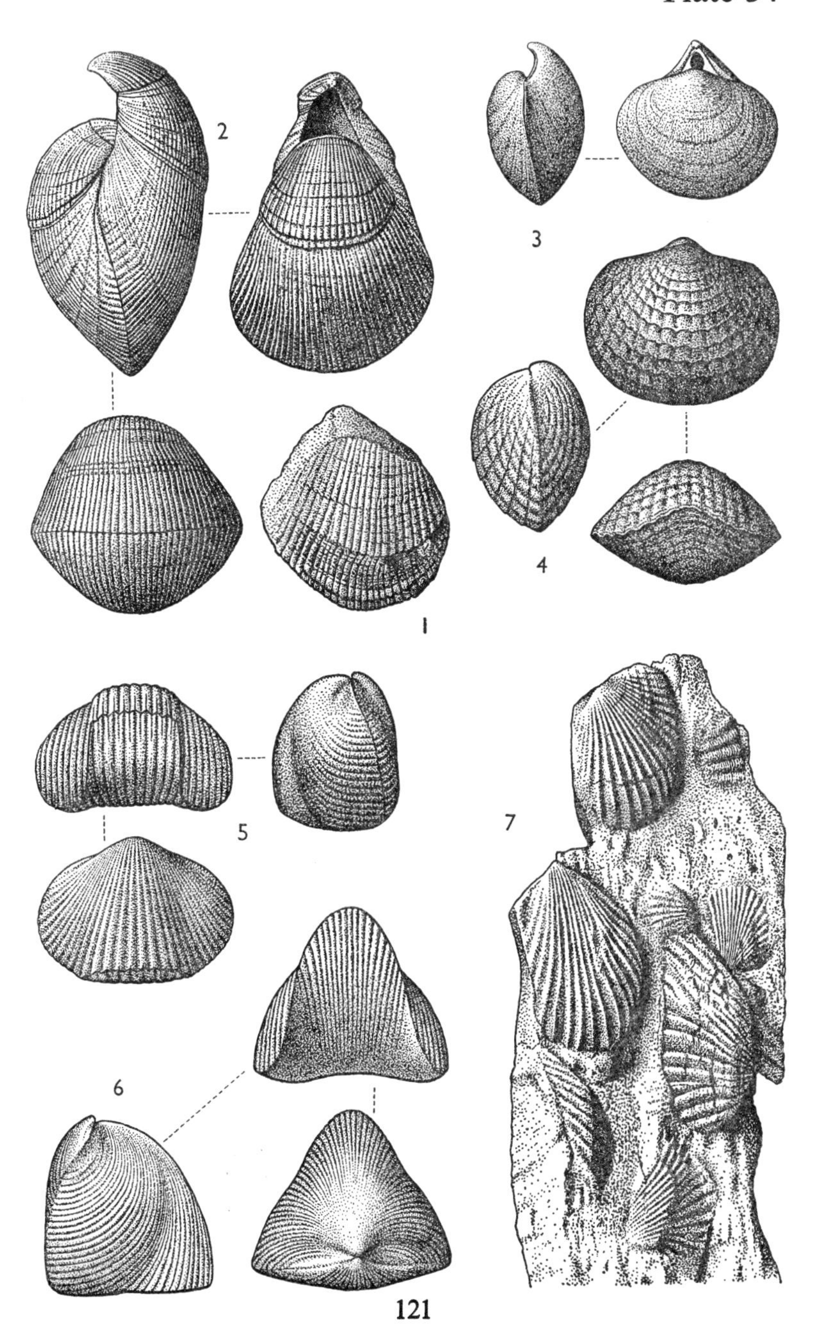

Plate 35
Devonian Bivalves (Figs. 1–3, 8), Gastropods (Figs. 4–6) and Goniatite (Fig. 7)

1.* **'Cucullaea' unilateralis** J. de C. Sowerby. (×½.) Upper Devonian; near Braunton, North Devon. RANGE: Upper Devonian.

2. **Buchiola retrostriata** (Buch). (×3.) Upper Devonian; Saltern Cove, near Paignton, South Devon. RANGE: Upper Devonian.

3.* **Actinopteria placida** (Whidborne). (×1½.) Middle Devonian; Lummaton Hill, Barton, Torquay, South Devon. RANGE: Genus, Silurian, Wenlock Series–Lower Carboniferous; Species, Middle–Upper Devonian.

4.* **Serpulospira militaris** (Whidborne). (×1.) Middle Devonian; Newton Abbot, South Devon. RANGE: Genus, Devonian–Lower Carboniferous; Species, Middle Devonian. [Syn., *Phanerotinus militaris.*]

5.* **Murchisonia bilineata** (Dechen). (×1.) Middle Devonian; Chudleigh, South Devon. RANGE: Genus, Devonian–Lower Carboniferous; Species, Middle Devonian. [Syn., *Murchisonia turbinata* of authors.]

6. **Euryzone delphinuloides** (Schlotheim). (×1.) Middle Devonian; Chudleigh, South Devon. RANGE: Middle–Upper Devonian.

7.* **Manticoceras intumescens** (Beyrich). (×¾.) a, septal suture. Upper Devonian; Lower Dunscombe, near Chudleigh, South Devon. RANGE: Upper Devonian, *Manticoceras* Zone. [Syn., *Gephyroceras intumescens.*]

8.* **Archanodon jukesi** (Baily). (×½.) Upper Old Red Sandstone; Kiltorcan, Kilkenny, Eire. RANGE: Upper Old Red Sandstone.

Plate 35

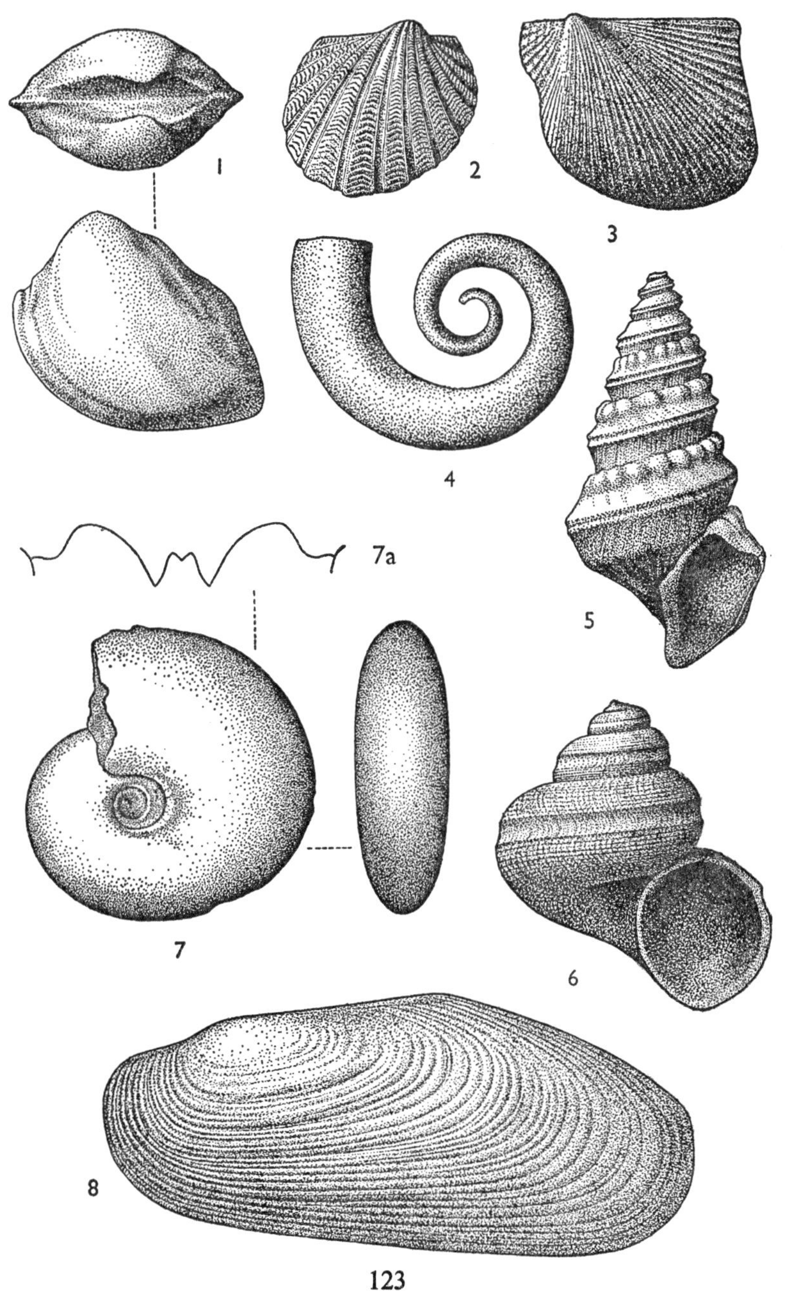

Plate 36

Devonian Trilobites (Figs. 1–7), Conodont (Fig. 8), Goniatite (Fig. 9) and Fish (Fig. 10)

1, 2.* **Trimerocephalus mastophthalmus** (Richter). (×1.) Upper Devonian; Knowle Hill, near Newton Abbot, South Devon. RANGE: Upper Devonian. [Syn., *Phacops laevis* (Münster).]

3. **Scutellum granulatum** (Goldfuss). (×¾.) Middle Devonian; Newton Abbot, South Devon. RANGE: Genus, Silurian–Devonian; Species, Middle Devonian.

4, 5. **Dechenella setosa** (Whidborne). (×1.) Middle Devonian; Chircombe Bridge, Devon. RANGE: Middle Devonian.

6. **Phacops accipitrinus** (Phillips). (×1.) Upper Devonian; Shirwell, near Barnstaple, North Devon. RANGE: Genus, Silurian–Devonian; Species, Upper Devonian.

7. **Crotalocephalus pengellii** (Whidborne). (×1.) Middle Devonian; Wolborough near Newton Abbot, South Devon. RANGE: Genus, Ordovician–Devonian; Species, Middle Devonian. [Syn., *Cheirurus pengellii.*]

8. **Icriodus** sp. (×20.) Upper Devonian; Lower Dunscombe, near Chudleigh, South Devon. RANGE: Upper Devonian.

9. **Tornoceras psittacinum** (Whidborne). (×1.) Middle Devonian; Wolborough near Newton Abbot, South Devon. RANGE: Middle Devonian.

10.* **Coccosteus cuspidatus** Miller. Median dorsal plate, posterior spine uppermost (×1). Middle Old Red Sandstone; Tynet Burn, near Portgordon, Banff. (*a*) Longitudinal section (×⅔), (*b*) Transverse section (×⅔). RANGE: Genus, Middle-Upper Devonian; Species, Middle Devonian. [Syn., *Coccosteus decipiens* Agassiz.]

Plate 36

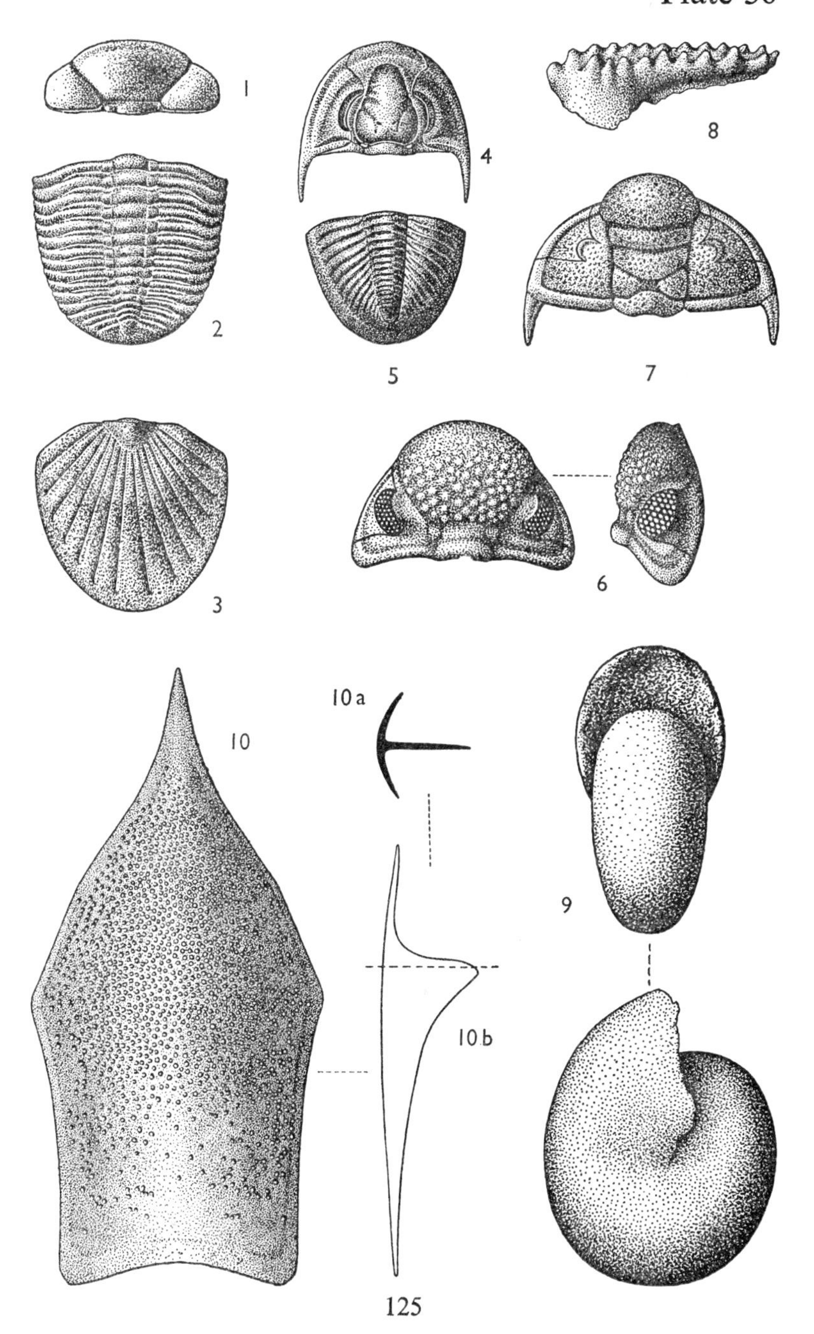

Plate 37

Devonian Agnathans (Figs. 1–3) and Fishes (Figs. 4, 5)

1. Thelodont scale. (×20.) Lower Old Red Sandstone; Hudwick Dingle, Monkhopton, near Much Wenlock, Shropshire. RANGE: Silurian, Llandovery Series–Devonian, Lower Old Red Sandstone.

2. **Cephalaspis lyelli** Agassiz. (×¾.) Lower Old Red Sandstone; Glamis, Angus. RANGE: Genus, Lower-Middle Devonian; Species, Lower Old Red Sandstone.

3. **Pteraspis rostrata** (Agassiz) subsp. **trimpleyensis** White. Dorsal Shield (×¾). Lower Old Red Sandstone, Dittonian Stage; Trimpley, near Kidderminster, Worcestershire. RANGE: Genus, Lower Devonian; Species, Dittonian.

4. **Holoptychius giganteus** Agassiz. Scale (×¾). Upper Old Red Sandstone; Elgin, Morayshire. RANGE: Genus and Species, Upper Devonian.

5.* **Asterolepis maxima** (Agassiz). Head Shield (×½). Upper Old Red Sandstone; King's Steps, east of Nairn (Scotland). RANGE: Genus and Species, Middle Devonian.

Plate 37

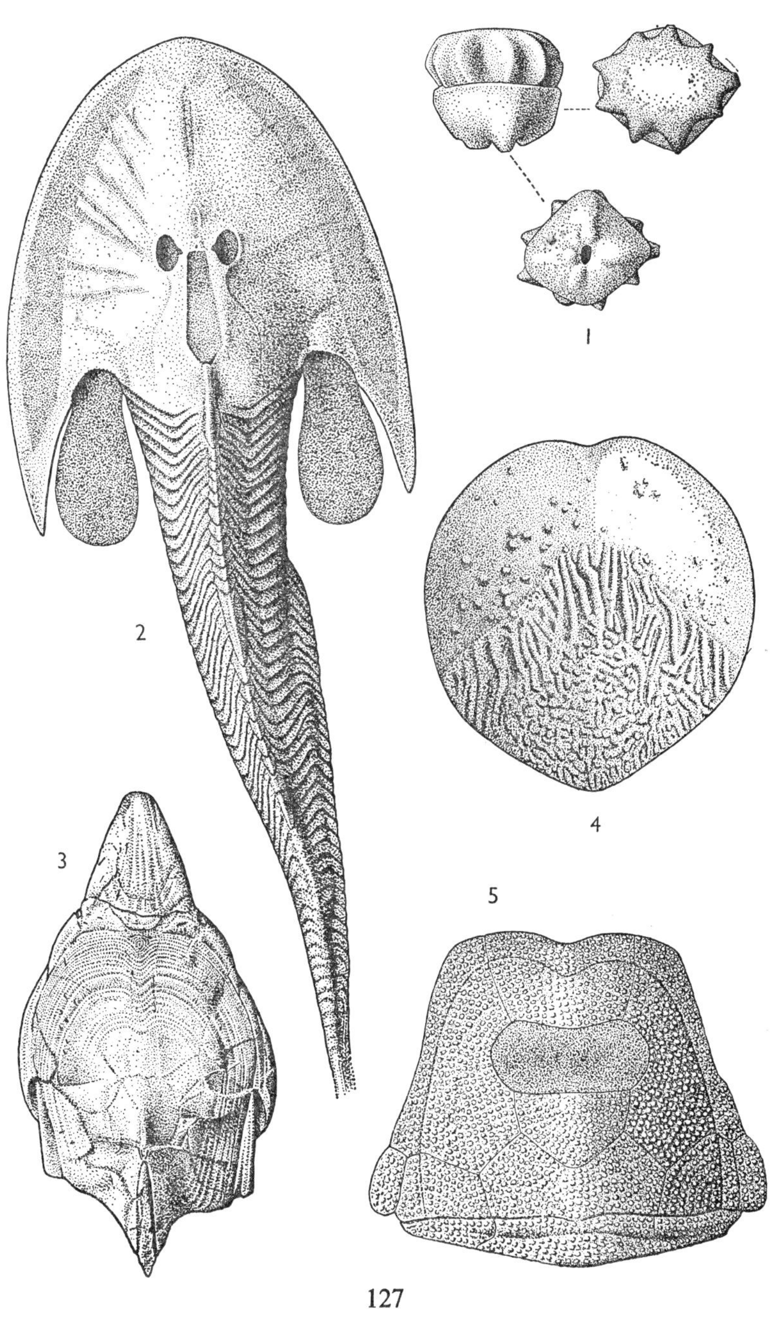

Plate 38

Carboniferous Plants. Articulates (Figs. 1, 2, 4, 5) and Lycopod (Fig. 3)

1. **Annularia stellata** (Schlotheim). Foliage ($\times\frac{3}{4}$.) Upper Carboniferous; Clandown, Radstock, Somerset. RANGE: Genus, Carboniferous–Permian ?; Species, Westphalian Stage.

2. **Sphenophyllum emarginatum** Brongniart. Foliage ($\times$1.) Upper Carboniferous; Forest of Dean, Gloucestershire. RANGE: Genus, Carboniferous; Species, Westphalian Stage.

3.* **Stigmaria ficoides** Brongniart. Part of rootstock ($\times\frac{1}{2}$.) Upper Carboniferous; Dudley, Worcestershire. RANGE: Carboniferous.

4. **Asterophyllites equisetiformis** (Schlotheim). Foliage ($\times$1.) Upper Carboniferous; Radstock, Somerset. RANGE: Genus, Carboniferous; Species, Westphalian Stage.

5.* **Calamites suckowi** Brongniart. Pith cast ($\times\frac{1}{2}$.) Upper Carboniferous; Gosforth, near Newcastle-on-Tyne, Northumberland. RANGE: Genus, Carboniferous; Species, Westphalian Stage.

Plate 38

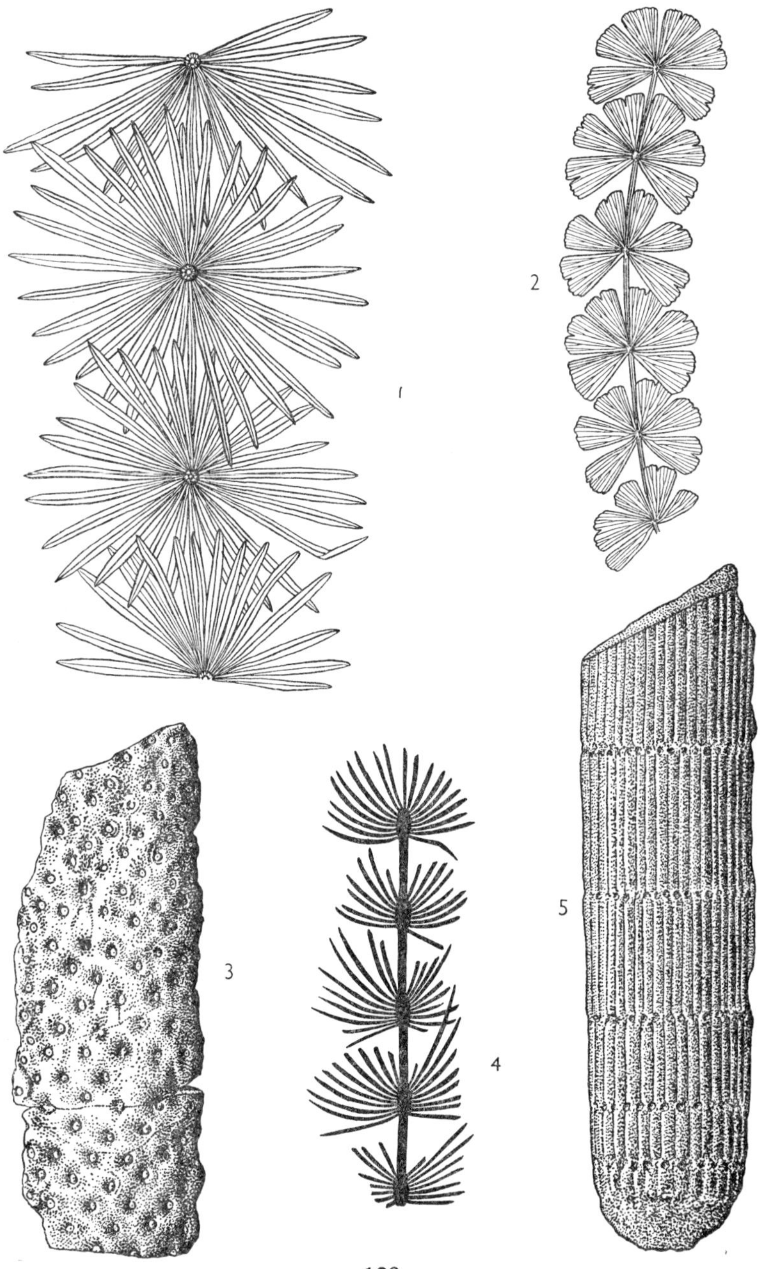

Plate 39

Carboniferous Plants. Pteridosperms (Figs. 1-3) and Lycopods (Figs. 4-6)

1. **Telangium affine** (Lindley & Hutton). Part of frond (×1); *a*, detail of pinnules (×3). Lower Carboniferous; West Calder, Midlothian, Scotland. RANGE: Genus, Devonian–Permian; Species, Viséan Stage. [Syn., *Sphenopteris affinis*.)

2. **Sphenopteris alata** Brongniart. Part of frond (×1.) Upper Carboniferous; Radstock, Somerset. RANGE: Genus, Devonian–Permian; Species, Westphalian Stage. [Syn., *Sphenopteris grandini* Goeppert.]

3. **Trigonocarpus** sp. Seed (×1.) Upper Carboniferous; Stevenston, Ayrshire. RANGE: Upper Carboniferous.

4. **Sigillaria mamillaris** Brongniart. Part of stem (×½.) Upper Carboniferous; Darton, near Barnsley, Yorks. RANGE: Genus, Carboniferous–Permian; Species, Westphalian Stage.

5.* **Lepidodendron aculeatum** Sternberg. Part of stem or large branch (×¾.) Upper Carboniferous; Sunderland, Co. Durham. RANGE: Genus, Carboniferous; Species, Namurian–Westphalian Stages.

6. **Lepidodendron sternbergi** Brongniart. Leafy branch (×1.) Upper Carboniferous; Coseley, Bilston, Staffordshire. RANGE: Genus, Carboniferous; Species, Westphalian Stage.

Plate 39

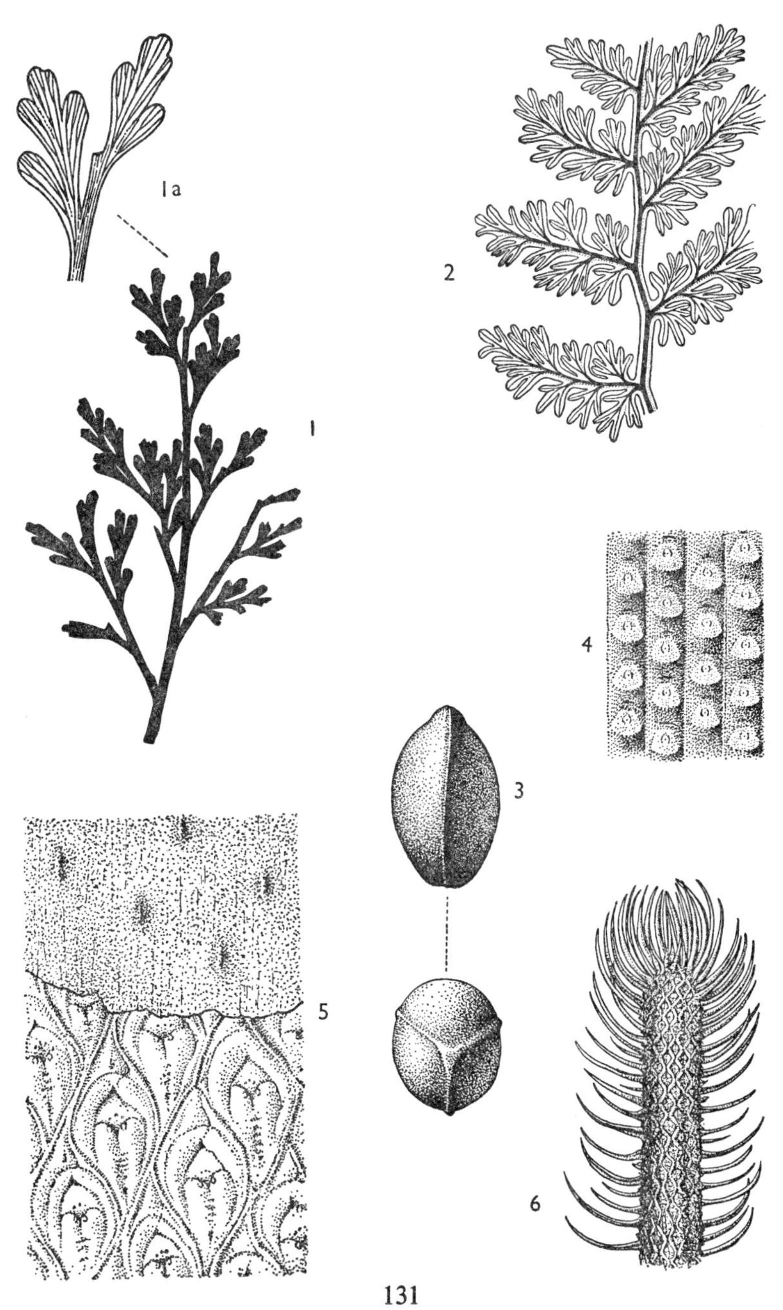

Plate 40

Carboniferous Plants. Ferns (Figs. 1, 5), Fern-like Foliage (Figs. 2, 3) and Pteridosperm (Fig. 4)

1. **Pecopteris polymorpha** Brongniart. Part of frond (×1); *a*, detail of sterile pinnules (×3.) Upper Carboniferous; Radstock, Somerset. RANGE: Genus, Upper Carboniferous; Species, Westphalian Stage. [Syn., *Acitheca polymorpha.*]

2, 3.* **Mariopteris nervosa** (Brongniart). Part of frond (×1.) Upper Carboniferous, Coal Measures; Netherton, near Dudley, Worcestershire. RANGE: Genus, Upper Carboniferous; Species, Westphalian Stage.

4. **Rhodea tenuis** Gothan. Part of frond (×1.) Lower Carboniferous; Gwaenysgor, near Rhyl, Flintshire. RANGE: Genus, Carboniferous; Species, Viséan Stage.

5.* **Alethopteris serli** Brongniart. Part of frond (×½); *a*, detail of pinnules (×3). Upper Carboniferous; Newcastle-on-Tyne, Northumberland. RANGE: Genus, Carboniferous; Species, Westphalian Stage.

Plate 40

Plate 41

Carboniferous Sponge (Fig. 1) and Plants, Pteridosperms ? (Figs. 2–4), Cordaite (Fig. 5)

1. **Hyalostelia smithi** Young & Young. (×1.) Lower Carboniferous; near Richmond, Yorkshire. RANGE: Lower Carboniferous.

2. **Rhacopteris petiolata** Goeppert. Part of frond (×1.) Lower Carboniferous; Teilia, near Prestatyn, Flintshire. RANGE: Genus, Carboniferous; Species, Viséan Stage.

3.* **Neuropteris gigantea** Sternberg. Part of frond (×½); *a*, detail of pinnule (×2½.) Upper Carboniferous; Coseley, near Bilston, Staffordshire. RANGE: Genus, Carboniferous; Species, Westphalian Stage.

4. **Cyclopteris trichomanoides** Brongniart. pinnule (×¾.) Upper Carboniferous; Coalbrookdale, near Ironbridge, Shropshire. RANGE: Genus, Upper Carboniferous; Species, Westphalian Stage.

5.* **Cordaites angulosostriatus** Grand'Eury. Part of leaf (×¾.) Upper Carboniferous; Camerton, Somerset. RANGE: Genus, Carboniferous-Permian; Species, Westphalian Stage.

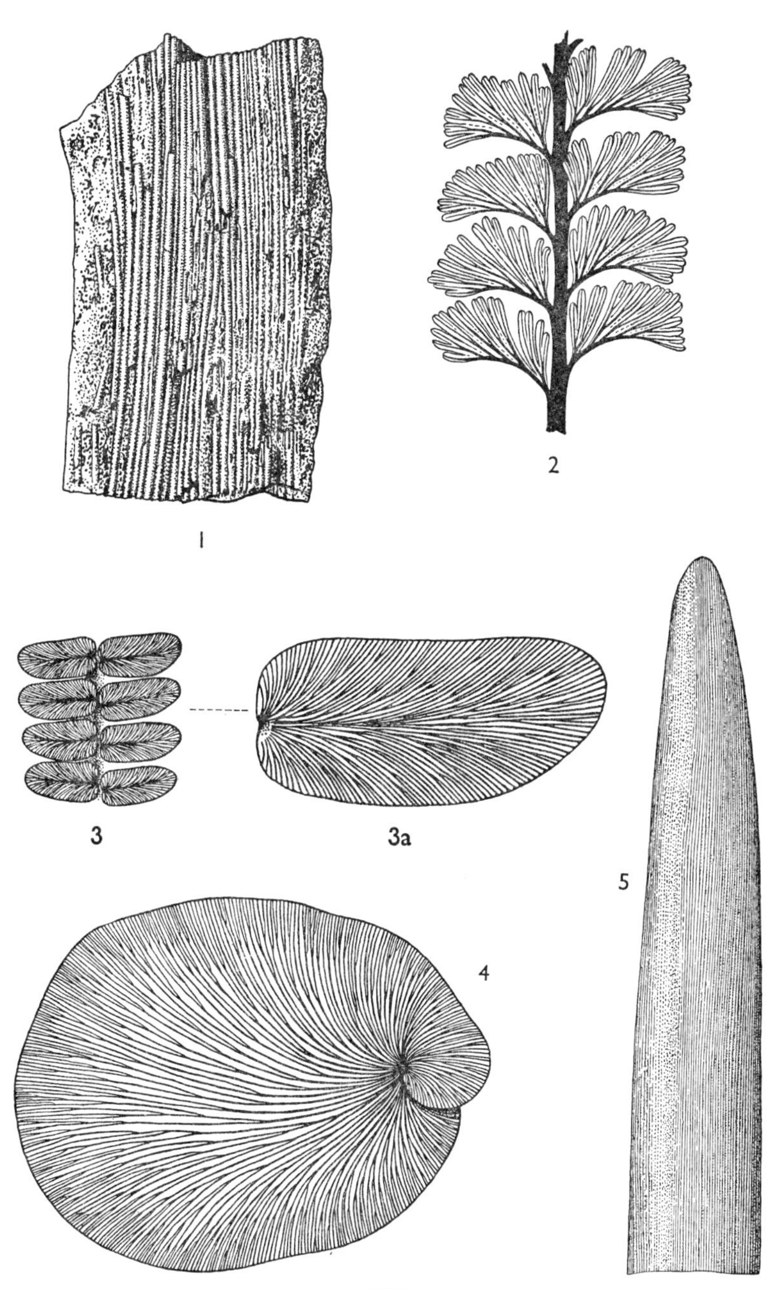
1
2
3
3a
4
5

Plate 42
Carboniferous Foraminifera

1, 2. **Archaediscus karreri** Brady. (×30.) Lower Carboniferous; Brockley, Lanarkshire. RANGE: Viséan Stage.

3, 4. **Tetrataxis conica** Ehrenberg. 3 (×25.) Lower Carboniferous; Colster Clough, near Elsdon, Northumberland. 4, Section (×40). Brockley, Lanarkshire. RANGE: Viséan–Namurian Stages. [Syn., *Valvulina palaeotrochus* Ehrenberg.]

5. **Endothyranopsis crassus** (Brady). (×15.) Carboniferous Limestone; Great Ormes Head, Llandudno, Carnarvonshire. RANGE: Viséan Stage. [Syn., *Endothyra crassa.*]

6. **Plectogyra bradyi** (Mikhailov). Section (× 40.) Viséan Stage; Locality unknown. RANGE: Viséan Stage. [Syn., *Endothyra bowmani* of authors.]

7. **Stacheoides polytremoides** (Brady). (× 10.) Viséan Stage; Hairmyres, near East Kilbride, Lanarkshire. RANGE: Viséan–Namurian Stages. [Syn., *Stacheia polytremoides.*]

8, 9. **Stacheia pupoides** Brady. (× 50.) Viséan Stage. 8, Downholme, near Richmond, Yorks. 9, Section. Fourstones, Northumberland. RANGE: Viséan Stage.

10, 11. **Howchinia bradyana** (Howchin). Lower Carboniferous, Viséan Stage; 10 (× 60.) Tipalt, Northumberland. 11, Section (× 85.) Aldfield, near Ripon, Yorkshire. RANGE: Middle–Upper Viséan Stage.

12, 13. **Climacammina antiqua** Brady. Lower Carboniferous. 12 (×25.) 13, Section (×20.) Brockley, Lanarkshire. RANGE: Upper Viséan.

14. **Lugtonia concinna** (Brady). (× 50.) Viséan Stage; Hurst, Reeth, near Richmond, Yorkshire. RANGE: Upper Viséan–Namurian Stages. [Syn., *Nodosinella concinna.*]

Plate 42

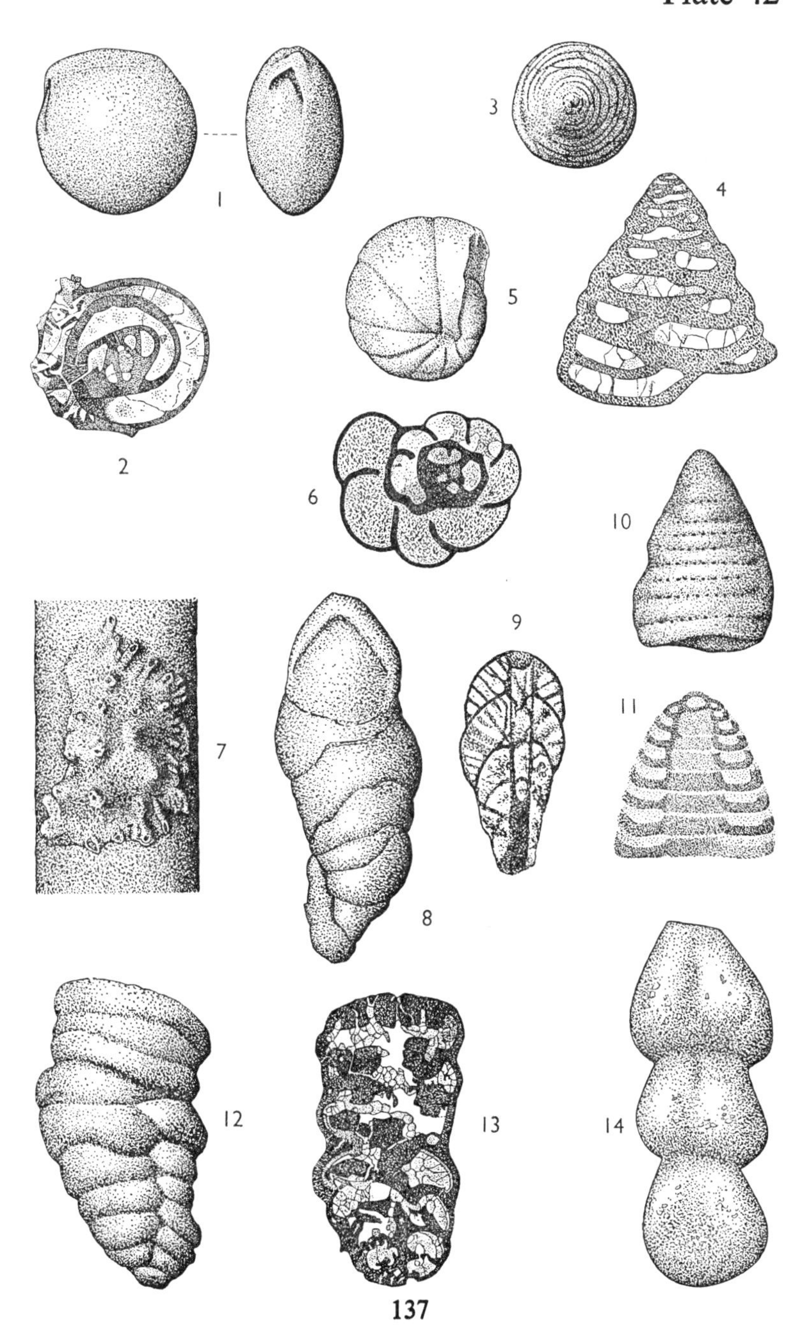

Plate 43
Carboniferous Corals

1.* **Dibunophyllum bipartitum** (M'Coy). (×1.) Viséan Stage; Avon Gorge, Bristol. RANGE: Genus, Carboniferous; Species, Viséan –Namurian Stages.

2, 3.* **Lithostrotion junceum** (Fleming). 2 (×1.) Viséan Stage; Birtley, south-east of Bellingham, Northumberland. 3, Section (×3.) Locality unknown. RANGE: Genus, Carboniferous; Species, Viséan–Namurian Stages.

4, 5.* **Lithostrotion vorticale** (Parkinson). Viséan Stage. 4, (×1.) Locality unknown. 5, (×3.) Avon Gorge, Bristol. RANGE: Genus, Carboniferous; Species, Viséan Stage.

Plate 43

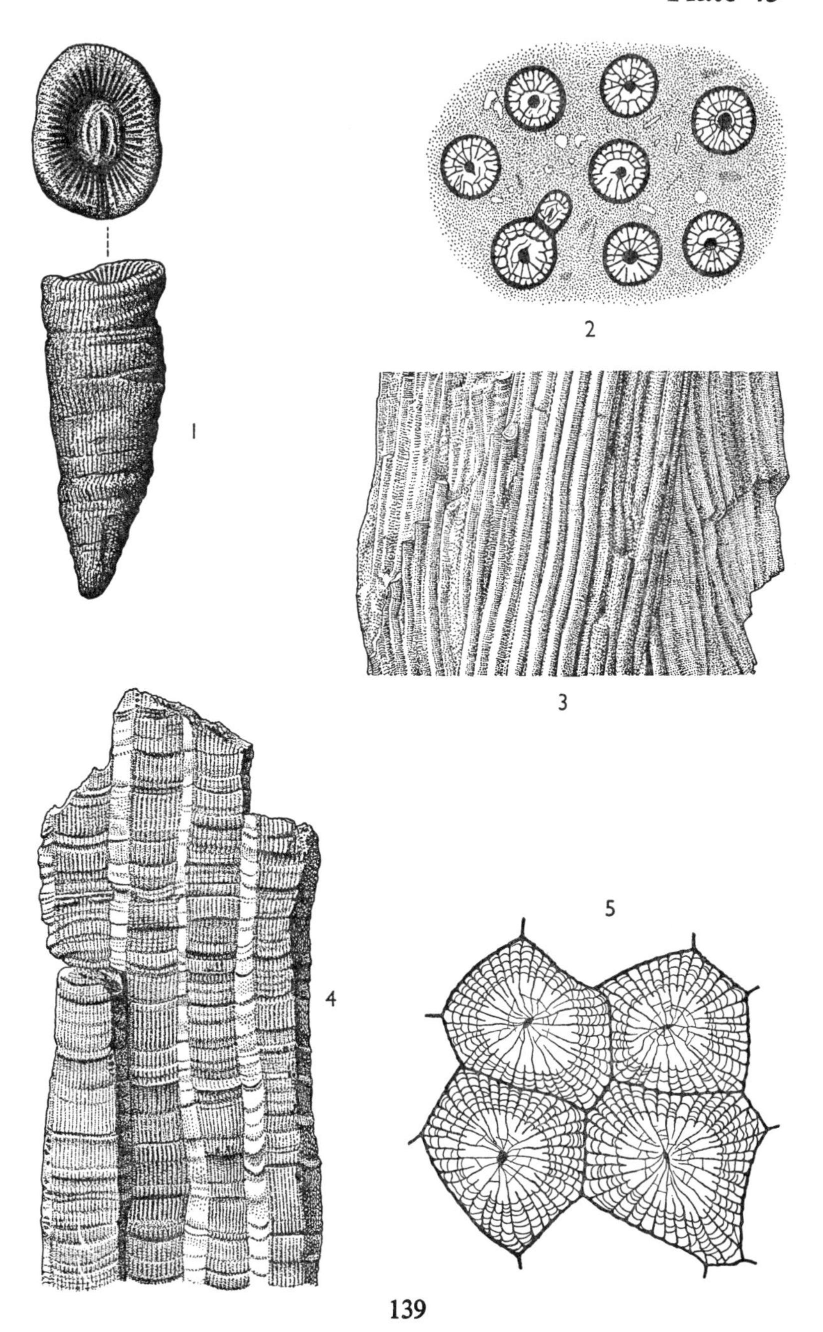

Plate 44
Carboniferous Corals

1. **Amplexus coralloides** J. Sowerby. (×¾.) Viséan Stage; Derbyshire. RANGE: Genus, Lower Carboniferous; Species, Viséan Stage.

2. **Aulophyllum fungites** (Fleming). (×1.) Viséan Stage; Oswestry, Shropshire. RANGE: Genus, Lower Carboniferous; Species, Viséan Stage.

3. **Amplexizaphrentis enniskilleni** (Edwards & Haime) var. **derbiensis** Lewis. Section (×2.) Viséan Stage; Matlock, Derbyshire. RANGE: Genus, Carboniferous; Species, Viséan Stage. [Syn., *Zaphrentis enniskilleni.*]

4.* **Lonsdaleia floriformis** (Fleming). (×1½.) Carboniferous; Coalbrookdale, Shropshire. RANGE: Genus, Carboniferous; Species, Viséan–Namurian Stages.

5.* **Palaeosmilia regium** (Phillips). (×1.) Viséan Stage; Clifton, Bristol. RANGE: Genus, Carboniferous; Species, Viséan–Namurian Stages.

6, 7.* **Palaeosmilia murchisoni** Edwards & Haime. Viséan Stage, 6, (×¾.) Clifton, Bristol. 7, Section (×1.) Narrowdale Grange, Alstonfield, Staffordshire. RANGE: Genus, Lower Carboniferous; Species, Viséan Stage.

Plate 44

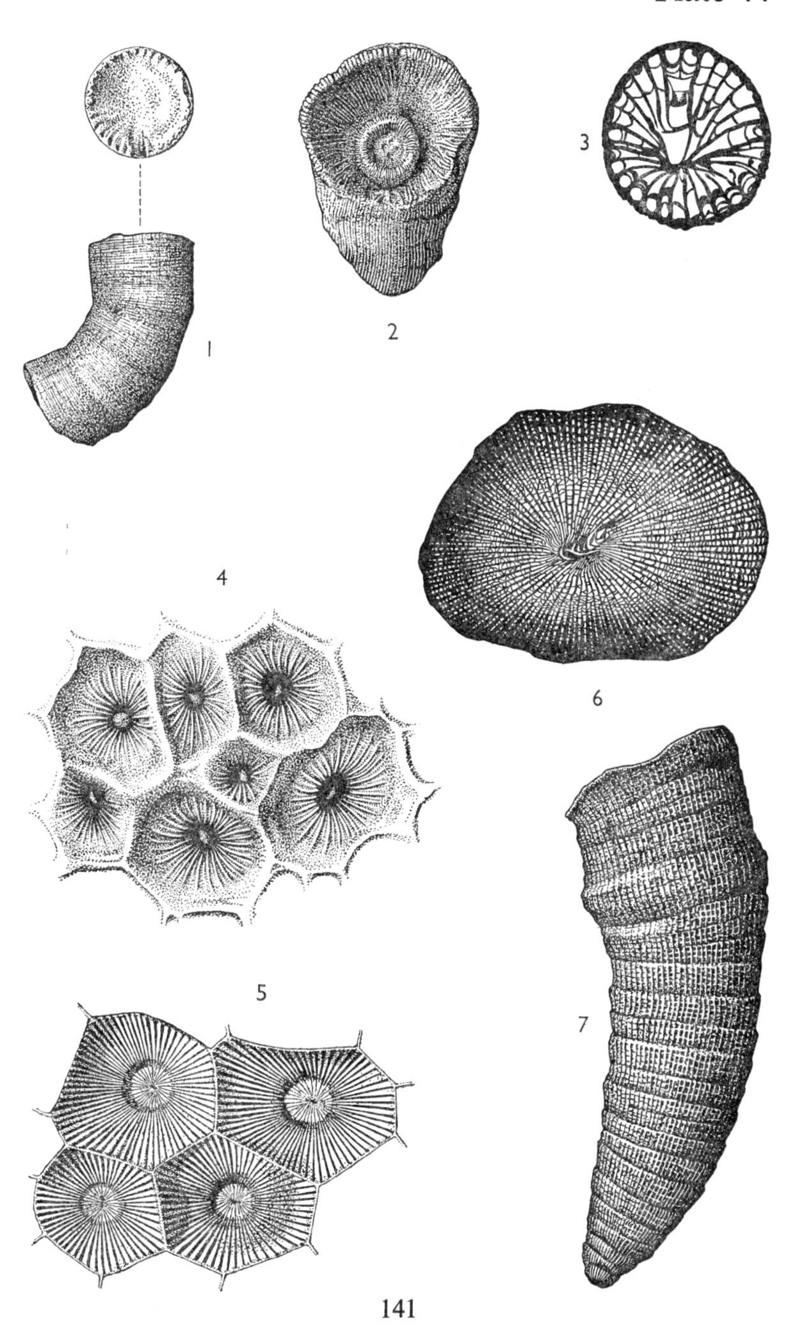

Plate 45

Carboniferous Polyzoan (Fig. 1), Corals (Figs. 2–4) and Class Uncertain (Fig. 5)

1.* **Fenestella plebeia** M'Coy. (×2); *a* (×3.) Lower Carboniferous; Ravenstonedale, Westmorland. RANGE: Genus, Ordovician–Permian; Species, Carboniferous, Tournaisian–Viséan Stages.

2.* **Siphonophyllia gigantea** (Michelin). (×¾); *a*, polished surface. Lower Carboniferous; south-western England. RANGE: Lower Carboniferous. [Syn., *Caninia gigantea*.]

3.* **Syringopora geniculata** Phillips. (×1½.) Lower Carboniferous; near Limerick, Eire. RANGE: Genus, Silurian–Carboniferous; Species, Viséan Stage.

4.* **Michelinia tenuisepta** (Phillips). (×¾.) Tournaisian Stage; St. Thomas' Head, north of Weston-super-Mare, Somerset. RANGE: Genus, Upper Devonian–Permian; Species, Tournaisian–Viséan Stages.

5.* **Conularia quadrisulcata** J. Sowerby. (×1.) Upper Carboniferous, Coal Measures; Coalbrookdale, near Ironbridge, Shropshire. RANGE: Genus, Ordovician–Carboniferous; Species, Carboniferous.

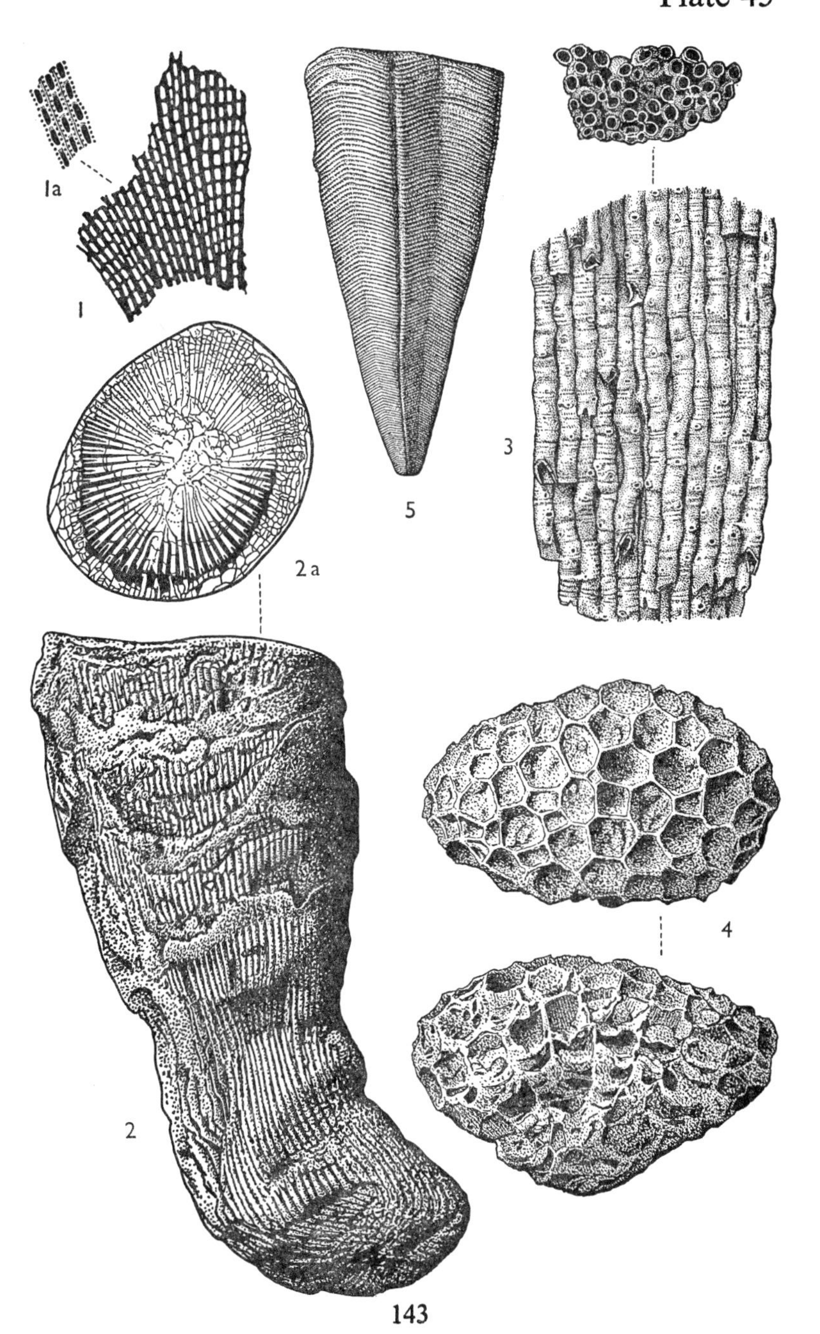
1a
1
2a
2
3
4
5

Plate 46

Carboniferous Brachiopods (Figs. 1–10) and Worm (Fig. 11)

1. **Overtonia fimbriata** (J. de C. Sowerby). (×1.) Viséan stage; Faulds Brow, Caldbeck, Cumberland. RANGE: Viséan-Namurian Stages. [Syn., *Productus fimbriatus.*]

2–4. **Productus productus** (Martin). 2, 3 (×1.) 4 (×⅔.) Viséan Stage; Beresford Hall, near Longnor, Staffordshire. RANGE: Genus, Viséan–Westphalian Stages; Species, Viséan–Namurian Stages.

5, 6. **Eomarginifera setosa** (Phillips). (×1¼.) Viséan Stage. 5. Gorbeck, Settle, Yorkshire. 6. Carluke, Lanarkshire. RANGE: Viséan–Namurian Stages.

7. **Orbiculoidea nitida** (Phillips). (×2.) Viséan Stage; near Woodburn, Redesdale, Northumberland. RANGE: Genus, Ordovician–Permian (?-Upper Jurassic); Species, Viséan–Namurian Stages.

8.* **Lingula mytiloides** J. Sowerby. (×1½.) Ammanian Stage; Ystalyfera, near Swansea, Glamorganshire. RANGE: Genus, Ordovician–Recent; Species, Viséan–Westphalian Stages.

9.* **Lingula squamiformis** Phillips. (×1½.) Viséan Stage; Budle Bay, Bamburgh, Northumberland. RANGE: Genus, Ordovician–Recent; Species, Viséan–Namurian Stages.

10. **'Linoproductus' corrugatus** (M'Coy). (×¾.) (*a*), surface ornamentation (×1½). Viséan Stage; Settle, Yorkshire. RANGE: Species, Viséan Stage. [Syn., *Productus corrugatus.*]

11. **Spirorbis pusillus** (Martin). (×6.) Viséan Stage; Linhouse Water, Mid-Calder, Midlothian. RANGE: Genus, Silurian–Recent; Species, Carboniferous. [Syn., *Microconchus carbonarius* (Giebel).]

Plate 46

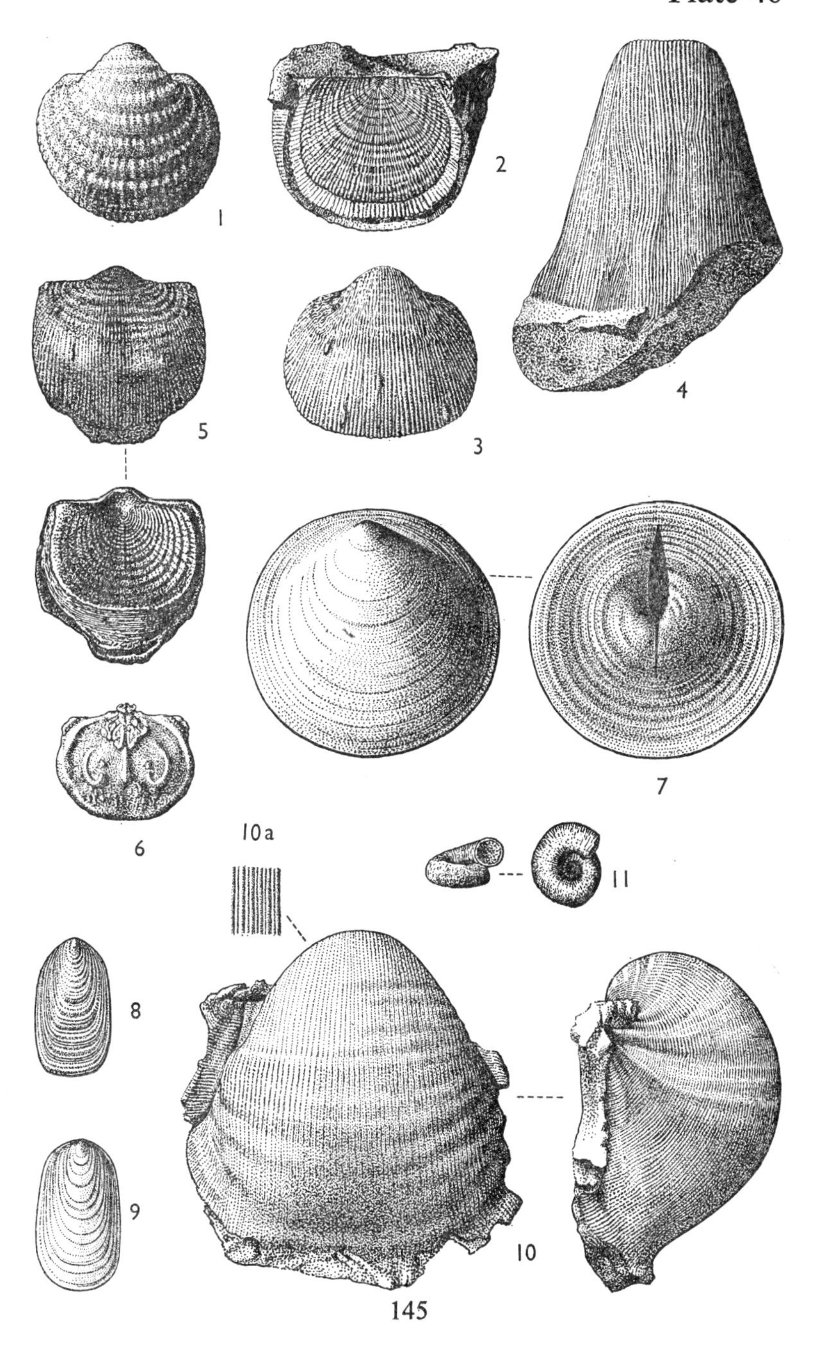

Plate 47
Carboniferous Brachiopods

1. **Rugosochonetes hardrensis** (Phillips). (×1½.) Viséan Stage; Craignant, Chirk, near Wrexham, Denbighshire. RANGE: Genus, Tournaisian–Namurian Stages; Species, Viséan Stage. [Syn., *Chonetes hardrensis.*]

2. **'Productus' craigmarkensis** (Muir-Wood). (×1½.) Westphalian Stage; Smallthorne, Staffordshire. RANGE: Westphalian Stage.

3. **Krotovia spinulosa** (J. Sowerby). (×1.) Lower Carboniferous; Faulds Brow, Caldbeck, Cumberland. RANGE: Genus, Lower Carboniferous–Permian; Species, Viséan–Namurian Stages. [Syn., *Productus spinulosus.*]

4. **Antiquatonia hindi** (Muir-Wood). (×1.) Viséan Stage; Narrowdale, near Longnor, Staffordshire. RANGE: Genus, Carboniferous; Species, Viséan Stage. [Syn., *Dictyoclostus hindi, Productus hindi.*]

5.* **Dictyoclostus semireticulatus** (Martin). (×¾.) Viséan Stage; Bowland, near Clitheroe, Lancashire. RANGE: Tournaisian–Namurian Stages. [Syn., *Productus semireticulatus.*]

6.* **Gigantoproductus giganteus** (J. Sowerby). (×½.) Viséan Stage; Llangollen, Denbighshire. RANGE: Genus, Viséan–Namurian Stages; Species, Viséan Stage. [Syn., *Gigantella gigantea, Productus giganteus.*]

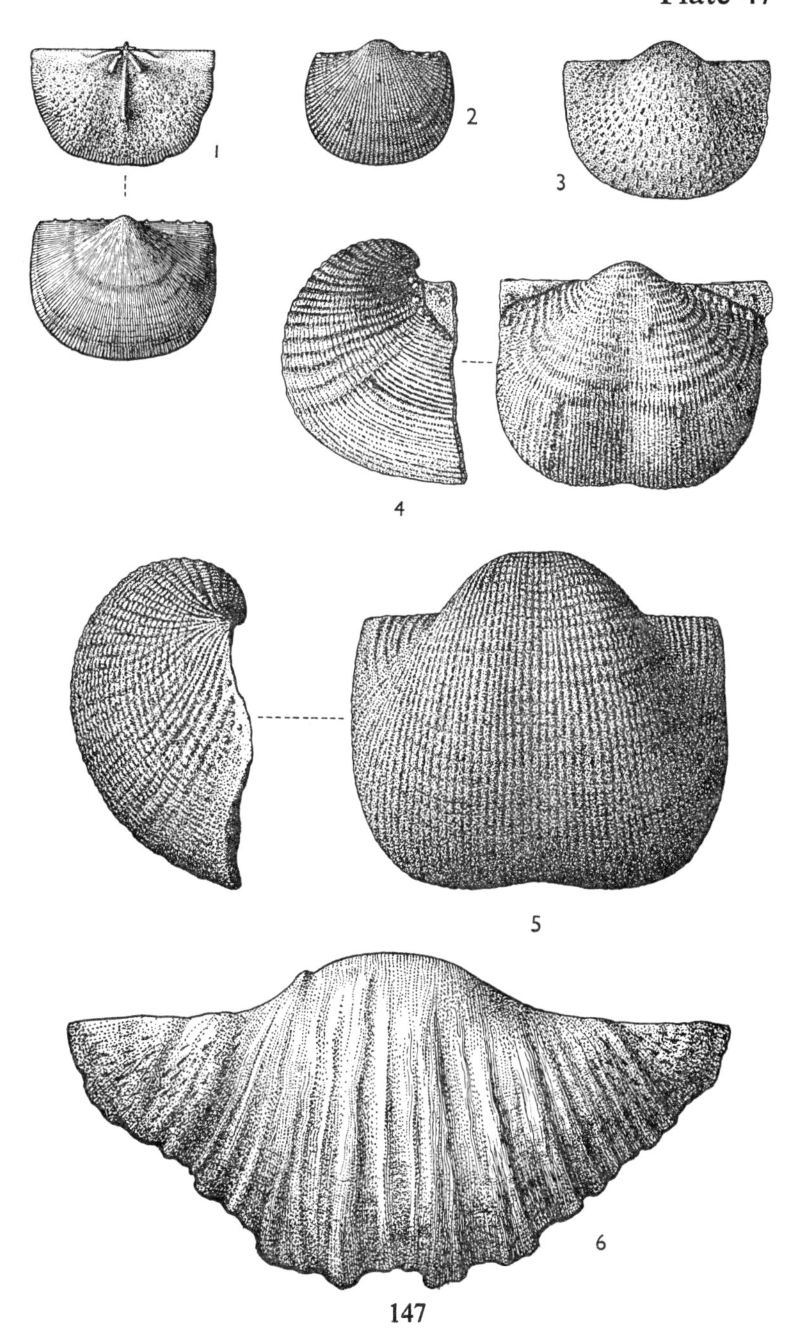
1
2
3
4
5
6

Plate 48
Carboniferous Brachiopods

1, 2. **Leptagonia analoga** (Phillips). (×1.) 1. Viséan Stage; Bowland, near Clitheroe, Lancashire. 2. Viséan Stage; ironstone workings, Redesdale, Northumberland. RANGE: Tournaisian–Namurian Stages. [Syn., *Leptaena analoga, Strophomena analoga.*]

3, 4. **Pustula pustulosa** (Phillips). Carboniferous Limestone. 3 (×1.) Bowland, near Clitheroe, Lancashire. 4 (×1); 4*a* (×3). Viséan Stage; Narrowdale, near Longnor, Staffordshire. RANGE: Genus, Tournaisian–Viséan Stages; Species, Viséan Stage. [Syn., *Productus pustulosus.*]

5, 6. **Rhipidomella michelini** (Léveillé). (×1.) 5. Viséan Stage; Congleton Edge, Cheshire. 6. Beith, Ayrshire. RANGE: Genus, Silurian –Permian; Species, Viséan–Namurian Stages. [Syn., *Orthis michelini.*]

7, 8. **Phricodothyris lineata** (J. Sowerby). 7 (×1.) Viséan Stage; Whitewell, Settle, Yorkshire. 8 (×10.) Ornamentation. RANGE: Genus, Lower Carboniferous–Permian; Species, Viséan– Namurian Stages. [Syn., *Reticularia lineata.*]

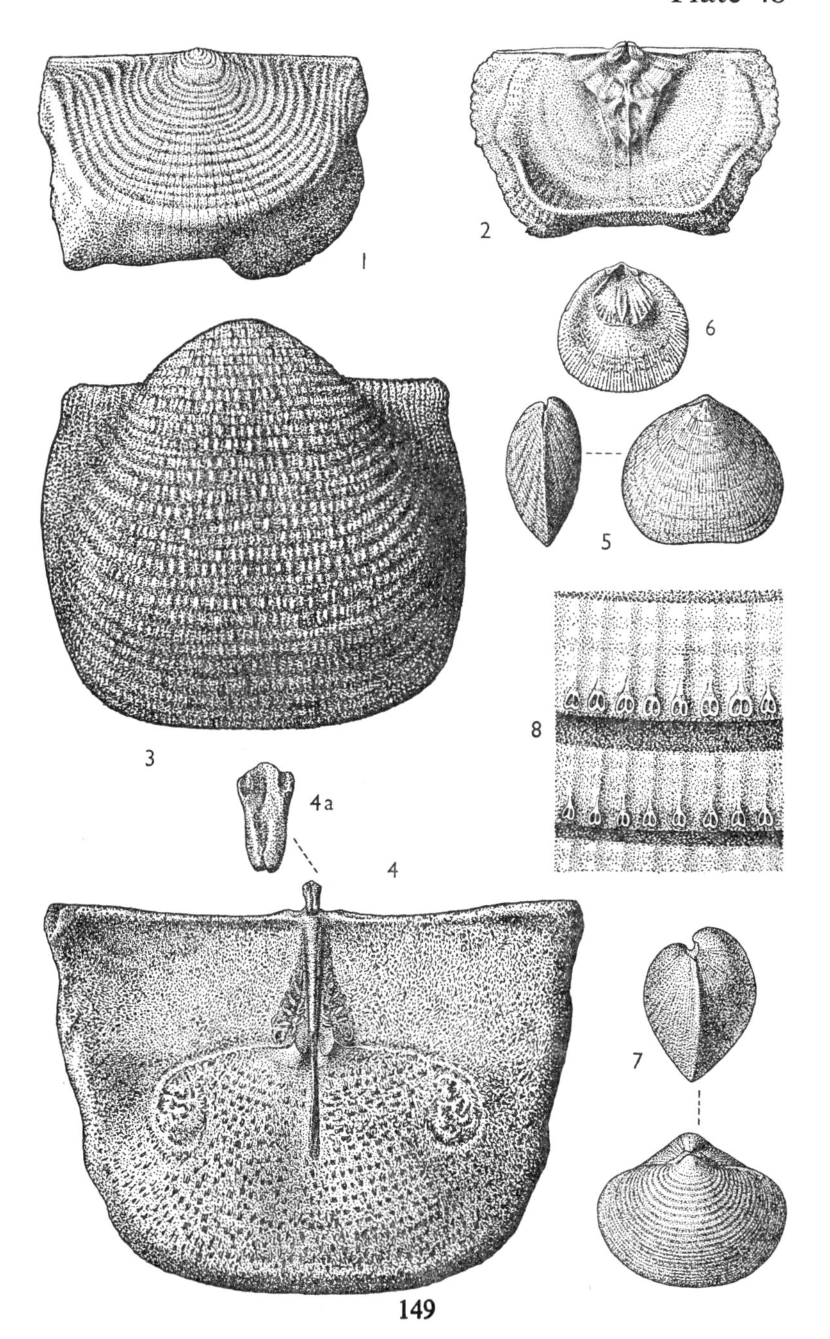
1
2
6
5
8
3
4a
4
7

Plate 49
Carboniferous Brachiopods

1. **Schizophoria resupinata** (Martin). (×½.) Viséan Stage; Narrowdale Hill, near Longnor, Staffordshire. RANGE: Genus, Silurian –Permian; Species, Viséan–Namurian Stages. [Syn., *Orthis resupinata.*]

2.* **Schellwienella crenistria** (Phillips). (×1.) 2. Dorsal view. 2*a*. Ventral view of internal mould. Viséan Stage; Elbolton, Yorkshire. RANGE: Genus, Tournaisian–Namurian Stages; Species, Viséan–Namurian Stages. [Syn., *Orthis crenistria.*]

3. **Brachythyris pinguis** (J. Sowerby). (×1.) Viséan Stage; Millicent, County Kildare, Eire. RANGE: Genus, Viséan–Westphalian Stages; Species, Viséan Stage. [Syn., *Spirifer pinguis.*]

4. **Daviesiella llangollensis** (Davidson). (×½.) Viséan Stage; Llangollen, Denbighshire. RANGE: Viséan Stage. [Syn., *Productus llangollensis.*]

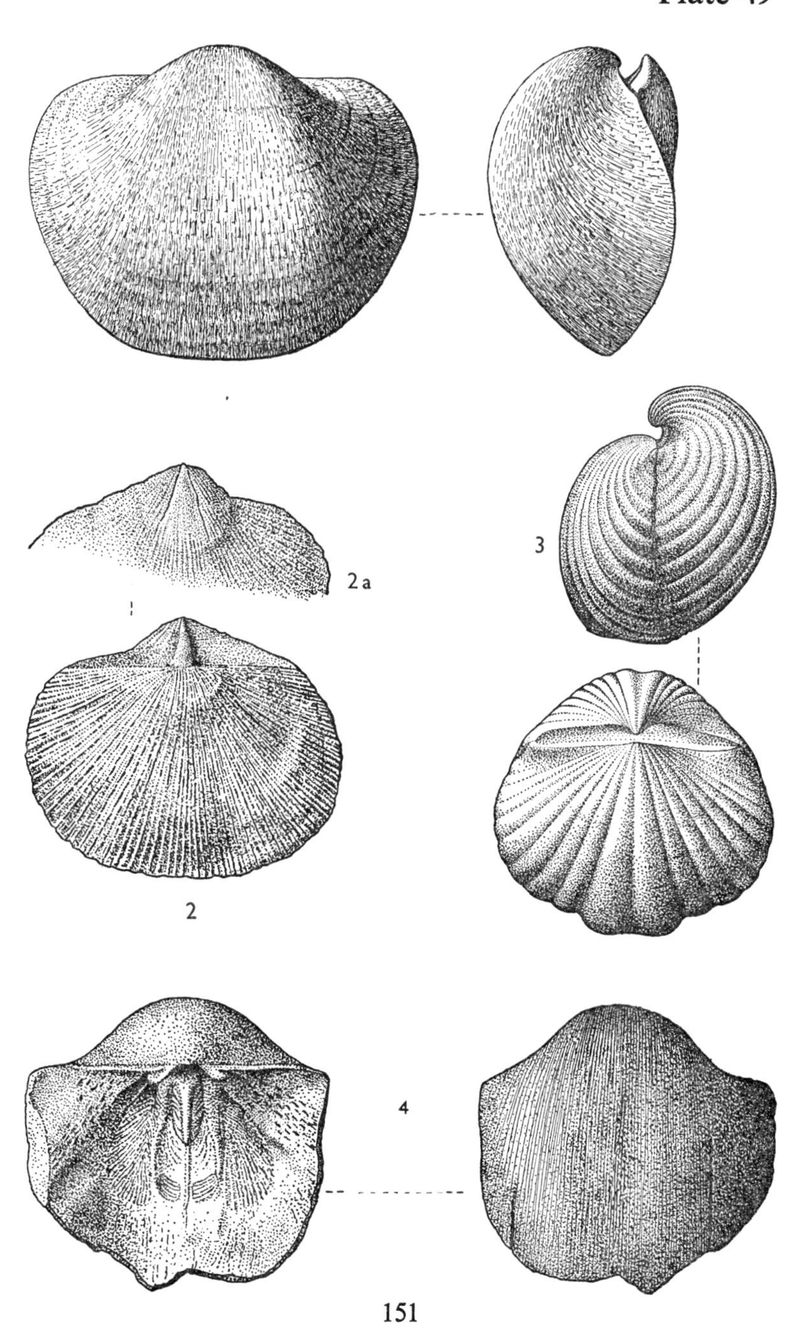
2a
2
3
4

Plate 50
Carboniferous Brachiopods

1. **Composita ambigua** (J. Sowerby). (×1.) Lower Carboniferous; Settle, Yorkshire. RANGE: Genus, Carboniferous, Viséan Stage –Permian; Species, Viséan–Namurian Stages. [Syn., *Athyris ambigua.*]

2. **Martinia glabra** (Martin). (×1.) Lower Carboniferous; Elden Hill, near Castleton, Derbyshire. RANGE: Viséan–Namurian Stages. [Syn., *Spirifer glaber.*]

3.* **Spirifer striatus** (Martin). (×½.) Viséan Stage; Derbyshire. RANGE: Genus, Carboniferous; Species, Tournaisian–Viséan Stages.

Plate 50

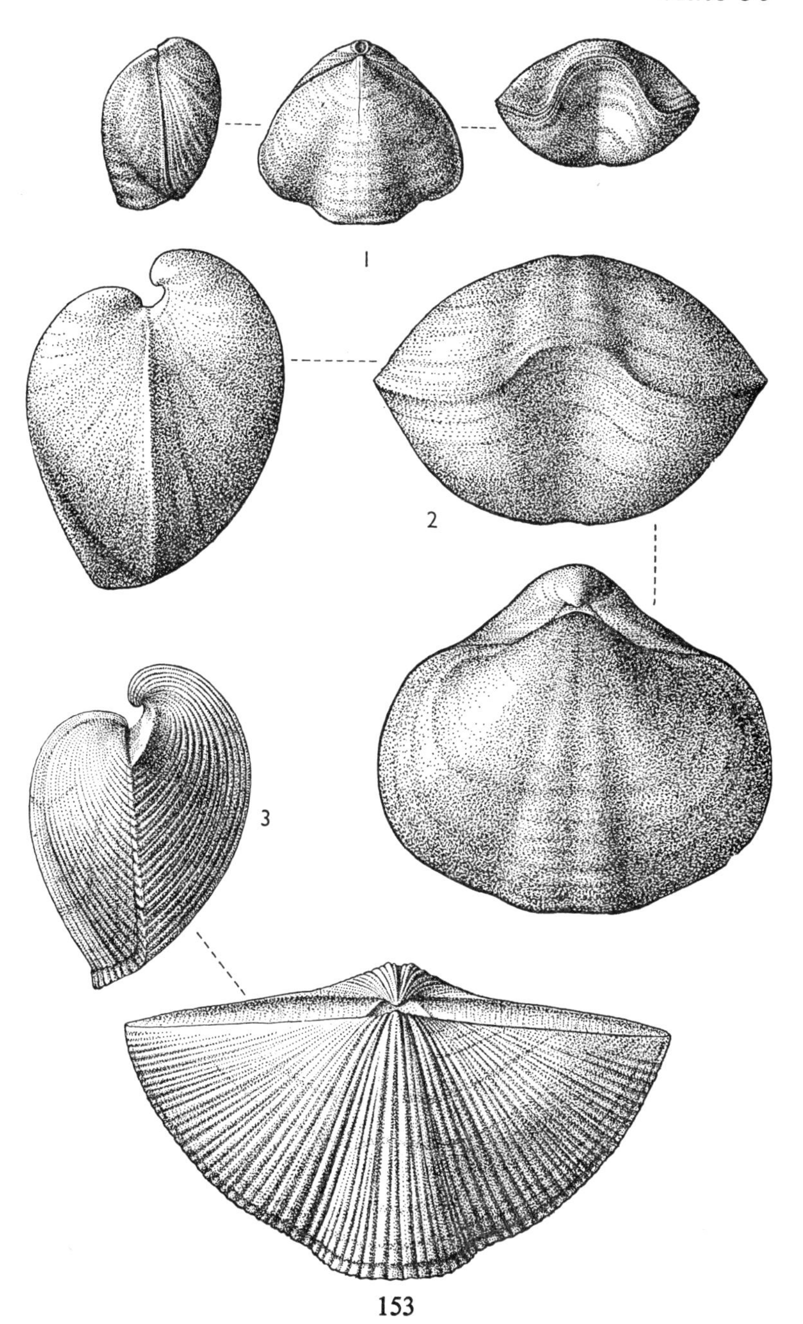

Plate 51
Carboniferous Brachiopods

1.* **Brachythyris pennystonensis** (George). (×1.) Upper Carboniferous; near Ironbridge, Shropshire. RANGE: Genus, Viséan–Westphalian Stages; Species, Westphalian Stage. [Syn., *Spirifer pennystonensis.*]

2. **Pugnoides pleurodon** (Phillips). (×1½.) Viséan Stage; Axton, near Prestatyn, Flintshire. RANGE: Viséan–Namurian Stages. [Syn., *Pugnax pleurodon, Rhynchonella pleurodon.*]

3.* **Syringothyris cuspidata** (J. Sowerby). (×¾.) Lower Carboniferous; Rathkeale, County Limerick, Eire. RANGE: Genus, Carboniferous; Species, Tournaisian–Viséan Stages. [Syn., *Spirifer cuspidatus.*]

Plate 51

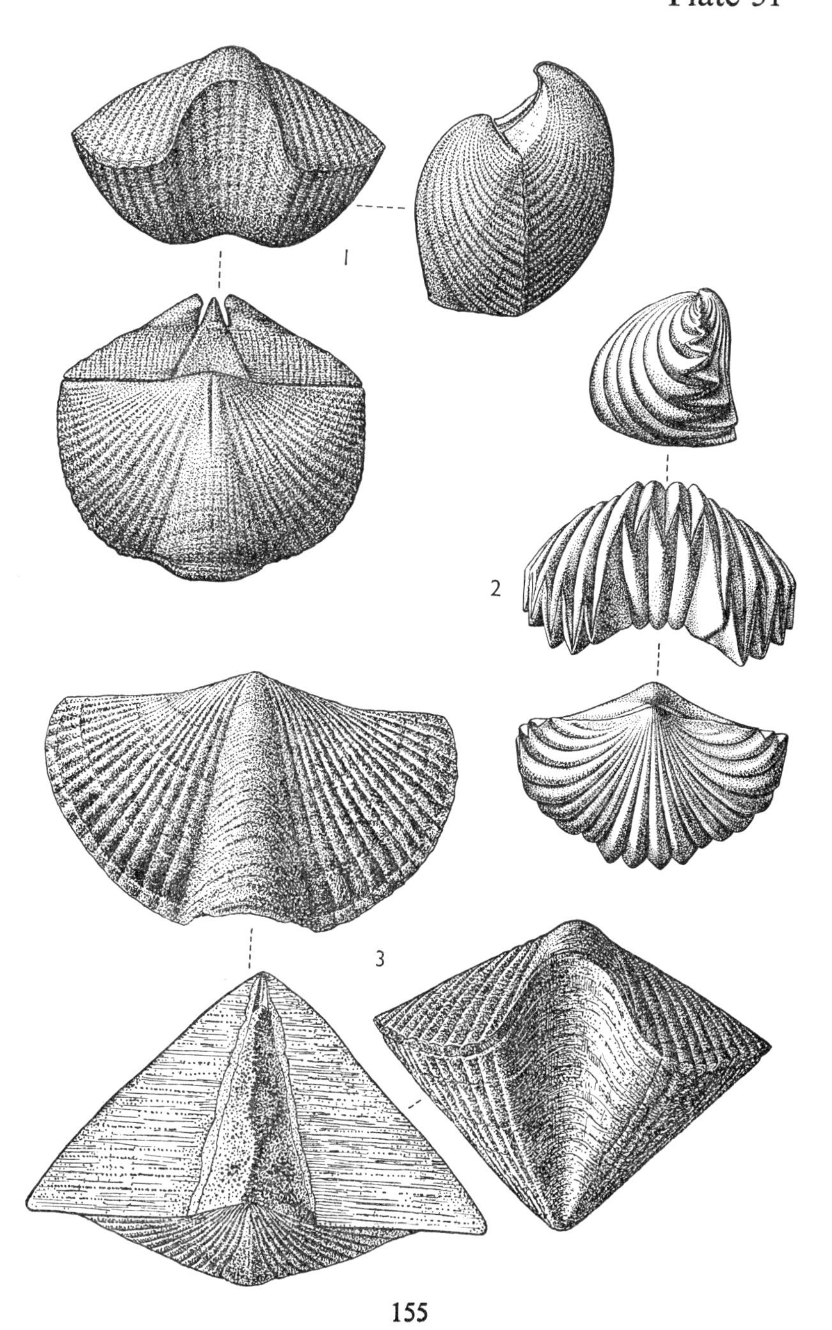

Plate 52
Carboniferous Brachiopods

1. **Punctospirifer scabricostus** North subsp. **ashfellensis** North. (×2.) Viséan Stage; Ash Fell, near Kirkby Stephen, Westmorland. RANGE: Genus, Carboniferous, Viséan Stage–Permian; Species, Viséan Stage.

2. **Spirifer attenuatus** J. de C. Sowerby. (×1.) Lower Carboniferous; Kildare, Eire. RANGE: Genus, Carboniferous; Species, Tournasian Stage.

3.* **Pugnax acuminatus** (J. Sowerby). (×1.) Viséan Stage; Derbyshire. RANGE: Genus, Middle Devonian–Lower Carboniferous; Species, Viséan Stage.

4. **Actinoconchus lamellosus** (Léveillé). (×1.) Showing marginal expansions. Viséan Stage; Axton, near Prestatyn, Flintshire. RANGE: Tournaisian–Namurian Stages. [Syn., *Athyris lamellosa*.]

5.* **Dielasma hastatum** (J. de C. Sowerby). (×1.) Carboniferous; Eire. RANGE: Genus, Carboniferous, Viséan Stage–Permian; Species, Viséan–Namurian Stages. [Syn., *Terebratula hastata*.]

Plate 52

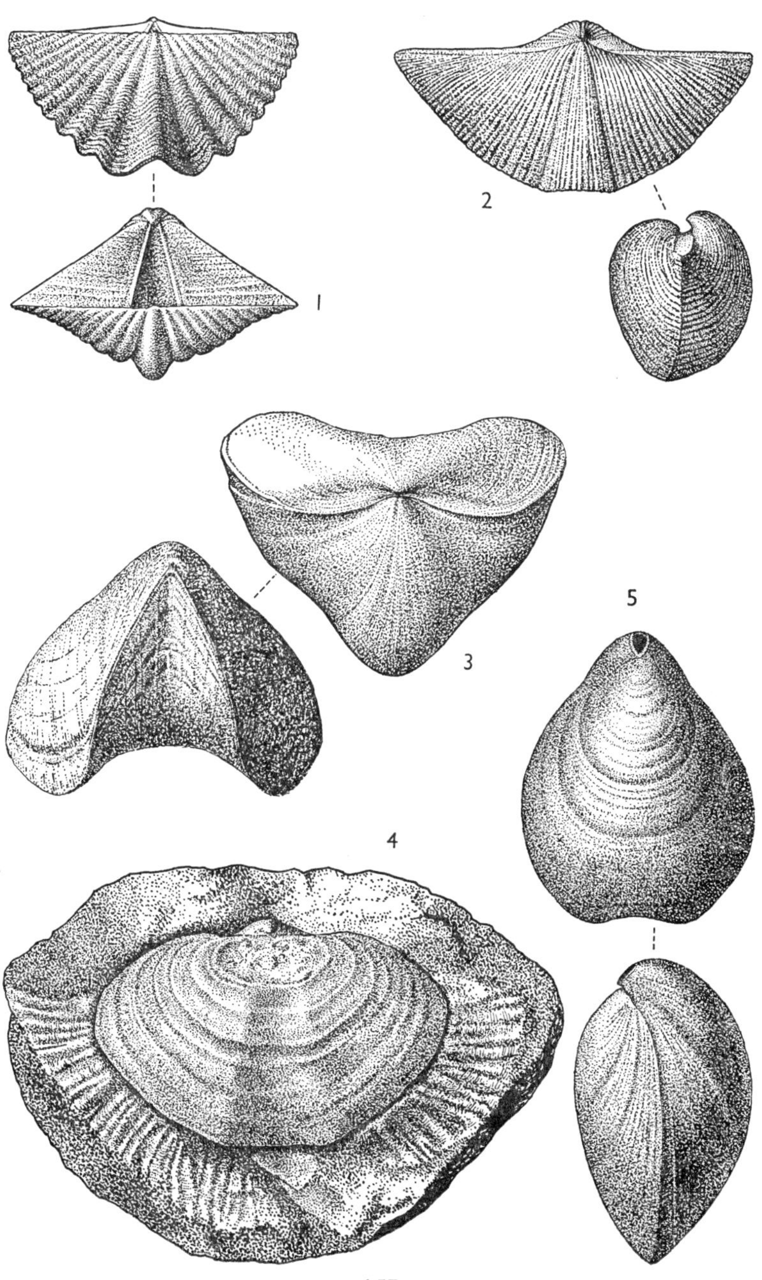

Plate 53
Carboniferous Bivalves

1. **Polidevcia attenuata** (Fleming). ($\times 1\frac{1}{2}$.) Lower Carboniferous; Woodmill, near Dunfermline, Fifeshire. RANGE: Carboniferous. [Syn., *Nuculana attenuata.*]

2.* **Lithophaga lingualis** (Phillips). ($\times \frac{3}{4}$.) Viséan Stage; Beith, Ayrshire. RANGE: Genus, Carboniferous–Recent; Species, Lower Carboniferous.

3. **Posidonia becheri** Bronn. ($\times 1$.) Lower Carboniferous; Budle, near Bamburgh, Northumberland. RANGE: Genus, Devonian–Carboniferous; Species, Lower Carboniferous. [Syn., *Posidonomya becheri.*]

4. **Posidoniella vetusta** (J. de. C. Sowerby). ($\times 1$.) Viséan Stage; near Castleton, Derbyshire. RANGE: Genus, Carboniferous; Species, Lower Carboniferous.

5, 6. **Conocardium hibernicum** J. Sowerby. Lower Carboniferous. 5 ($\times 1$.) Clitheroe, Lancashire. 6. Partly restored specimen ($\times \frac{1}{2}$). Kildare, Eire. RANGE: Genus, Ordovician–Permian; Species, Lower Carboniferous.

Plate 53

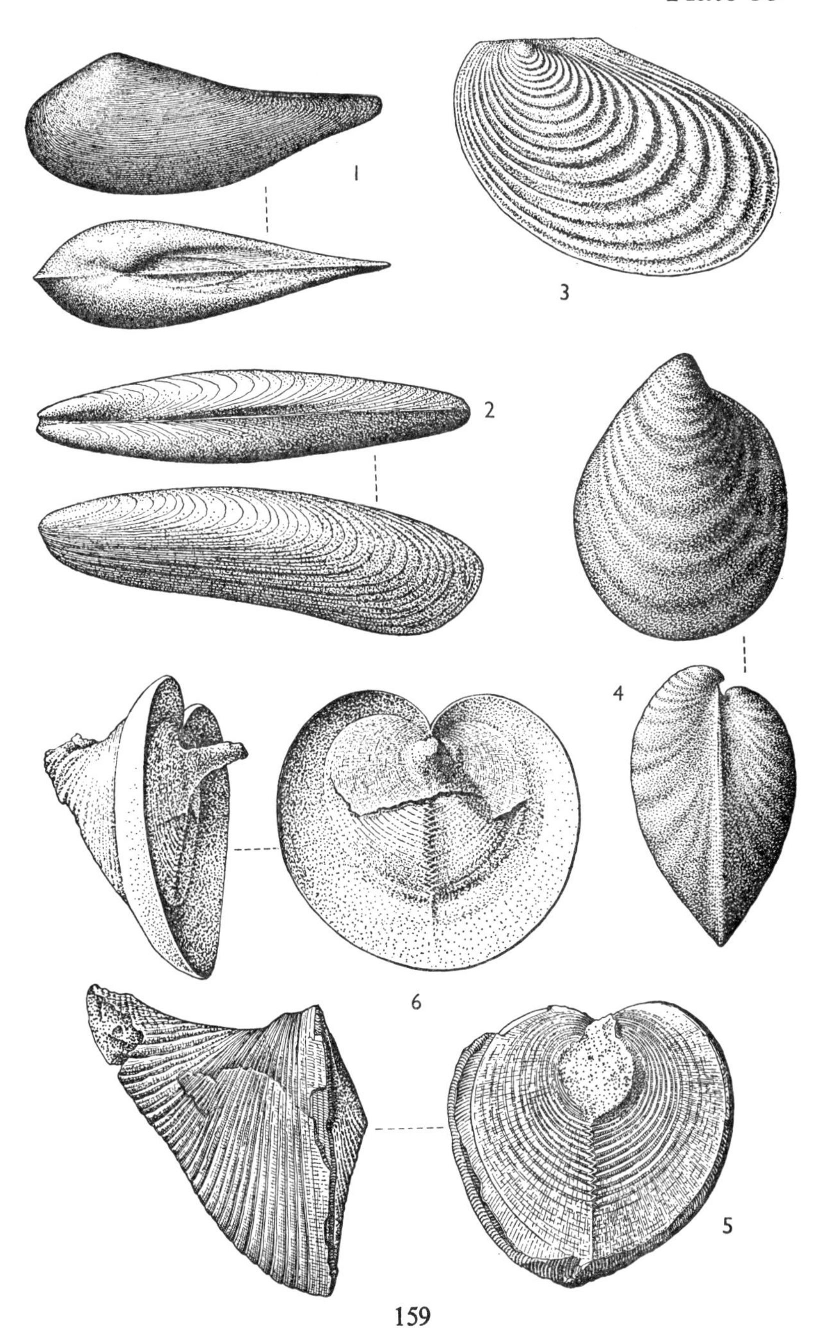

Plate 54
Carboniferous Bivalves

1.* **Schizodus carbonarius** (J. de C. Sowerby). ($\times\frac{3}{4}$.) Upper Carboniferous, Coal Measures; Madeley, Shropshire. RANGE: Genus, Carboniferous–Permian; Species, Coal Measures.

2.* **Edmondia sulcata** (Phillips). ($\times\frac{3}{4}$.) Lower Carboniferous; Poolvash, near Castletown, Isle of Man. RANGE: Genus, Devonian–Permian; Species, Lower Carboniferous.

3.* **Wilkingia elliptica** (Phillips). (×1.) Upper Carboniferous, Coal Measures; Coalbrookdale, near Ironbridge, Shropshire. RANGE: Genus, Carboniferous–Permian; Species, Carboniferous. [Syn., *Allorisma sulcata* (Fleming).]

4. **Sanguinolites costellatus** M'Coy. (×1.) Lower Carboniferous, Viséan Stage; Gurdy, near Beith, Ayrshire. RANGE: Genus, Devonian–Carboniferous; Species, Carboniferous.

5.* **Pterinopectinella granosa** (J. de C. Sowerby). (×1.) Lower Carboniferous; Kildare, Eire. RANGE: Lower Carboniferous. [Syn., *Pterinopecten granosus* of authors.]

6.* **Dunbarella papyracea** (J. de C. Sowerby). (×1.) Upper Carboniferous, Coal Measures; Leeds, Yorkshire. RANGE: Upper Carboniferous. [Syn., *Pterinopecten papyraceus.*]

7.* **Aviculopecten plicatus** (J. de C. Sowerby). (×1.) Lower Carboniferous; locality unknown. RANGE: Genus, Devonian ?–Carboniferous; Species, Lower Carboniferous.

Plate 54

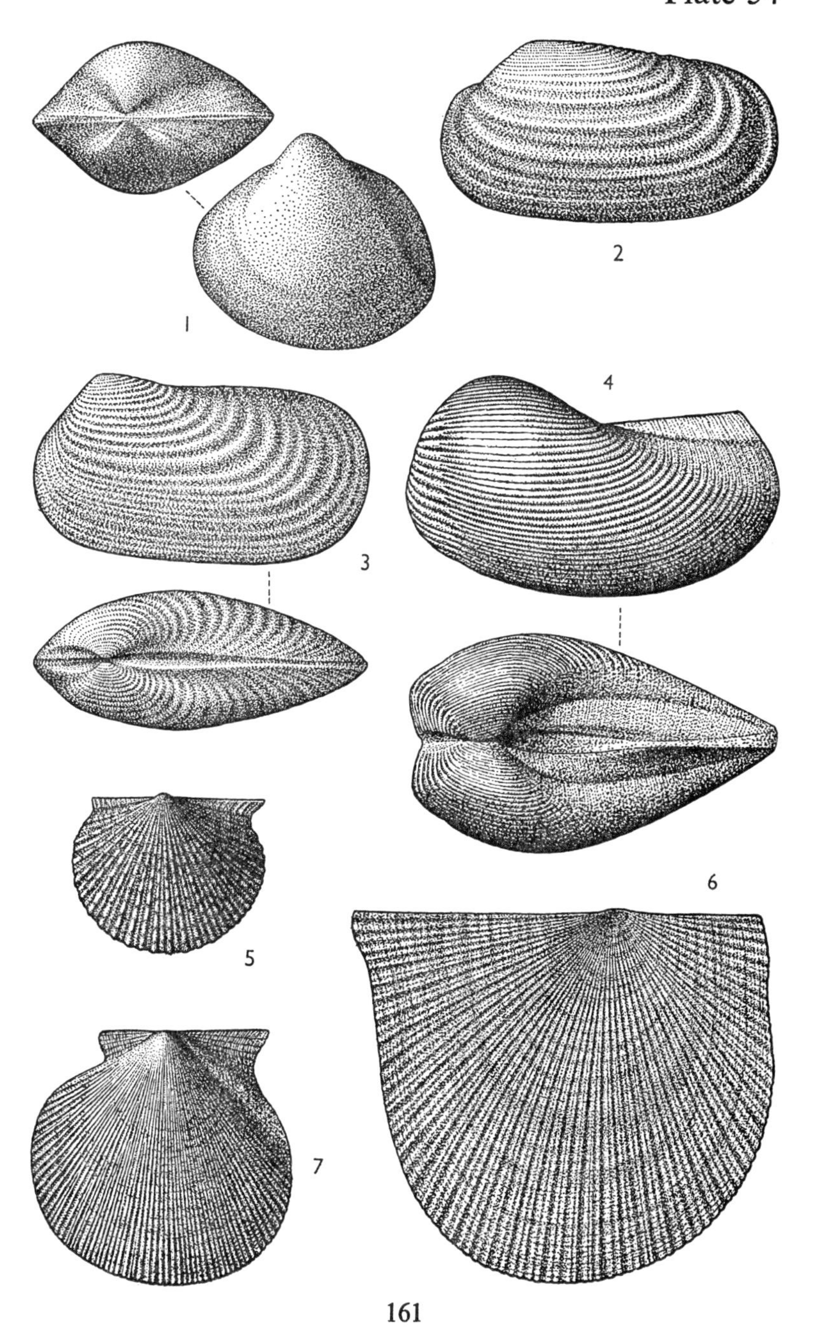

Plate 55
Carboniferous Bivalves

1.* **Naiadites modiolaris** J. de C. Sowerby. (×1.) Coal Measures, Ammanian Stage; Adderley Green, Longton, Stoke-on-Trent, Staffordshire. RANGE: Genus, Carboniferous, Tournaisian–Ammanian Stages; Species, Ammanian Stage, *modiolaris*–Lower *similis–pulchra* Zones.

2. **Anthracosphaerium exiguum** (Davies & Trueman). (×1.) Coal Measures, Ammanian Stage; Ystalyfera, near Swansea, Glamorgan. RANGE: Genus, Carboniferous, Ammanian–Stephanian Stages; Species, Ammanian Stage, *modiolaris*–Lower *similis–pulchra* Zones.

3. **Anthracosia atra** (Trueman). (×1.) Coal Measures, Ammanian Stage; Ystalyfera, near Swansea, Glamorgan. RANGE: Genus, Carboniferous, Ammanian Stage; Species, Lower *similis–pulchra* Zone.

4. **Anthracosia planitumida** (Trueman). (×1½.) Coal Measures, Ammanian Stage;Ystalyfera, near Swansea, Glamorgan. RANGE: Genus, Carboniferous, Ammanian Stage; Species, Lower *similis–pulchra* Zone.

5.* **Carbonicola communis** Davies & Trueman. (×1.) Coal Measures, Ammanian Stage; Black Mountain Colliery, Twrch Valley, Carmarthenshire. RANGE: Genus, Carboniferous, Tournaisian –Ammanian Stages; Species, Ammanian Stage, *communis* Zone.

6.* **Carbonicola pseudorobusta** Trueman. (×½.) Coal Measures, Ammanian Stage; Halifax, Yorkshire. RANGE: Genus, Carboniferous, Tournaisian–Ammanian Stages; Species, Ammanian Stage, *communis* Zone.

7.* **Anthraconaia adamsi** (Salter). (×¾.) Coal Measures, Ammanian Stage; near Fenton, Stoke-on-Trent, Staffordshire. RANGE: Genus, Carboniferous, Ammanian–Stephanian Stages; Species, Ammanian Stage, Upper *similis-pulchra* Zone.

Plate 55

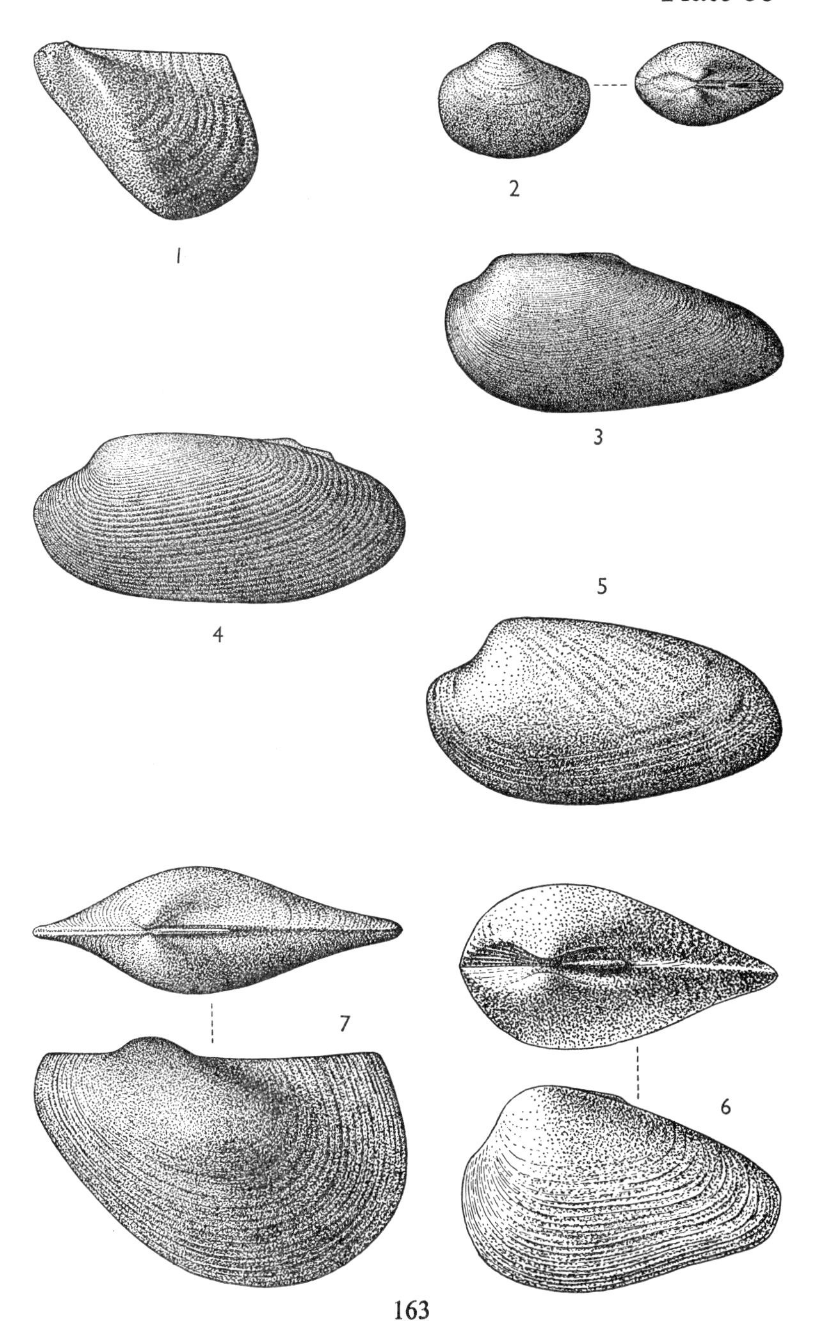

Plate 56
Carboniferous Gastropods

1.* **Euphemites urii** (Fleming). (×1½.) Lower Carboniferous; Gare, Carluke, Lanarkshire. RANGE: Genus, Carboniferous; Species, Lower Carboniferous. [Syn., *Euphemus urii.*]

2.* **Euconospira conica** (Phillips). (×1.) 2*a*, Surface ornamentation (×2). Lower Carboniferous; Bowland, near Clitheroe, Lancashire. RANGE: Lower Carboniferous. [Syn., *Mourlonia conica.*]

3.* **Straparollus dionysii** Montfort. (×¾.) Lower Carboniferous, Viséan Stage; Wedber Knoll, near Malham, Yorkshire. RANGE: Genus, Devonian–Carboniferous; Species, Lower Carboniferous.

4. **Glabrocingulum atomarium** (Phillips). (×2¼.) 4*a*, Surface ornamentation (×5). Viséan Stage; Woodmill, near Dunfermline, Fifeshire. RANGE: Genus, Viséan–Namurian Stages; Species, Viséan Stage.

5. **Platyceras vetustum** (J. de C. Sowerby). (×1.) Lower Carboniferous; Ireland. RANGE: Genus, Silurian–Carboniferous; Species, Lower Carboniferous.

6.* **Soleniscus acutus** (J. de C. Sowerby). (×¾.) Lower Carboniferous; Kildare, Eire. RANGE: Genus, Lower Carboniferous–Permian; Species, Lower Carboniferous. [Syn., *Macrochilina acuta.*]

7. **Mourlonia carinata** (J. Sowerby). (×½.) Lower Carboniferous; Bowland, near Clitheroe, Lancashire. RANGE: Genus, Devonian–Permian; Species, Lower Carboniferous.

8.* **Straparollus pentangulatus** (J. Sowerby). (×1.) Lower Carboniferous; Bowland, near Clitheroe, Lancashire. RANGE: Genus, Devonian–Carboniferous; Species, Lower Carboniferous. [Syn., *Euomphalus pentangulatus.*]

9. **Glabrocingulum armstrongi** Thomas. (×2.) *a*, Surface ornamentation (×5.) Lower Carboniferous; Wilkieston, Kirknewton, Midlothian. RANGE: Viséan–Namurian Stages.

Plate 56

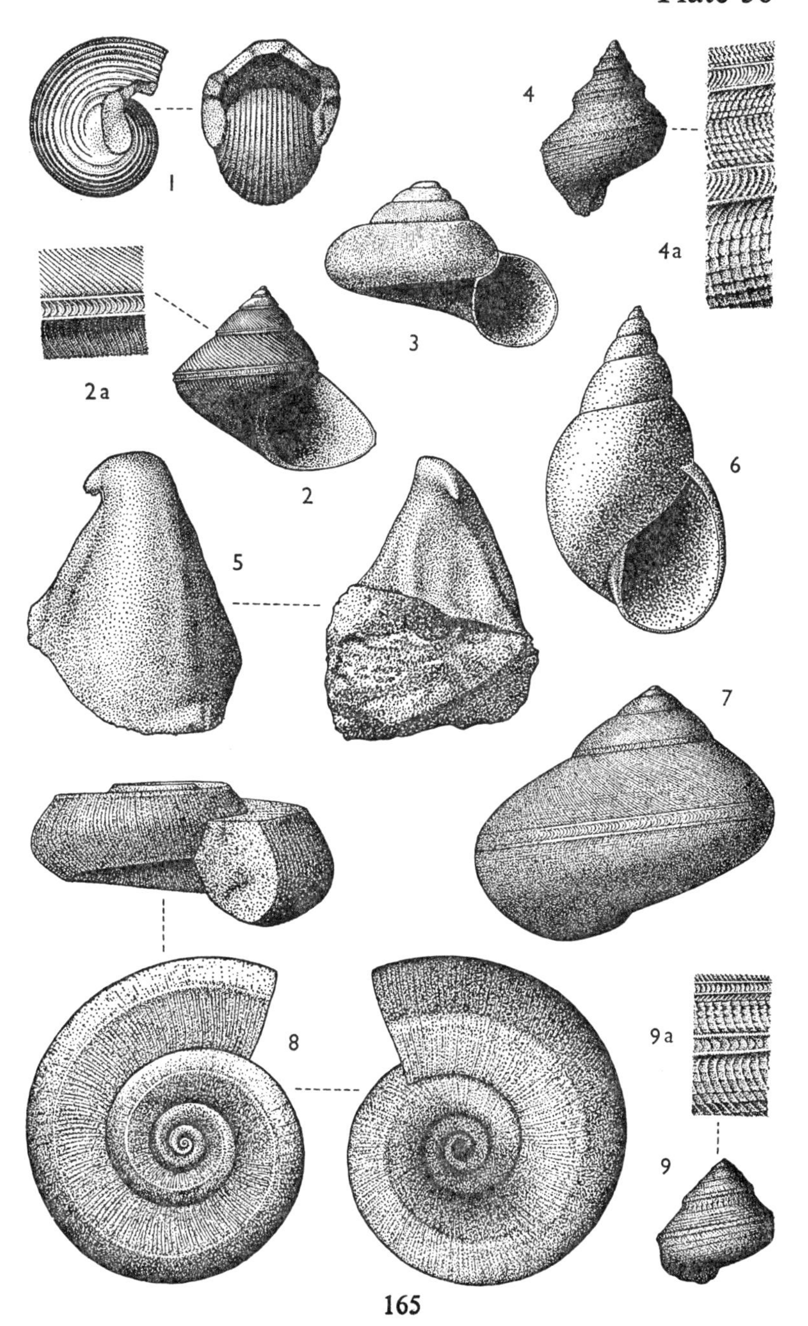

Plate 57
Carboniferous Gastropods (Figs. 1, 2) and Goniatites (Figs. 3, 4)

1.* **Naticopsis elliptica** (Phillips). (×¾.) Lower Carboniferous; Kildare, Eire. RANGE: Genus, Devonian–Permian (? Trias); Species, Lower Carboniferous.

2.* **Palaeostylus rugiferus** (Phillips). (×1.) Lower Carboniferous; Craigenglen, Campsie, Stirlingshire. RANGE: Carboniferous. [Syn., *Zygopleura rugifera.*]

3. **Reticuloceras reticulatum** (Phillips). (×1½.) Namurian Stage; Hebden Bridge, Yorkshire. RANGE: Genus, Namurian Stage, Zone R; Species, Zone R_1.

4. **Reticuloceras bilingue** (Salter). (×1.) 4*a*, Ornamentation (×2½). Namurian Stage; Hebden Bridge, Yorkshire. RANGE: Genus, Namurian Stage, Zone R; Species, Zone R_2. [Syn., *Reticuloceras reticulatum* mut. *β*.]

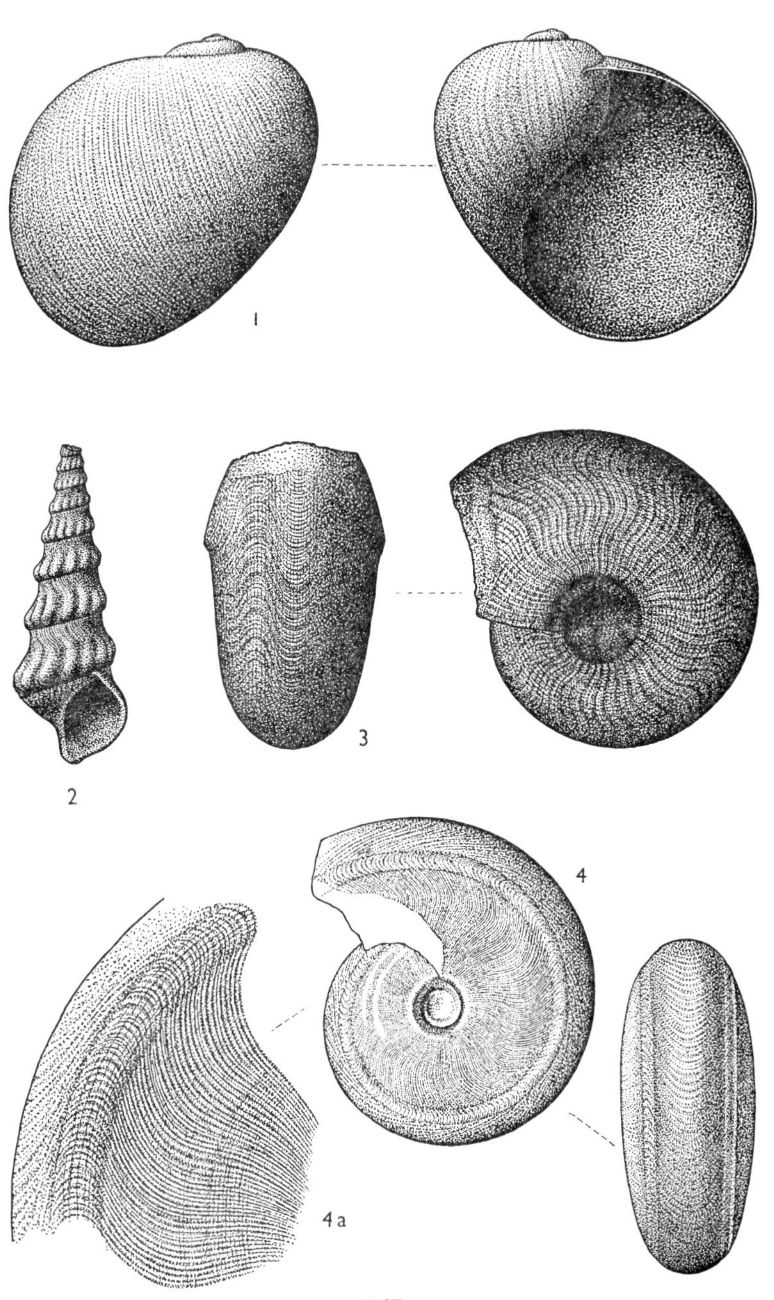
1
2
3
4
4 a

Plate 58
Carboniferous Goniatites

1.* **Homoceras diadema** (Beyrich). (×1½.) Namurian Stage; Halifax, Yorkshire. RANGE: Namurian Stage, Zone H.

2, 3.* **Muensteroceras truncatum** (Phillips). (×1.) 3, Septal suture. Viséan Stage; Bowland, near Clitheroe, Lancashire. RANGE: Viséan Stage, Zone P. [Syn., *Beyrichoceratoides truncatum.*]

4, 5. **Beyrichoceras obtusum** (Phillips). (×1.) 5, Septal suture. Viséan Stage; Bowland, near Clitheroe, Lancashire. RANGE: Viséan Stage. Genus, Zones B_1–P_1; Species, Zone P_1.

6. **Gastrioceras carbonarium** (Buch). (×1.) Upper Carboniferous; Churnet Valley, near Leek, Staffordshire. RANGE: Namurian–Ammanian Stages. Genus, Zone G; Species, Zone G_2.

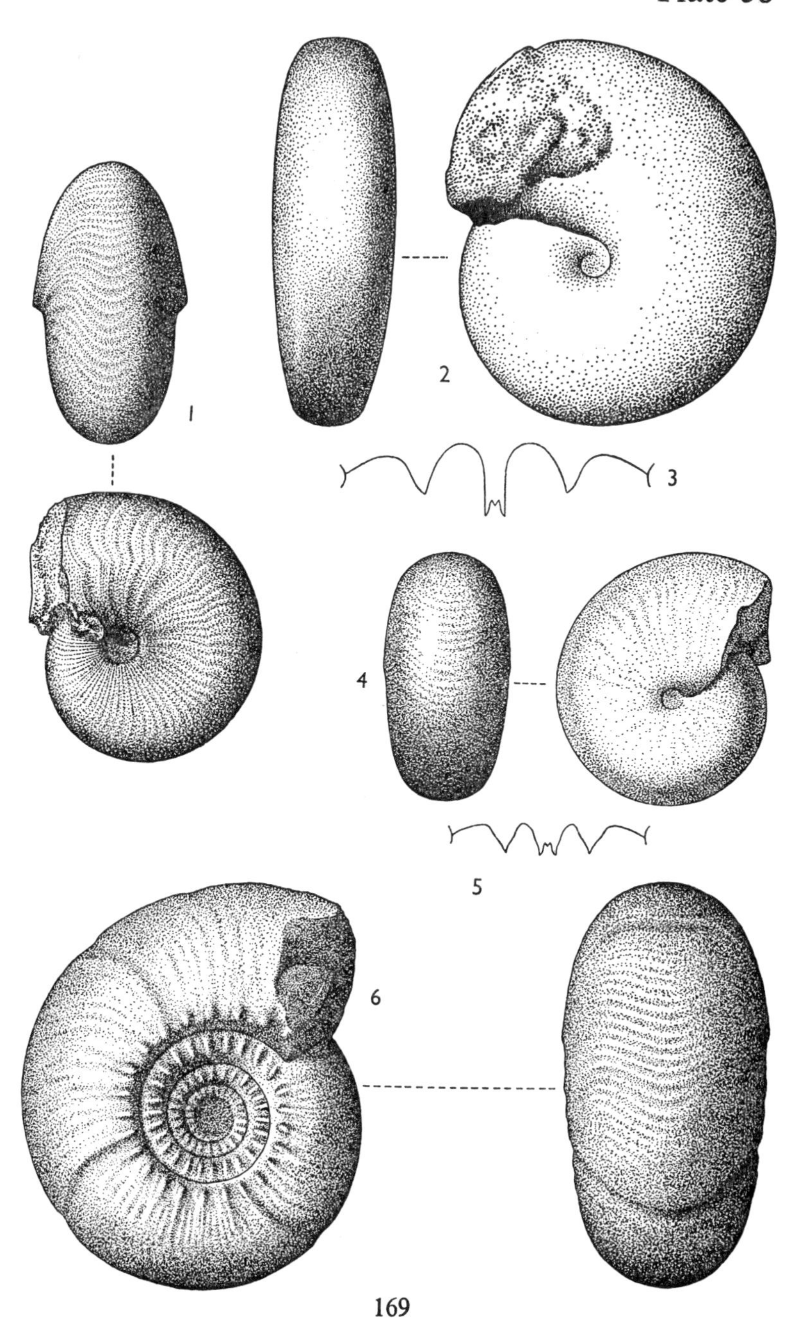
1
2
3
4
5
6

Plate 59

Carboniferous Goniatites (Figs. 1, 2), Blastoids (Figs. 3–7) and Echinoids (Figs. 8–10)

1.* **Goniatites crenistria** Phillips. (×1.) *a*, septal suture. Lower Carboniferous; Dinckley Ferry, River Ribble, near Blackburn, Lancashire. RANGE: Genus, Viséan Stage; Species, Zone P.

2.* **Neoglyphioceras spirale** (Phillips). (×1.) Viséan Stage; Waddon Barton, near Chudleigh, South Devon. RANGE: Viséan Stage. [Syn., *Goniatites spiralis.*]

3, 4.* **Codaster acutus** M'Coy. (×1½.) 3, upper surface. 4, side view. Lower Carboniferous; Settle, Yorkshire. RANGE: Lower Carboniferous. [Syn., *Codastertrilobatus* M'Coy, *Codonaster trilobatus.*]

5, 6. **Orbitremites ellipticus** (G. B. Sowerby). (×1½.) Viséan Stage; Lancashire. RANGE: Genus, Carboniferous; Species, Viséan Stage. [Syn., *Granatocrinus ellipticus.*]

7. **Orophocrinus verus** (Cumberland). (×1½.) Viséan Stage; Whitewell, Bowland, near Clitheroe, Lancashire. RANGE: Genus, Lower Carboniferous; Species, Viséan Stage.

8. **Archaeocidaris** sp. Radiole (×1). Lower Carboniferous; Chrome Hill, near Buxton, Derbyshire. RANGE: Genus, Carboniferous.

9. **Archaeocidaris urii** (Fleming). Plate (×3). Lower Carboniferous; Roscobie, near Dunfermline, Fifeshire. RANGE: Species, Tournaisian ?–Viséan Stages. [Syn., *Cidaris benburbensis* Portlock.]

10. **Lovenechinus lacazei** (Julien). (×¾.) Tournaisian Stage; near Kirkby Stephen, Westmorland. RANGE: Genus, Tournaisian–Viséan Stages; Species, Tournaisian Stage. [Syn., *Palaeechinus sphaericus* Koninck *non* M'Coy.]

Plate 59

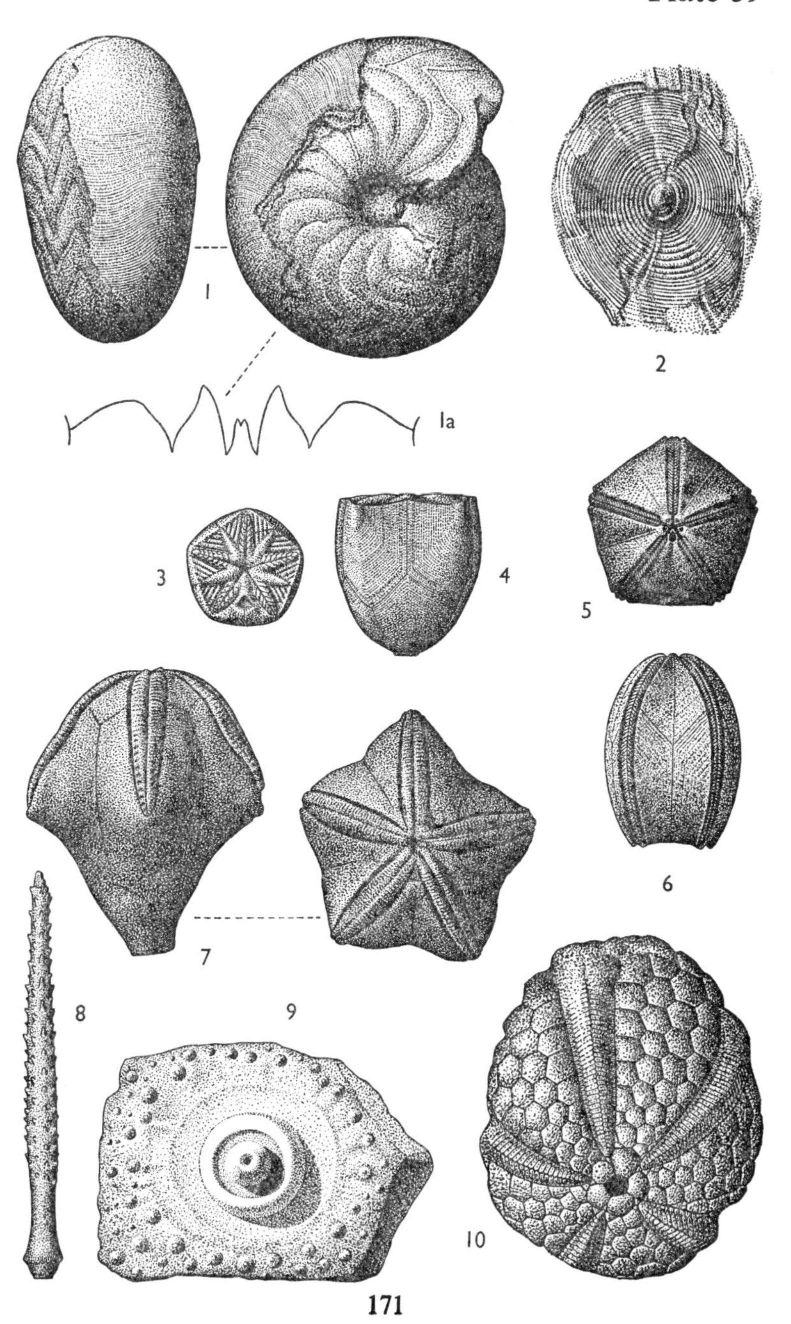

Plate 60
Carboniferous Echinoid (Fig. 1 and Crinoids (Figs. 2–4)

1.* **Melonechinus etheridgei** (Keeping). Fragments of test (×1). Lower Carboniferous; Thor's Cave, Manifold Valley, near Wetton, Staffordshire. RANGE: Lower Carboniferous.

2.* **Woodocrinus macrodactylus** Koninck. (×1.) Namurian Stage; Richmond, Yorkshire. RANGE: Genus, Carboniferous, Viséan–Namurian Stages; Species, Namurian Stage.

3. **Amphoracrinus gigas** Wright. ($\times\frac{3}{4}$.) Tournaisian Stage; Balnaleck, near Florence Court, Enniskillen, Co. Fermanagh, Northern Ireland. RANGE: Genus, Lower Carboniferous; Species, Tournaisian Stage.

4.* **Platycrinites gigas** Phillips. ($\times 1\frac{1}{4}$.) Viséan Stage; Bowland, near Clitheroe, Lancashire. RANGE: Genus, Devonian–Carboniferous; Species, Viséan Stage.

Plate 60

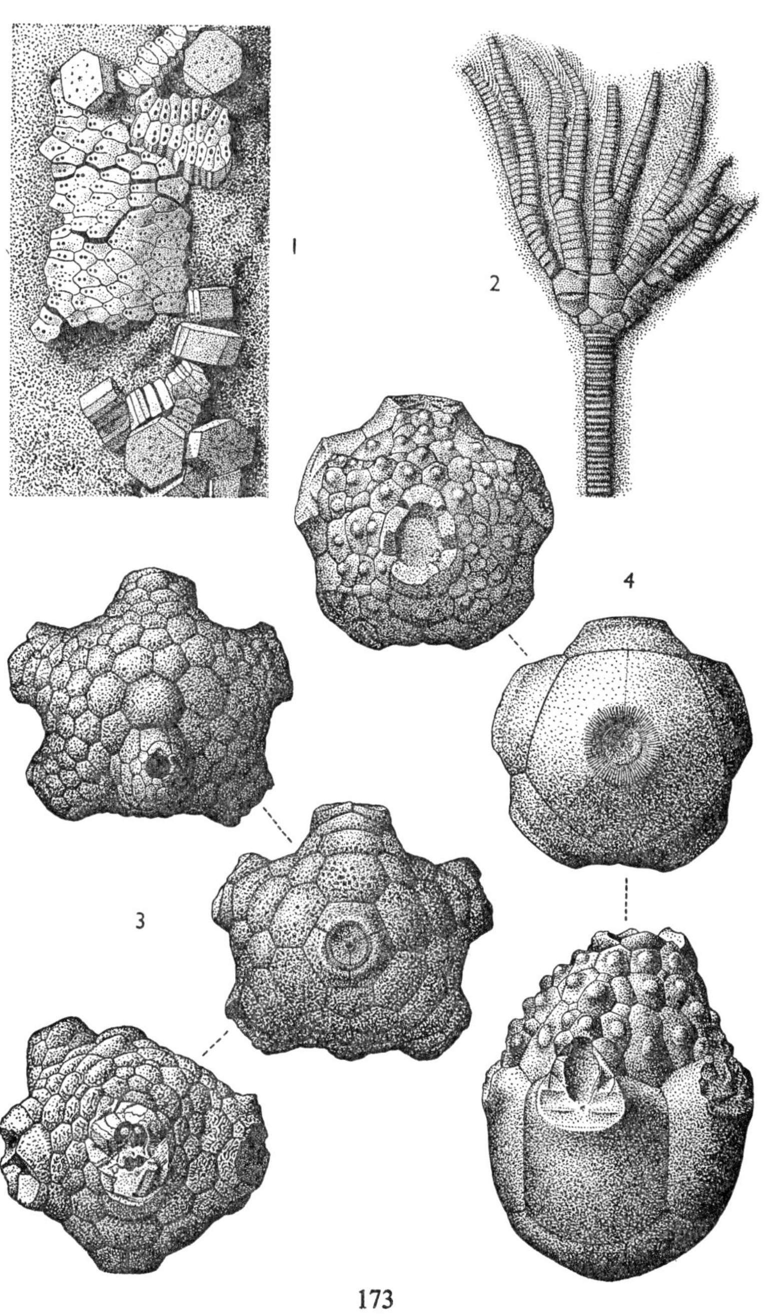

Plate 61
Carboniferous Crinoids

1.* **Actinocrinites triacontadactylus** Miller. (×1.) *a*, tegminal; *b*, basal; *c*, side view. Lower Carboniferous; locality unknown. RANGE: Genus, Carboniferous; Species, Viséan Stage.

2.* **Gilbertsocrinus konincki** Grenfell. (×1.) *a*, tegminal, *b*, basal, *c*, side view. Lower Carboniferous; Yorkshire. RANGE: Genus, Middle Devonian–Lower Carboniferous; Species, Viséan Stage. [Syn., *Gilbertsocrinus calcaratus* Bather *non* Phillips.]

Plate 61

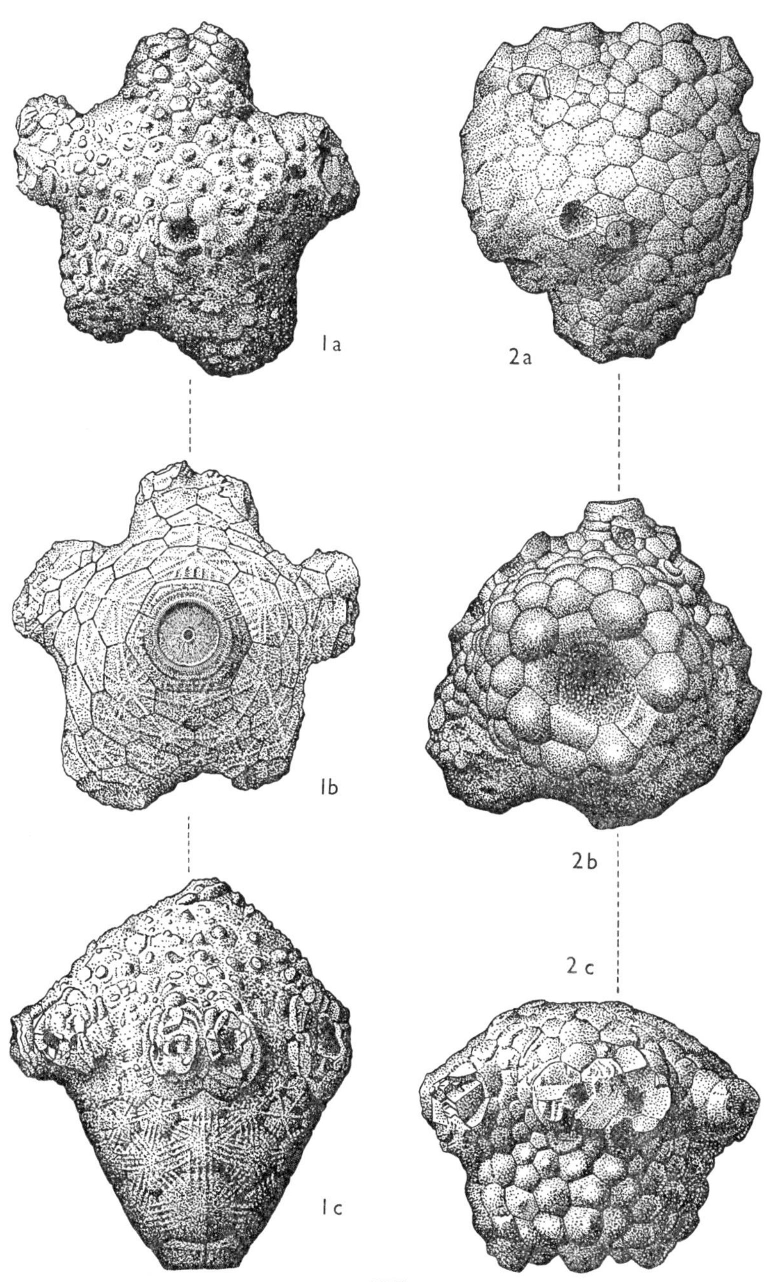

Plate 62
Carboniferous Trilobites (Figs. 1–9) and Crustacean (Fig. 10)

1.* **Griffithides seminiferus** (Phillips). (×1.) Lower Carboniferous, Viséan Stage; Matlock, Derbyshire. RANGE: Lower Carboniferous.

2. **Cummingella jonesi** (Portlock). (×1.) Lower Carboniferous; Bowland, near Clitheroe, Lancashire. RANGE: Lower Carboniferous. [Syn., *Phillipsia derbiensis* of authors.]

3, 4.* **Brachymetopus ouralicus** (Verneuil). (×2.) Lower Carboniferous. 3, Viséan Stage; Peakshill Farm, Mam Tor, near Castleton, Derbyshire. 4, Derbyshire. RANGE: Lower Carboniferous.

5. **Phillipsia gemmulifera** (Phillips). (×2.) Lower Carboniferous; Bowland, near Clitheroe, Lancashire. RANGE: Lower Carboniferous. [Syn., *Asaphus gemmuliferus.*]

6, 7.* **Spatulina spatulata** (Woodward). (×1½.) Lower Carboniferous, Viséan Stage; Coddon Hill, near Barnstaple, Devonshire. RANGE: Viséan Stage. [Syn., *Phillibole* (*Cystispina*) *spatulata*, *Phillipsia spatulata.*]

8, 9. **'Phillipsia' laticaudata** Woodward. (×4.) Lower Carboniferous; Bowland, near Clitheroe, Lancashire. RANGE: Lower Carboniferous.

10.* **Perimecturus parki** (Peach). (×1.) Lower Carboniferous, Viséan Stage, Calciferous Sandstone Series; near Langholm, Eskdale, Dumfriesshire. RANGE: Genus, Carboniferous; Species, Lower Carboniferous.

Plate 62

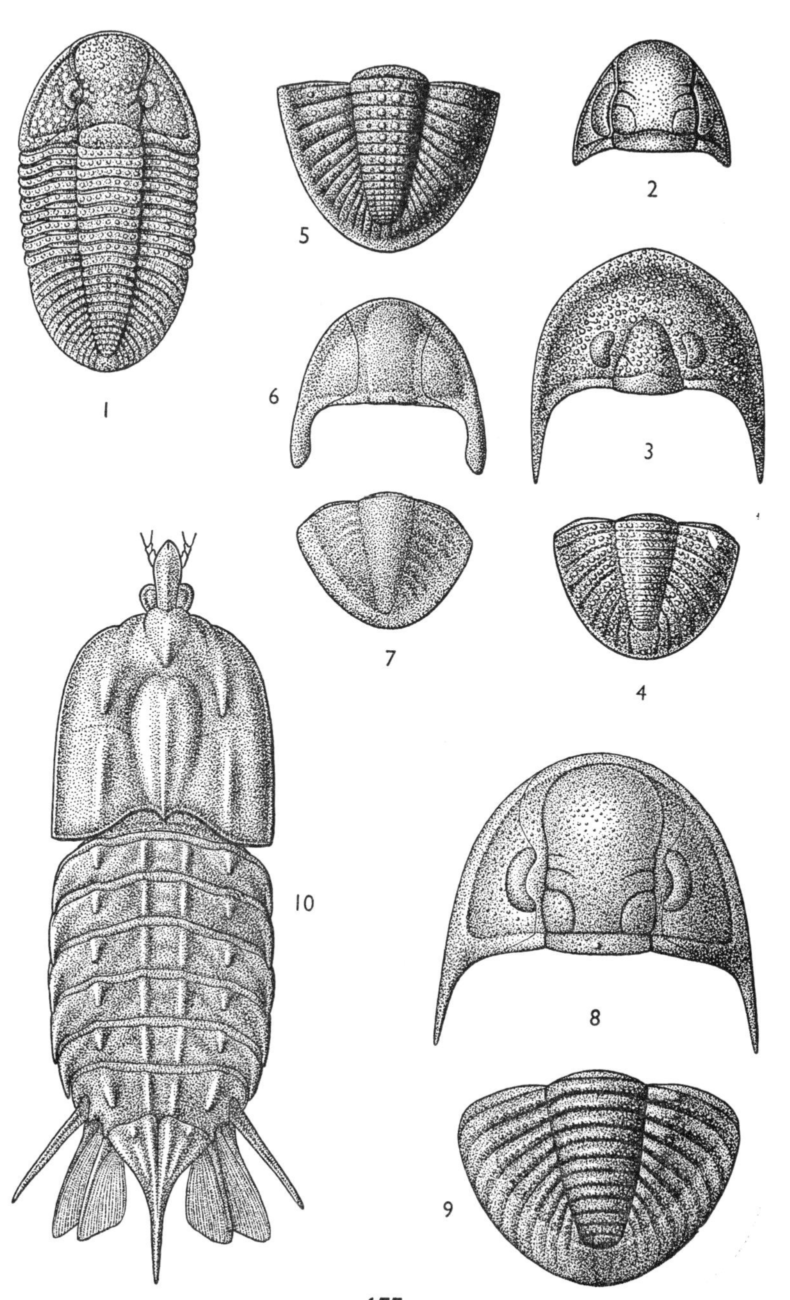

Plate 63

Carboniferous Arthropods (Figs. 1–6), Conodonts (Figs. 7, 8) and Fish (Fig. 9)

1. **Entomoconchus scouleri** M'Coy. (×1.) Lower Carboniferous; Clitheroe, Lancashire. RANGE: Lower Carboniferous.

2. **Richteria biconcentrica** (Jones). (×4.) Lower Carboniferous; Little Island, near Cork, Eire. RANGE: Genus, Devonian–Lower Carboniferous; Species, Lower Carboniferous. [Syn., *Entomis biconcentrica.*]

3. **Amphissites bipartitus** (Vine). (×25.) Lower Carboniferous; Orchard, near Glasgow. RANGE: Genus, Carboniferous–Permian; Species, Lower Carboniferous. [Syn., *Ectodemites bipartitus, Kirkbya bipartita.*]

4.* **Euproops rotundatus** (Prestwich). (×$\frac{3}{4}$.) Upper Carboniferous, Coal Measures; Coseley, Staffordshire. RANGE: Upper Carboniferous. [Syn., *Prestwichia rotundata, Prestwichianella rotundata.*]

5.* **Euphoberia ferox** (Salter). (×1.) Upper Carboniferous, Coal Measures; Coseley, Staffordshire. RANGE: Upper Carboniferous.

6. **Eophrynus prestvici** (Buckland). (×2.) Upper Carboniferous, Coal Measures; Dudley, Worcestershire. RANGE: Upper Carboniferous.

7. **Idiognathoides corrugata** (Harris & Hollingworth). (×35.) Upper Carboniferous, Namurian Stage; Oakamoor, near Cheadle, Staffordshire. RANGE: Namurian Stage.

8. **Gnathodus bilineatus** (Roundy). (×18.) Upper Carboniferous, Namurian Stage; Waterhouses, near Leek, Staffordshire. RANGE: Namurian Stage.

9.* **Cladodus mirabilis** Agassiz. Tooth (×1). Lower Carboniferous; Armagh, N. Ireland. RANGE: Genus, Carboniferous; Species, Lower Carboniferous.

Plate 63

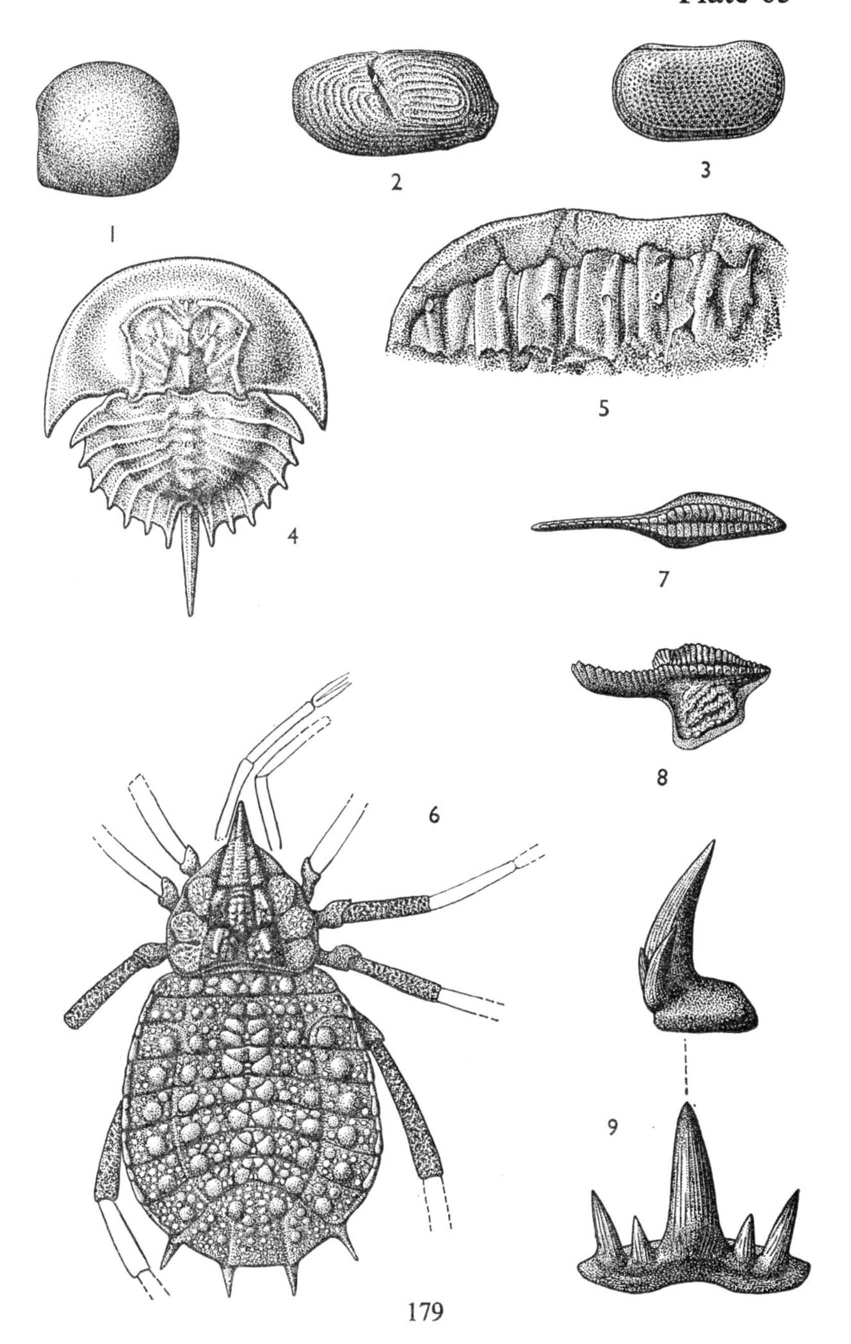

Plate 64
Carboniferous Fishes

1.* **Psephodus magnus** (Portlock). Tooth-plate (×1). Lower Carboniferous; Armagh, N. Ireland. RANGE: Genus, Carboniferous; Species, Lower Carboniferous.

2.* **Psammodus rugosus** Agassiz. Tooth-plate (×¾). 2*a*, surface (×10). Lower Carboniferous; Armagh, N. Ireland. RANGE: Lower Carboniferous.

3.* **Helodus turgidus** (Agassiz). Tooth-plate (×1). Lower Carboniferous; Bristol. RANGE: Genus, Carboniferous; Species, Lower Carboniferous.

4.* **Orodus ramosus** Agassiz. Tooth (×¾). Lower Carboniferous; Oreton, near Ludlow, Shropshire. RANGE: Genus and Species, Lower Carboniferous.

5.* **Gyracanthus formosus** Agassiz. Fin-spine (×½). Coal Measures; Dalkeith, Midlothian. RANGE: Genus and Species, Carboniferous.

6.* **Xenacanthus laevissimus** (Agassiz). Head-spine (×½). *a*, margin (×1½). Upper Carboniferous; Dalkeith, Midlothian. RANGE: Genus, Carboniferous; Species, Upper Carboniferous. [Syn., *Pleuracanthus laevissimus*.]

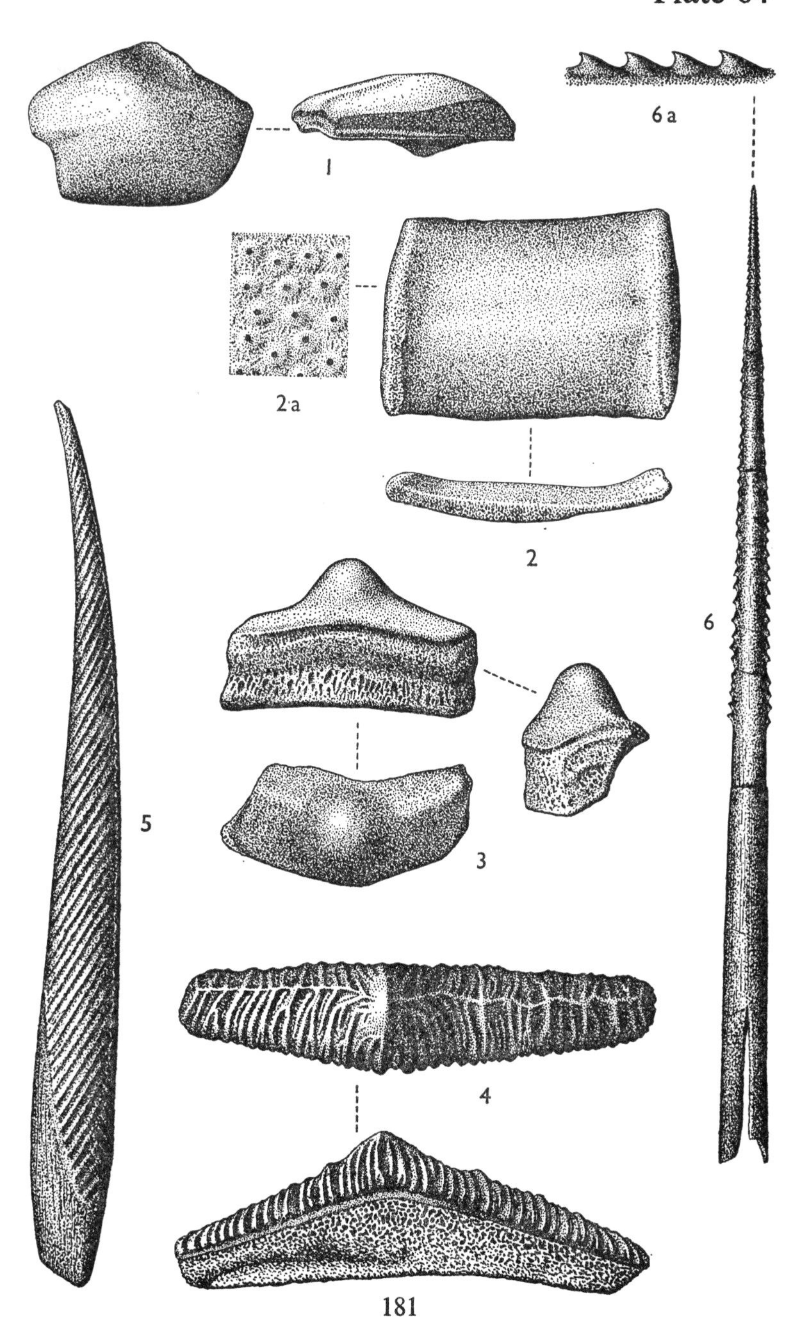
6 a
1
2 a
2
3
5
6
4

Plate 65
Carboniferous Fishes

1, 2. **Megalichthys hibberti** Agassiz. 1, skull ($\times\frac{1}{4}$); dorsal view above, ventral view below. 2, restoration of skull in lateral view ($\times\frac{1}{6}$), (after Moy-Thomas). Upper Carboniferous; near Wakefield, Yorkshire. RANGE: Genus, Carboniferous; Species, Upper Carboniferous. [Syn., *Megalichthys clackmannensis* (Fleming).]

3. **Rhabdoderma tingleyense** (Davis). Gular (throat) plate ($\times\frac{1}{2}$). Upper Carboniferous; Tingley, near Wakefield, Yorkshire. RANGE: Genus, Carboniferous; Species, Upper Carboniferous.

4.* **Rhizodus hibberti** (Agassiz). Tooth ($\times\frac{1}{2}$). *a*, section. Lower Carboniferous; Lochgelly, Fife. RANGE: Genus, Carboniferous; Species, Lower Carboniferous.

Plate 65

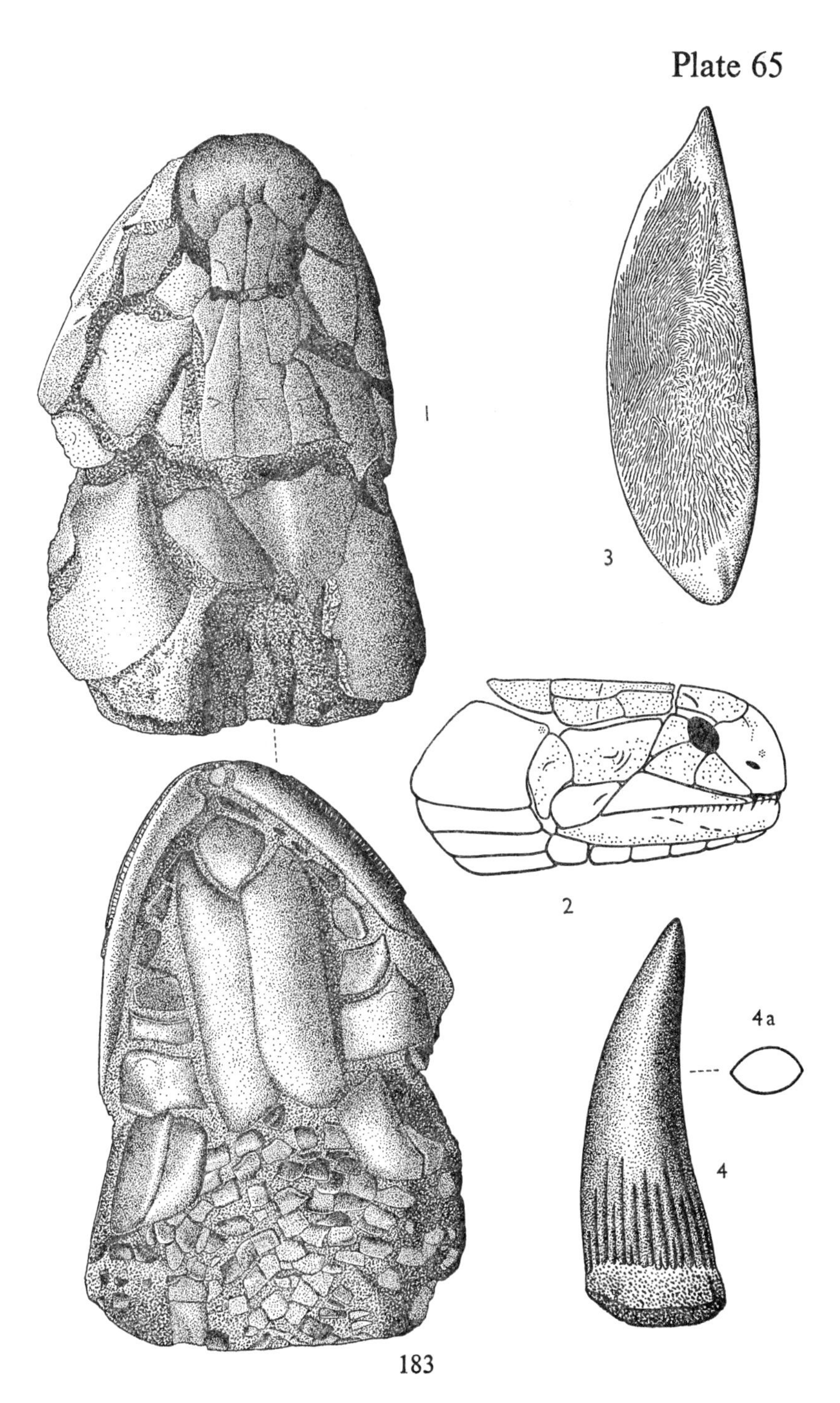

Plate 66
Carboniferous Fish (Fig. 1) and Amphibians (Figs. 2–4)

1. **Sagenodus inaequalis** Owen. Palato-pterygoid with dental plate ($\times\frac{3}{4}$). Upper Carboniferous, Coal Measures; Newsham, Newcastle, Northumberland. RANGE: Genus, Carboniferous; Species, Upper Carboniferous.

2.* Anthracosaurian vertebra ($\times\frac{1}{2}$). Upper Carboniferous, Coal Measures; Lowmoor, Bradford, Yorkshire. RANGE: Upper Carboniferous.

3. **Keraterpeton galvani** Huxley. ($\times\frac{1}{2}$.) Upper Carboniferous, Middle Coal Measures; Jarrow Colliery, near Kilkenny, Eire. RANGE: Middle Coal Measures.

4. **Megalocephalus** cf. **macromma** Barkas. Skull ($\times\frac{1}{4}$). Upper Carboniferous, Coal Measures, *modiolaris* Zone; Dawley, Shropshire. RANGE: Genus, Coal Measures; Species, Ammanian –Morganian Stages. [Syn., *Loxomma allmani* Huxley.]

Plate 66

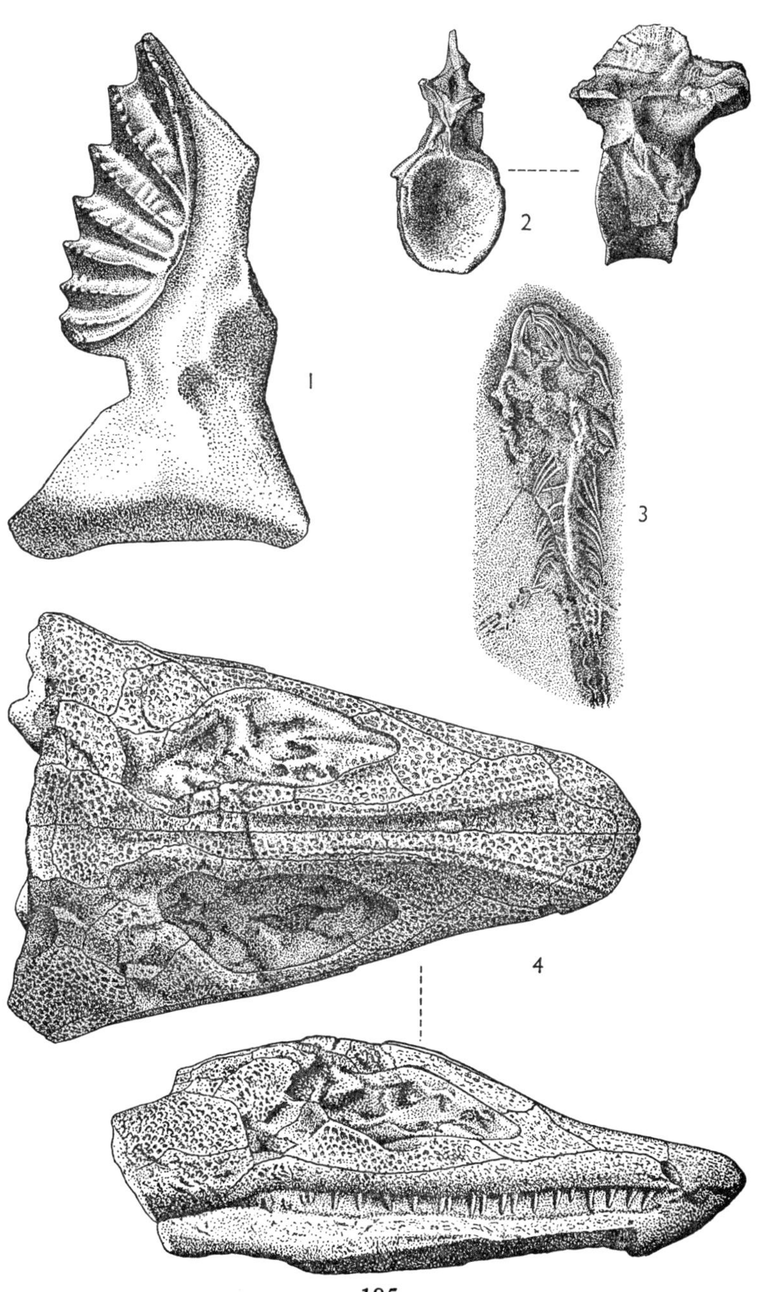

Plate 67

Permian Brachiopods (Figs. 1–4), Foraminifer (Figs. 5, 6) and Polyzoan (Figs. 7, 8)

1, 2.* **Orthothrix excavata** (Geinitz). 1 (×1); *a*, spine bases (×5). 2, valve with spines (×2). Magnesian Limestone; Humbleton Hill, near Sunderland, Co. Durham. RANGE: Upper Permian. [Syn., *Orthis excavata*, *Strophalosia excavata*.]

3, 4.* **Stenoscisma humbletonensis** (Howse). Magnesian Limestone. 3 (×1). Humbleton Hill, near Sunderland, Co. Durham. 4 (×$\frac{3}{4}$). Blackhall Colliery Sinking, near Hartlepool, Co. Durham. RANGE: Genus, Lower Carboniferous–Permian; Species, Upper Permian. [Syn., *Camarophoria humbletonensis*, *C. multiplicata* King.]

5, 6. **Nodosinella digitata** Brady. 5, exterior (×30). 6, section (×15). Magnesian Limestone; Tunstall Hill, near Sunderland, Co. Durham. RANGE: Upper Permian.

7, 8.* **Fenestella retiformis** (Schlotheim). Magnesian Limestone. 7 (×1). Humbleton Hill, near Sunderland, Co. Durham. 8 (×2). East Thickley, near Bishop Auckland, Co. Durham. RANGE: Genus, Ordovician–Permian; Species, Permian.

Plate 67

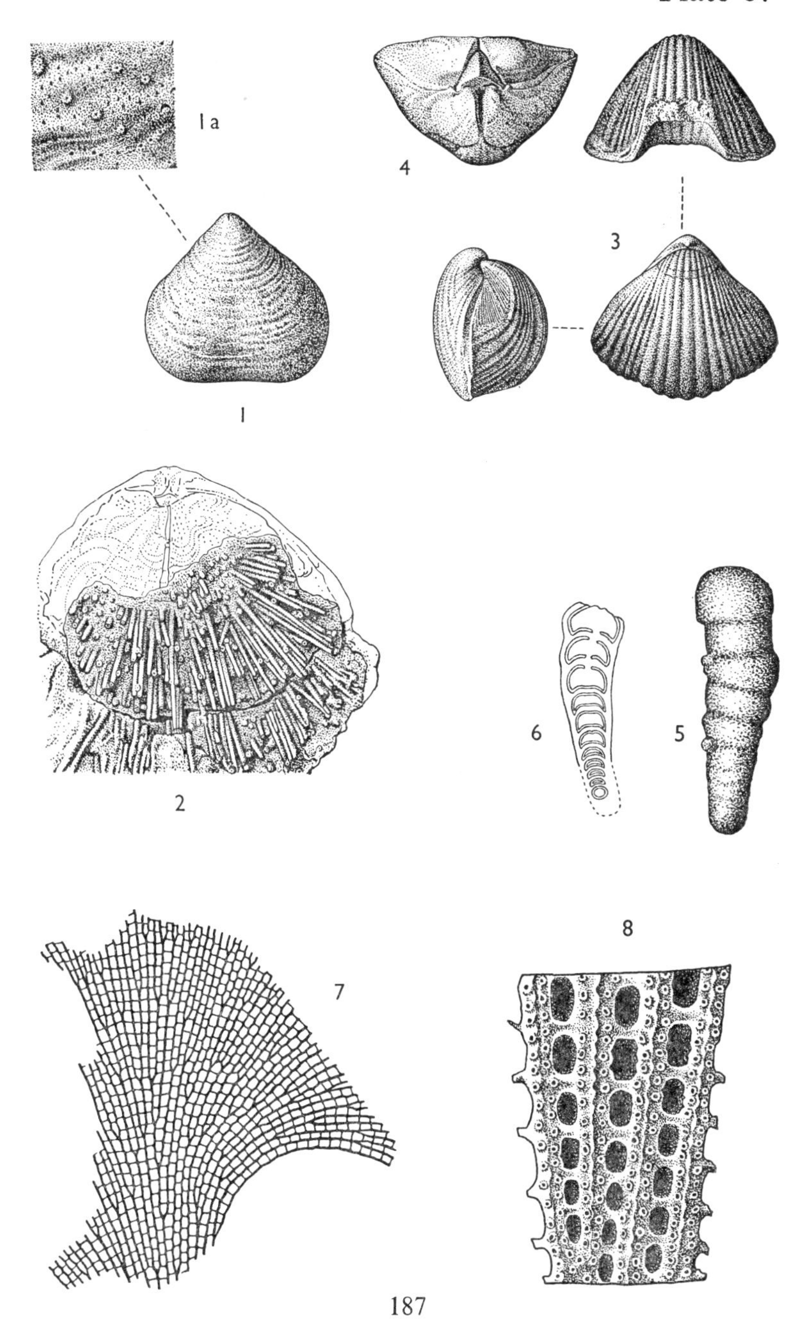

Plate 68
Permian Brachiopods

1.* **Pterospirifer alatus** (Schlotheim). (×1.) Magnesian Limestone; Humbleton Hill, near Sunderland, Co. Durham. RANGE: Genus, Devonian–Permian; Species, Upper Permian. [Syn., *Spirifer alatus*.]

2.* **Dielasma elongatum** (Schlotheim). (×2.) Magnesian Limestone; Sunderland, Co. Durham. RANGE: Genus, Carboniferous, Viséan Stage–Permian; Species, Upper Permian. [Syn., *Terebratula elongata*.]

3. **Spiriferellina cristata** (Schlotheim). (×3.) Magnesian Limestone; Humbleton Hill, near Sunderland, Co. Durham. RANGE: Genus, Devonian–Permian; Species, Upper Permian. [Syn., *Spiriferina cristata*.]

4, 5.* **Horridonia horrida** (J. Sowerby). (×1.) Magnesian Limestone. 4, ventral valve, near Bishop Auckland, Co. Durham. 5, mould of interior of ventral valve, Humbleton Hill, near Sunderland, Co. Durham. RANGE: Genus, Permian; Species, Upper Permian. [Syn., *Productus horridus*.]

Plate 68

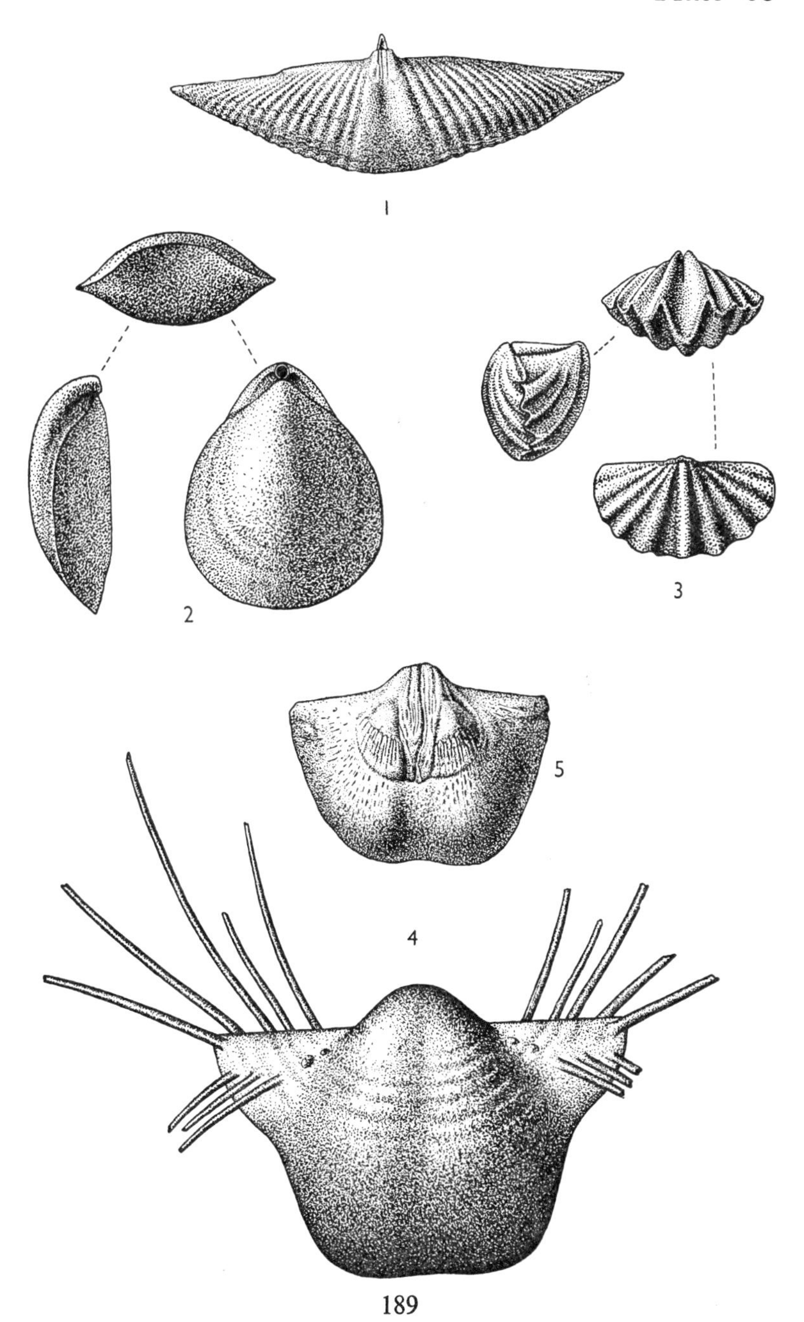

Plate 69

Permian Bivalves (Figs. 1–6) and Fish (Fig. 7)

1. **Parallelodon striatus** (Schlotheim). (×1½.) Magnesian Limestone; near Hartlepool, Co. Durham. RANGE: Genus, Devonian–Jurassic; Species, Permian. [Syn., *Byssoarca striata.*]

2.* **Permophorus costatus** (Brown). (×1½.) Magnesian Limestone; Ford Lime Quarry, south of Claxheugh Rock, Sunderland, Co. Durham. RANGE: Permian. [Syn., *Pleurophorus costatus.*]

3, 4.* **Bakevellia binneyi** (Brown). (×2.) 4, internal mould. Magnesian Limestone; Co. Durham. RANGE: Genus, Permian–Cretaceous; Species, Permian.

5.* **Schizodus obscurus** (J. Sowerby). (×¾.) Magnesian Limestone; Garforth Cliff, near Leeds, Yorkshire. RANGE: Genus, Carboniferous–Permian; Species, Permian.

6.* **Pseudomonotis speluncularia** (Schlotheim). (×2.) Magnesian Limestone; Sunderland, Co. Durham. RANGE: Permian.

7.* **Palaeoniscus freieslebenensis** Blainville. Tail (×1.) Marl Slate; Ferry Hill, south of Durham City. RANGE: Genus and Species, Upper Permian.

Plate 69

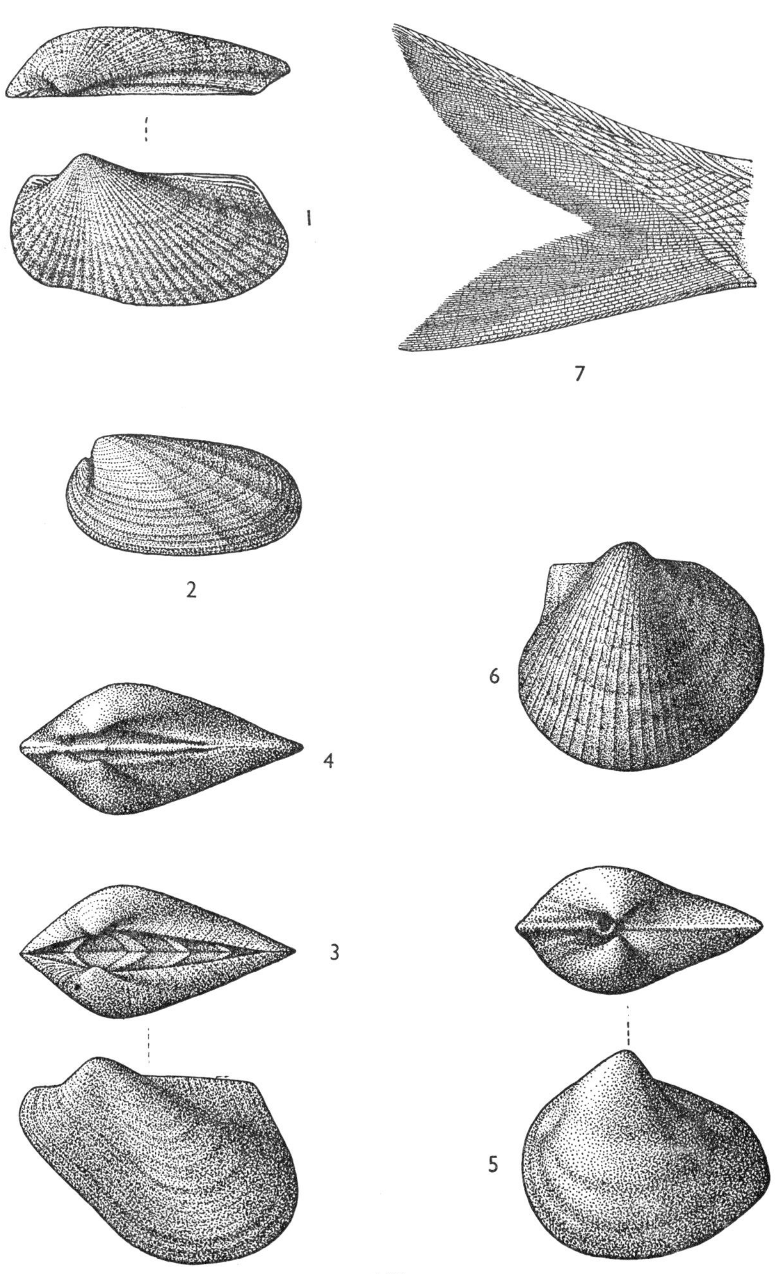

Bibliography

The following is a list of the most important works of reference, including illustrated monographs, in which further information on British Palaeozoic fossils can be found.

BRITISH MUSEUM (NATURAL HISTORY) PUBLICATIONS

BALL, H. W., DINELEY, D. L. & WHITE, E. I. 1961. The Old Red Sandstone of Brown Clee Hill and the adjacent area. *Bull. Brit. Mus. (Nat. Hist.) Geol.*, **5**, 7.

BATHER, F. A. 1899. *The Genera and Species of Blastoidea, with a list of the specimens in the British Museum (Natural History).*

DEAN, W. T. 1959–1963. The Ordovician Trilobite faunas of south Shropshire. *Bull. Brit. Mus. (Nat. Hist.) Geol.*, **4**, 4; **5**, 8; **7**, 8; **9**, 2.

DEAN, W. T. 1962. The Trilobites of the Caradoc Series in the Cross Fell Inlier of Northern England. *Bull. Brit. Mus. (Nat. Hist.) Geol.*, **7**, 3.

ETHERIDGE, R. & CARPENTER, P. H. 1886. *Catalogue of the Blastoidea in the Geological Department of the British Museum (Natural History).*

FOORD, A. H. 1888–1891. *Catalogue of the fossil Cephalopoda in the British Museum (Natural History).* Parts, 1, 2.

HINDE, G. J. 1883. *Catalogue of the fossil Sponges in the Geological Department of the British Museum (Natural History).*

MUIR-WOOD, H. M. 1955. *A history of the classification of the Phylum Brachiopoda.*

MUIR-WOOD, H. M. 1962. *On the morphology and classification of the brachiopod Suborder Chonetoidea.*

STENSIO, E. A. 1932. *The Cephalaspids of Great Britain.*

WHITTARD, W. F. 1955. Cyclopygid Trilobites from Girvan and a note on *Bohemilla. Bull. Brit. Mus. (Nat. Hist.) Geol.*, **1**, 10.

WILLIAMS, A. 1963. The Caradocian brachiopod faunas of the Bala District, Merionethshire. *Bull. Brit. Mus. (Nat. Hist.) Geol.*, **8**, 7.

WOODWARD, A. S. 1889–1901. *Catalogue of the Fossil Fishes in the British Museum (Natural History).* 4 Vols.

PALAEONTOGRAPHICAL SOCIETY MONOGRAPHS

BRADY, H. B. 1876. *A Monograph of Carboniferous and Permian Foraminifera (the genus* FUSULINA *excepted).*

BULMAN, O. M. B. 1927– . *A Monograph of British Dendroid Graptolites.* (In course of publication.)

BULMAN, O. M. B. 1944–1947. *A Monograph of the Caradoc (Balclatchie) Graptolites from limestones in Laggan Burn, Ayrshire.*

DAVIDSON, T. 1851–1886. *A Monograph of the British Fossil Brachiopoda.*

EDWARDS, H. M. & HAIME, J. 1850–1855. *A Monograph of the British Fossil Corals.*

ELLES, G. L. & WOOD, E. M. R. 1901–1918. *A Monograph of British Graptolites.* Edited by C. Lapworth.

FOORD, A. H. 1897–1903. *Monograph of the Carboniferous Cephalopoda of Ireland.*

HILL, D. 1938–1941. *A Monograph on the Carboniferous Rugose Corals of Scotland.*

HIND, W. 1894–1896. *A Monograph on Carbonicola, Anthracomya and Naiadites.*

HIND, W. 1896–1905. *A Monograph of the British Carboniferous Lamellibranchiata.*

HINDE, G. J. 1887–1912. *A Monograph of the British Fossil Sponges.*

JONES, T. R. 1862. *A Monograph of the Fossil Estheriae.*

JONES, T. R., KIRBY, J. W. & BRADY, G. S. 1874–1884. *A Monograph of the British Fossil Bivalved Entomostraca from the Carboniferous Formations.*

JONES, T. R. & WOODWARD, H. 1888–1899. *A Monograph of the British Palaeozoic Phyllopoda (Phyllocarida, Packard).*

KING, W. 1850. *A Monograph of the Permian Fossils of England.*

LAKE, P. 1906–1946. *A Monograph of the Cambrian Trilobites.*

NICHOLSON, H. A. 1886–1892. *A Monograph of the British Stromatoporoids.*

POCOCK, R. I. 1911. *A Monograph of the Terrestrial Carboniferous Arachnida of Great Britain.*

POWRIE, J., LANKESTER, E. R. & TRAQUAIR, R. H. 1868–1914. *A Monograph of the Fishes of the Old Red Sandstone of Britain.*

RAMSBOTTOM, W. H. C. 1961 *A Monograph on British Ordovician Crinoidea.*

REED, F. R. C. 1903–1935. *The Lower Palaeozoic Trilobites of the Girvan District, Ayrshire.*

REED, F. R. C. 1920–1921. *A Monograph of the British Ordovician and Silurian Bellerophontacea.*

SALTER, J. W. 1864–1883. *A Monograph of the British Trilobites from the Cambrian, Silurian and Devonian Formations.*

SLATER, I. L. 1907. *A Monograph of British Conulariae.*

SPENCER, W. K. 1914–1940. *A Monograph of the British Palaeozoic Asterozoa.*

TRAQUAIR, R. H. 1877–1914. *The Ganoid Fishes of the British Carboniferous Formations.*

TRUEMAN, A. E. & WEIR, J. 1946– . *A Monograph of British Carboniferous Non-marine Lamellibranchia.* (In course of publication.)

WHIDBORNE, G. F. 1889–1907. *A Monograph of the Devonian fauna of the south of England.*

WHITTARD, W. F. 1955– . *The Ordovician Trilobites of the Shelve Inlier, west Shropshire.* (In course of publication.)

WHITTINGTON, H. B. 1950. *A Monograph of the British Trilobites of the Family Harpidae.*

WHITTINGTON, H. B. 1962– . *A Monograph of the Ordovician Trilobites of the Bala Area, Merioneth.* (In course of publication.)

WOODWARD, H. 1866–1878. *A Monograph of the British Fossil Crustacea belonging to the Order Merostomata.*

WOODWARD, H. 1883–1884. *A Monograph of the British Carboniferous Trilobites.*

WRIGHT, J. 1950–1960. *A Monograph on the British Carboniferous Crinoidea.*

OTHER PUBLICATIONS

ANDREWS, H. N. 1961. *Studies in Paleobotany.* New York & London.

ARBER, E. A. N. 1921. *Devonian Floras: a study of the origin of Cormorphyta.* Cambridge.

BAKER, E. W. & WHARTON, G. W. 1952. *An Introduction to Acarology.* New York.

BATHER, F. A. 1890–1892. British Fossil Crinoids, Pts. I–VIII (scattered through) *Ann. Mag. Nat. Hist.*, London (6) **5–7, 9.** Chiefly Silurian.

BATHER, F. A. 1913. Caradocian Cystidea from Girvan. *Trans. Roy. Soc. Edinb.*, **49:** 359–529.

BERG, L. S. 1947. *Classification of Fishes.* Ann Arbor.

BISAT, W. S. 1924. The Carboniferous goniatites of the north of England and their zones. *Proc. Yorks. Geol. Soc.*, **20**: 40–124.

BISAT, W. S. 1934. The goniatites of the *Beyrichoceras* Zone in the north of England. *Proc. Yorks. Geol. Soc.*, **22** : 280–309.

BISAT, W. S. & HUDSON, R. G. S. 1943. The lower Reticuloceras (R_1) goniatite succession in the Namurian of the north of England. *Proc. Yorks. Geol. Soc.*, **24** : 383–440.

BULMAN, O. M. B. 1955. Graptolithina. Treatise on Invertebrate Palaeontology, Pt. V. Edit. by R. C. Moore. Lawrence & Meriden.

CROFT, W. N. & LANG, W. H. 1942. The Lower Devonian Flora of the Senni Beds of Monmouthshire and Breconshire. *Philos. Trans.*, London (B) **231** : 131–163.

CROOKALL, R. 1929. *Coal Measure Plants.* London.

CUMMINGS, R. H. 1955. *Nodosinella* Brady, 1876 and associated Upper Palaeozoic genera. *Micropaleontology*, New York, **1** : 221–238, pls. 1–10.

— 1955. New genera of Foraminifera from the British Lower Carboniferous. *J. Wash. Acad. Sci.*, **45**: 1–8.

— 1955. *Stacheoides*, a new foraminiferal genus from the British Upper Palaeozoic. *J. Wash. Acad. Sci.*, **45**: 342–346, pl. 1.

— 1958. The faunal analysis and stratigraphical application of Upper Palaeozoic smaller Foraminifera. *Micropaleontology*, New York, **4**: 1–24, pl. 1.

DAVIS, A. G. 1951. *Howchinia bradyana* (Howchin) and its distribution in the Lower Carboniferous of England. *Proc. Geol. Ass. Lond.*, **62**: 248–253, pl. 10.

DIENER, C. 1924. *Eurypterida: Fossilium Catalogus, I. Animalia,* **25.** Berlin.

ELLES, G. L. 1922. The graptolite faunas of the British Isles. *Proc. Geol. Ass. Lond.*, **33** : 168–200.

FORBES, E. 1848. On the Cystideae of the Silurian rocks of the British Islands. *Mem. Geol. Surv. Gt Brit.*, **2,** 2: 483–538.

GEORGE, T. N. 1933. Principles in the classification of the Spiriferidae. *Ann. Mag. Nat. Hist.*, London (10) **11**: 423–456.

GOLDRING, R. 1955. The Upper Devonian and Lower Carboniferous trilobites of the Pilton Beds in North Devon. *Senckenbergiana*, Frankfurt a.M., **36**: 27–48.

HARPER, J. C. 1940. The Upper Valentian Ostracod fauna of Shropshire. *Ann. Mag. Nat. Hist.*, London (11) **5** : 385–400.

HIGGINS, A. C. 1961. Some Namurian Conodonts from North Staffordshire. *Geol. Mag., Lond.*, **98**: 210–224.

HIRST, S. 1923. On some arachnid remains from the Old Red Sandstone (Rhynie Chert Bed, Aberdeenshire). *Ann. Mag. Nat. Hist.*, London (9) **12**: 455–474.

HUDSON, R. G. S. 1925–1945. Series of papers on Carboniferous corals in *Ann. Mag. Nat. Hist.*, *Proc. Leeds Phil. Soc.*, *Proc. Yorks. Geol. Soc.*, *Geol. Mag.*, and *Quart. J. Geol. Soc. Lond.*

HUXLEY, T. H. & SALTER, J. W. 1859. On the anatomy and affinities of the genus *Pterygotus* (Huxley) and description of the species of *Pterygotus* (Salter). *Mem. Geol. Surv. U.K.*, *Mon.* **1** : 1–105.

JONES, O. T. 1928. *Plectambonites* and some allied genera. *Mem. Geol. Surv. Gt. Brit.*, Palaeontology, **1**: 367–527.

JONES, T. R. 1890. On some Palaeozoic Ostracoda from North America, Wales and Ireland. *Quart. J. Geol. Soc. Lond.*, **46** : 1–31.

KIDSTON, R. 1923–1925. Fossil plants of the Carboniferous rocks of Great Britain. *Mem. Geol. Surv. Gt. Brit.*, Palaeontology, **2**, 1–6.

KJELLESVIG-WAERING, E. N. 1961. Silurian Eurypterida of the Welsh Borderland. *J. Paleont.*, Chicago, **35** : 789–835.

KOZLOWSKI, R. 1947. Les affinités des graptolithes. *Biol. Rev.*, **22**: 93–108.

LANG, W. D. & SMITH, S. 1927. A critical revision of the Rugose Corals described by W. Lonsdale in Murchison's 'Silurian System'. *Quart. J. Geol. Soc. Lond.*, **83**: 448–491.

LANG, W. D. & SMITH, S. 1935. *Cyathophyllum caespitosum* Goldfuss, and other Devonian Corals considered in a revision of that species. *Quart. J. Geol. Soc. Lond.*, **91**: 538–590.

LAPWORTH, C. 1873. On an improved classification of the Rhabdophora. *Geol. Mag., Lond.* (1) **10**: 500–504, 555–560.

LAPWORTH, C. 1879–1880. On the geological distribution of the Rhabdophora *Ann. Mag. Nat. Hist.*, London (5) **4, 5.**

MOORE, E. W. J. 1939. The goniatite genus *Dimorphoceras* and its development in the British Carboniferous. *Proc. Yorks. Geol. Soc.*, **24** : 103–128.

MOORE, E. W. J. 1946. The Carboniferous goniatite genera *Girtyoceras* and *Eumorphoceras*. *Proc. Yorks. Geol. Soc.*, **25** : 387–445.

MOY-THOMAS, J. A. 1939. *Palaeozoic Fishes.* London.

MUIR-WOOD, H. M. 1928. The British Carboniferous Producti. II. *Productus* (sensu stricto); *semireticulatus* and *longispinus* groups. *Mem. Geol. Surv. Gt. Brit.*, Palaeontology, **3**, 1.

MUIR-WOOD, H. M. & COOPER, G. A. 1960. Morphology, classification and life habits of the Productoidea (Brachiopoda). *Mem. Geol. Soc. Amer.*, **81**.

NICHOLAS, T. C. 1916. Notes on the trilobite fauna of the Middle Cambrian of the St. Tudwal's Peninsula (Carnarvonshire). *Quart. J. Geol. Soc. Lond.*, **71**: 451–472.

NICHOLSON, H. A. 1872. *Monograph of the British Graptolitidae.* Edinburgh & London.

NICHOLSON, H. A. 1881. *On the structure and affinities of the genus* Monticulipora *and its sub-genera.* Edinburgh & London.

NICHOLSON, H. A. & ETHERIDGE, R. Jnr. 1878–1880. *A Monograph of the Silurian Fossils of the Girvan district of Ayrshire.* Edinburgh & London.

NICHOLSON, H. A. & MARR, J. E. 1895. Notes on the phylogeny of the Graptolites. *Geol. Mag., Lond.* (4) **2**: 529–539.
PETRUNKEVITCH, A. 1949. A study of Palaeozoic Arachnida. *Trans. Conn. Acad. Arts Sci.*, **37**: 60–315.
PETRUNKEVITCH, A. 1952. Macroevolution and the fossil record of the Arachnida. *Amer. Scientist*, **40**: 99–122.
PETRUNKEVITCH, A. 1952. Principles of classification as illustrated by studies of Arachnida. *Systematic Zool.*, **1**: 1–19.
PETRUNKEVITCH, A. 1953. Palaeozoic and Mesozoic Arachnida of Europe. *Mem. Geol. Soc. Amer.*, **53**.
PHILLIPS, J. 1841. Figures and descriptions of the Palaeozoic fossils of Cornwall, Devon and West Somerset. *Mem. Geol. Surv. Gt. Brit.*
REED, F. R. C. 1917. The Ordovician and Silurian Brachiopoda of the Girvan district. *Trans. Roy. Soc. Edinb.*, **51**: 795–998.
REED, F. R. C. 1942. Some new Carboniferous Trilobites. *Ann. Mag. Nat. Hist.*, London (11) **9**: 649–672.
RHODES, F. H. T. 1953. Some British Lower Palaeozoic Conodont faunas. *Philos. Trans.* London (B) **237**: 261–334.
RHODES, F. H. T. & DINELEY, D. L. 1957. Devonian Conodont faunas from southwest England. *J. Paleont.*, Chicago, **31**: 353–369.
SCHUCHERT, C. & COOPER, G. A. 1932. Brachiopod Genera of the Suborders Orthoidea and Pentameroidea. *Mem. Peabody Mus.*, **4**.
SMITH, S. 1913–1955. Series of papers on Silurian, Devonian and Carboniferous corals in *Quart. J. Geol. Soc. Lond.*, *Ann. Mag. Nat. Hist.*, *Summ. Progr. Geol. Surv. Gt. Britain* & *Bull. Geol. Surv. Gt. Britain.*
STØRMER, L. 1944. On the relationships and phylogeny of fossil and Recent Arachnomorpha. *Skr. norske Vidensk Akad., Oslo. I.M.-N.Kl.*, **5**: 1–158.
STØRMER, L. 1952. Phylogeny and taxonomy of fossil horseshoe crabs. *J. Paleont.*, Chicago, **26**: 630–639.
STØRMER, L. PETRUNKEVITCH, A. & HEDGPETH, J. W. 1955. Arthropoda 2, Chelicerata. *Treatise on Invertebrate Paleontology*, Pt. P. Ed. by R. C. Moore. Lawrence & Meriden.
STUBBLEFIELD, C. J. 1929. Notes on some early British Graptolites. *Geol. Mag., Lond.*, **66**: 268–285.
STUBBLEFIELD, C. J. & BULMAN, O. M. B. 1927. The Shineton Shales of the Wrekin district. *Quart. J. Geol. Soc. Lond.*, **83**: 96–146,
WALCOTT, C. D. 1908. Cambrian Geology and Paleontology. No. 4. Classification and terminology of the Cambrian Brachiopoda. *Smithson. Misc. Coll.*, Washington, **53**: 139–165.
WALCOTT, C. D. 1912. Cambrian Brachiopoda. *Mon. U.S. Geol. Surv.*, Washington, **51**.
WALTON, J. 1933. *An introduction to the study of the fossil plants.* London.
WESTOLL, T. S. 1937. The Old Red Sandstone Fishes of the north of Scotland, particularly of Orkney and Shetland. *Proc. Geol. Ass. Lond.*, **48**: 13–45.
WHITTARD, W. F. 1938. The Upper Valentian Trilobite fauna of Shropshire. *Ann. Mag. Nat. Hist.*, London, (11) **1**: 85–140.
WHITTARD, W. F. & BARKER, G. H. 1950. The Upper Valentian brachiopod fauna of Shropshire. *Ann. Mag. Nat. Hist.*, London (12) **3**: 553–590.

WILLIAMS, A. 1949. New Lower Ordovician brachiopods from the Llandeilo-Llangadock district. *Geol. Mag., Lond.*, **86**: 161–174. 226–238.

WILLIAMS, A. 1951. Llandovery brachiopods from Wales with special reference to the Llandovery district. *Quart. J. Geol. Soc. Lond.*, **107**: 85–136.

WILLIAMS, A. 1962. The Barr and Lower Ardmillan Series (Caradoc) of the Girvan District, south-west Ayrshire, with descriptions of the Brachiopoda. *Mem. Geol. Soc. Lond.*, **3**.

WILLS, L. J. 1959–1960. The external anatomy of some Carboniferous 'Scorpions'. *Palaeontology*, London, **1**: 261–282; **3**: 276–332.

Index

Names of species in current use are printed in **heavy** type. Synonyms, or discarded names, are in *italics*. In the plate references, the figure in **heavy** type (**1**) refers to the plate; that in ordinary type (1) to the figure.